History
for the IB Diploma

PAPER 3

European States in the Interwar Years (1918-1939)

SECOND EDITION

Allan Todd, Sally Waller,
Jean Bottaro

Series editor: Allan Todd

CAMBRIDGE
UNIVERSITY PRESS

University Printing House, Cambridge CB2 8BS, United Kingdom

Cambridge University Press is part of the University of Cambridge.

It furthers the University's mission by disseminating knowledge in the pursuit of education, learning and research at the highest international levels of excellence.

Information on this title: education.cambridge.org

First published 2012
Second edition 2016

Printed in India by Multivista Global Pvt Ltd

A catalogue record for this publication is available from the British Library

ISBN 9781316506462 Paperback

Dedication
For Ken and Di
Friendship is a sheltering tree
(S. T. Coleridge)

Contents

1 Introduction

This book is designed to prepare students taking Paper 3, Topic 14, *European States in the Interwar Years, 1918–39* (in HL Option 4: History of Europe) in the IB History examination. It deals with the history of domestic developments in four key European states in the period between the First and Second World Wars. The four countries covered are:

- Germany
- Italy
- Spain
- France.

After examining the impact of the First World War on each of these four states, the various units will examine the main economic, social and cultural changes in these countries during the 1920s and 1930s. The book will also explore the impact of the problems resulting from the Great Depression in these four countries, and the rise of fascist and right-wing regimes in Italy, Germany and Spain.

Figure 1.1: Eastern Europe after the 1919–20 peace settlements.

Themes

To help you prepare for your IB History exams, this book will cover the main themes and aspects relating to *European States in the Interwar Years 1918–39*, as set out in the IB *History Guide*. In particular, it examines the main political, economic and social developments in the period 1918–39 in terms of:

- the political, constitutional, economic and social problems of Weimar Germany in the period 1918–33
- Hitler's rise to power in Germany, and his main domestic policies
- the rise and consolidation of fascism in Italy after 1918, and Mussolini's main domestic policies in the period 1922–39
- the main political and economic factors behind the outbreak of the Spanish Civil War in 1936, foreign involvement in the Civil War, and the reasons for its outcome
- the economic and political impact of the First World War on France, and social and cultural developments during the 1920s
- the impact of the Great Depression, the problems faced by the Popular Front government, and the collapse of the French Third Republic.

Key Concepts

Each unit will help you focus on the main issues in one of the four countries covered, and to compare and contrast the main developments that took place within them during the period 1918–39.

At various points in the units, there will be questions and activities which will help you focus on the six key concepts – these are:

- change
- continuity
- causation
- consequence
- significance
- perspectives.

Theory of Knowledge

In addition to the broad key themes, the units contain Theory of Knowledge links, to get you thinking about aspects that relate to history, which is a Group 3 subject in the IB Diploma. The topic *European states in the interwar years* has several clear links to ideas about knowledge and history. Many of the subjects covered are much debated by historians – for instance, the significance of the impact of the Great Depression, or the role of elites in the rise of fascism in countries such as Germany or Italy. Much of this is highly political, as it concerns, among other things, aspects of ideology – namely, a logically connected set of ideas which form the foundation of political beliefs and/or political theory. As far as this book is concerned, the main ideologies relevant to your study are **fascism** and **communism**.

At times, the controversial nature of these topics has affected the historians writing about these states, the leaders involved, and their policies and actions. Therefore, questions relating to how historians select and interpret sources have clear links to Theory of Knowledge.

For example, when trying to explain aspects of various political leaders' motives and actions, and the success or failure of their policies, historians must decide which evidence to select and use to make their case, and which evidence to leave out. But to what extent do the historians' personal political views influence them when selecting what they consider to be the most important or relevant sources, and when they make judgements about the value and limitations of specific sources or sets of sources? Is there such a thing as objective 'historical truth'? Or is there just a range of subjective historical opinions and interpretations about the past, which vary according to the political interests and leanings of individual historians?

You are therefore strongly advised to read a range of publications giving different interpretations of the rise of fascism in Europe after 1918, the various political, economic and social policies pursued by different leaders, and the significance of different historical events during the period covered by this book, in order to gain a clear understanding of the relevant historiographies (see Further Reading).

IB History and Paper 3 questions

Paper 3

In IB History, Paper 3 is taken only by Higher-level students. For this paper, IB History specifies that **three** sections of an Option should be selected for in-depth study. The examination paper will set two questions on each section – and you have to answer three questions in total.

Unlike Paper 2, where there were regional restrictions, in Paper 3 you will be able to answer *both* questions from one section, with a third chosen from one of the other sections. These questions are essentially in-depth analytical essays. It is therefore important to study *all* the bullet points set out in the IB *History Guide*, in order to give yourself the widest possible choice of questions.

Exam skills

Throughout the main units of this book, there are activities and questions to help you develop the understanding and the exam skills necessary for success in Paper 3. Your exam answers should demonstrate:

• factual knowledge and understanding
• awareness and understanding of historical interpretations
• structured, analytical and *balanced* arguments.

Before attempting the specific exam practice questions that come at the end of each main unit, you might find it useful to refer *first* to Chapter 6, the final Exam Practice unit. This suggestion is based on the idea that if you know where you are supposed to be going (gaining a good grade), and how to get there, you stand a better chance of reaching your destination!

Questions and mark schemes

To ensure that you develop the necessary skills and understanding, each unit contains comprehension questions and examination tips. For success in Paper 3, you need to produce essays that combine a number of features. In many ways, these require the same skills as the essays in Paper 2.

However, for the HL Paper 3, examiners will be looking for greater evidence of *sustained* analysis and argument, linked closely to the demands of the question. They will also be seeking more depth and precision with regard to supporting knowledge. Finally, they will be expecting a clear and well-organised answer, so it is vital to do a rough plan *before* you start to answer a question. Not only will this show you early on whether or not you know enough about the topic to answer the question, it will also provide a good structure for your answer.

So, it is particularly important to start by focusing *closely* on the wording of the question, so that you can identify its demands. If you simply take the view that a question is 'generally about this period/leader', you will probably produce an answer that is essentially a narrative or story, with only vague links to the question. Even if your knowledge is detailed and accurate, it will only be broadly relevant. If you do this, you will get half-marks at most.

The next important aspect of your answer is that you present a *well-structured* and *analytical argument that is clearly linked to **all** the demands of the question*. Each aspect of your argument/ analysis/ explanation then needs to be supported by carefully selected, precise and relevant own knowledge.

In addition, in order to access the highest bands and marks (see Chapter 6, 'Simplified mark scheme'), you need to show, where appropriate, awareness and understanding of relevant historical debates and interpretations. This does not mean simply paraphrasing what different historians have said. Instead, try to *critically evaluate* particular interpretations. For example, are there any weaknesses in some arguments put forward by certain historians? What strengths does a particular interpretation have?

Examiner's tips

To help you develop your examination skills, most units contain sample questions, with examiner's tips about what to do (and what *not* to do) in order to achieve high marks. These questions will focus on a specific skill, as follows:

1

- Skill 1 (Chapter 2, Unit 1) – understanding the wording of a question
- Skill 2 (Chapter 2, Unit 2) – planning an essay
- Skill 3 (Chapter 3, Unit 1) – writing an introductory paragraph
- Skill 4 (Chapter 3, Unit 2) – avoiding irrelevance
- Skill 5 (Chapter 4, Unit 2) – avoiding a narrative-based answer
- Skill 6 (Chapter 5, Unit 1) – using your own knowledge analytically and combining it with awareness of historical debate
- Skill 7 (Chapter 5, Unit 2) – writing a conclusion to your essay.

Some of these tips will contain parts of a student's answer to a particular question, with examiner's comments, to help you understand what examiners are looking for.

This guidance is developed further in Chapter 6, the Exam Practice chapter, where examiner's tips and comments will help you focus on the important aspects of questions and their answers. These examples will also help you avoid simple mistakes and oversights which, every year, result in some otherwise-good students failing to gain the highest marks.

For additional help, a simplified Paper 3 mark scheme is provided in the Exam Practice chapter. This should make it easier to understand what examiners are looking for in examination answers. The actual Paper 3 IB History mark scheme can be found on the IB website.

This book will provide you with the historical knowledge and understanding to help you answer all the specific content bullet points set out in the IB *History Guide*. Also, by the time you have worked through the various exercises, you should have the skills necessary to construct relevant, clear, well-argued and well-supported essays.

Background to the period

To understand developments in the period 1918–39 fully, it is necessary to have some knowledge of the First World War and its immediate impact. The war lasted from 1914 to 1918 and, at the time, it was the most destructive conflict the world had ever seen. Several factors contributed to the outbreak of the First World War, including a rise in nationalism, along with economic and colonial rivalries between the most powerful nations of Europe. These rivalries were accompanied by arms races and secret diplomacy, as countries tried to strengthen their position in Europe and around the world.

By 1914, two major alliances had formed. On one side was the Triple Alliance (Imperial Germany, Austria-Hungary and Italy) and on the other was the Triple Entente (*entente* is French for 'understanding' or 'agreement' and is applied to diplomatic agreements between states). The Triple Entente was made up of Britain, France and Tsarist Russia. In June 1914, a clash of imperial interests and the rise of nationalism in the Balkans (in south-eastern Europe) resulted in the assassination of the heir to the Austro-Hungarian throne. Within two months, the countries of the rival alliances were at war.

Revolution and the end of empires

In addition to widespread physical destruction, the First World War also had significant political effects. In particular, prewar nationalist tensions led to the break-up of the old Austro-Hungarian (or Habsburg) Empire, and to the emergence of nationalist groups demanding the right to form independent countries.

The Russian Empire also collapsed as revolution spread across the country. Russian soldiers mutinied against the horrors of modern warfare and overthrew the tsar (emperor). After a second revolution in October and November 1917 – led by the communist Bolsheviks – Russia withdrew from the First World War and a revolutionary Marxist government was established. The Bolsheviks called on soldiers and workers in countries around the world to overthrow their governments and end the war.

The Bolshevik Revolution inspired other revolutionary groups, including soldiers who were disillusioned by the effects of the First World War. They became determined to overthrow the capitalist system which – according to Marxist theories – was responsible for plunging the world into such a destructive conflict. There was a short-lived rebellion in Hungary, but perhaps most significant was the revolution in Germany, which led to the abdication of the German kaiser (emperor) and the emergence of a democratic government. The new German leaders were prepared to sign an armistice (ceasefire) in November 1918, thus ending the war. Later, a democratic constitution for Germany was drawn up in the town of Weimar; as a result, historians refer to the period 1919–33 as Weimar Germany.

Figure 1.2: The mutiny at the Petrograd garrison during the Bolshevik Revolution in Russia in 1917.

However, the emergence and growth of new communist parties in Europe in the years after 1918 caused varying degrees of panic among the capitalist bankers, industrialists and landowners, and among most political leaders. In several European states, these fears led to the emergence and rise to power of fascist parties which, alongside other actions and strategies, were determined to defeat and destroy all left-wing political movements.

Postwar problems in the 1920s and 1930s

As well as causing the break-up of old empires, the war had serious economic consequences for both the victors and the defeated. Countries in Europe used up both human and material resources, gained massive debts, and lost trade to countries such as the USA and Japan. In addition, huge agricultural areas of Europe – in both the west and the east – were destroyed, along with railways, roads and bridges.

As you study the period 1918–39, it is important to remember that both statesmen and the ordinary people of Europe who lived through the First World War were determined to avoid any future conflict. When they met in Paris in 1919–20, therefore, the leaders of the victorious nations attempted to create peace treaties that would ensure the First World War would be the 'war to end all wars'.

Yet, in attempting to deal with so many issues, the peace treaties themselves actually created new problems. This is particularly true of the Treaty of Versailles, which was imposed on the new democratic government of Germany. Such a view of these treaties is not one simply proposed by historians with the benefit of hindsight. Many observers at the time recognised the problems – and warned of a future war.

PEACE AND FUTURE CANNON FODDER

The Tiger: "Curious! I seem to hear a child weeping!"

Figure 1.3: A British cartoon from 1919 showing the Allied leaders Clemenceau (France), Wilson (USA), Lloyd George (Britain) and Orlando (Italy) after the peace conferences; the cartoon is predicting a new war in 1940.

As well as these problems, after the collapse of the US stock market in 1929, what became known as the Great Depression began to seriously affect the economies of most states across the globe – including all four of the European states examined in this book. The impact of these economic problems had significant effects on political and economic developments in the states affected by the Great Depression.

ACTIVITY

Using the internet and any other resources available to you, carry out some research on the various treaties that were signed in 1919 and 20. Then make notes about the problems the peacemakers faced at the Paris Peace Conferences, and the main decisions reached during the peace talks.

Terminology and definitions

In order to understand the history of the interwar years, you will need to be familiar with a few basic terms – both technical terms and those relating to political ideologies.

Capitalism

Essentially, capitalism is an ideology which is based on the belief that the most important parts of a country's economy – such as banks, industries and the land – should be owned and controlled by private individuals and/ or companies. An important part of this belief is the view that the state, or government, should not be involved in the economy. In fact, in its early 'liberal' or 'classical' phase in the Industrial Revolution, it was believed that, apart from providing an army and (grudgingly) a police force, the government should not even provide social welfare. This, it was argued, helped ensure 'freedom'. Although most capitalist states eventually developed as liberal political democracies, this was not always the case. Several capitalist states – such as Hitler's Germany in the 1930s – were decidedly undemocratic.

Such a social and economic system is often called a free-market or free-enterprise economy. In its early forms, capitalist firms and individuals argued that prices, wages and employment should be determined by 'market forces' or 'supply and demand', not by government policies.

Yet at the same time, many industrialists pushed for laws which either banned or restricted the formation of trade unions by employees. However, during the second half of the 19th century and the first half of the 20th century, these views were gradually modified in most European countries, and states began to provide such public services as education, old-age pensions, welfare benefits and a health service.

Communism

Communism refers to the far-left political ideology associated with **Karl Marx** and Friedrich Engels, which aimed to overthrow capitalism and replace it with a classless communist society.

Karl Marx (1818–83):

Marx was a German philosopher and historian who developed the materialist concept of history (meaning that historians should look to social and economic aspects rather than 'ideas' as the main causal factors in history). He argued that class struggle and conflict were the most (but not the only) important factors behind social and economic – as well as intellectual and political – change. He also identified various stages in the development of human societies. He worked closely with his friend and collaborator, Friedrich Engels (1820–95), and together, in 1847, they wrote *The Communist Manifesto*. Marx then went on to write an in-depth study of the workings of capitalism, entitled *Capital* (*Das Kapital*). His theories inspired many revolutionaries, including Lenin and Trotsky, who made the first attempt to put his ideas into practice in Russia, following the November 1917 Revolution. However, practice turned out to be very different from theory – and many have argued that communism has never yet been implemented anywhere.

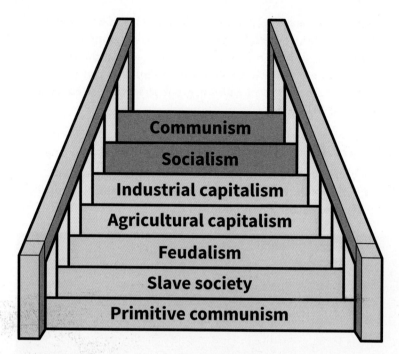

Figure 1.4: Marxist theory of the stages of development in a society.

The first attempt to apply these theories was made by the Bolsheviks in Russia. Under the leadership of **Vladimir Ilyich Lenin**, the Bolsheviks encouraged workers' uprisings in other parts of Europe and, in 1919, established the organisation Communist International (Comintern) in order to help spread revolution.

Vladimir Ilyich Lenin (1870–1924):

His real name was Vladimir Ilyich Ulyanov, and he had joined the Russian Social Democratic Labour Party (RSDLP, a Marxist party) when it was formed in 1898. He provoked a split in the RSDLP in 1903, and formed his own faction, known as the Bolsheviks. In exile until April 1917, he returned to Russia and immediately began to push for a revolution to overthrow the Provisional Government which had taken power following a revolution in February and March 1917. After the successful Bolshevik Revolution in October and November, he acted as prime minister until his death in 1924.

The Bolshevik regime was widely feared and hated and, in order to prevent the spread of revolution, other major European states tried to overthrow the Bolsheviks. When this failed, the European powers applied economic and trade embargoes in an attempt to isolate and weaken Russia (known as the Soviet Union, or USSR, after 1924). For many European politicians – even after the Nazis came to power in Germany in 1933 – the communist Soviet Union posed the most serious threat to stability in Europe.

Communism should not be confused with socialism. Although the two ideologies have some common aims, socialism focuses on achieving these aims entirely by peaceful means, such as holding elections. By contrast, communists believe some violence will be necessary to achieve a fairer society because capitalist classes will themselves use violence in order to protect their wealth and power.

Fascism

The term fascism is derived from the Italian word *fascio* (plural *fasci*), meaning a group, band, league or union. In 1919, Mussolini applied it to his *Fasci di Combattimento* ('Fighting' or 'Battle Group'), which was set up to oppose socialists and communists (see 3.3, Mussolini and the *Fasci di Combattimento*). Mussolini later formed the far-right ultra-nationalist Fascist Party. After October 1922, he began to turn Italy into a one-party fascist dictatorship. Other far-right nationalist politicians in interwar Europe tried to follow his lead, including Hitler and the Nazi Party in Germany. The term fascist was then used to describe this far-right political ideology, and all groups holding such views.

Fascism is opposed to liberalism, which is tolerant of different viewpoints and seeks non-violent and democratic solutions. Fascism is particularly opposed to left-wing political groups and tends to act in the interests of capitalist firms, especially the larger ones.

Inflation

Inflation is where prices rise – very often, this can lead to declines in living standards for ordinary people if they are unable to ensure that their incomes (real wages) keep up with price increases. When inflation is very high, currencies can become relatively worthless. During and after the First World War, there was considerable inflation in many countries.

Left wing and right wing

The origin of these terms can be traced back to the French Revolution. In 1792, the most radical political groups (those wanting the most fundamental changes to the system) sat on the left side of the National Convention, while the most conservative groups (those opposed to change) sat on the right. In the centre were moderates, who wanted smaller-scale changes at a gradual pace. Since then, the term 'left wing' has been applied to socialist or communist groups, while 'right wing' has been applied to conservative or fascist groups; those in the moderate centre are referred to as 'liberals'.

Figure 1.5: The political spectrum: Left/Centre/Right.

Proportional representation

Proportional representation (PR) is a method of voting whereby each party gains representation in parliament to a greater or lesser extent, according to the proportion of the total votes it receives in an election. Some PR systems are more closely linked to actual votes cast than other PR systems – the one that gives the closest correlation is the party list system; most states that have PR tend to use the Single Transferable Vote (STV), or some other combination (such as the Additional Member

System). Such systems also tend to have a percentage threshold, which parties must reach before they are allocated seats.

Stocks and shares

In order to raise extra money for investments, some companies sell part-ownership – a 'share' – of their business to investors by issuing stocks and shares. In return, the owners of these 'shares' expect to receive a higher rate of return (known as 'dividends') on their investment than the interest which could be gained by putting their funds in safe savings accounts. These shares in companies can then be bought and sold through the stock markets of different countries, for instance, the US stock market on Wall Street, La Bourse in France. The price of shares can rise and fall according to the confidence investors have in the ability of individual companies to pay a good rate of dividends. Share price can also fluctuate according to investors' confidence in the general economic situation.

Syndicalists

Syndicalists were originally people who believed that the workers, not the state or private owners, should control the economy through trade unions. This form of syndicalism was most often associated with left-wing anarcho-syndicalism (such as existed in Spain before and during the Spanish Civil War). However, some syndicalists were politically involved with early fascism.

Tariffs

Countries which are industrially advanced and economically powerful generally tend to favour 'free trade'. This means they are opposed to less-developed countries placing taxes – or tariffs – on imported goods. Yet developing countries often see tariffs (or import duties) as the only way to protect their agriculture or emerging industries from competition from foreign countries which have more advanced economies. After the First World War, tariffs were used by many countries as a way to re-grow their economies after the destruction and dislocation caused by war. In fact, the US itself played a big part in the general increased use of tariffs in the 1920s.

The Wall Street Crash

Wall Street in New York was, and still is, the location of the US Stock Exchange, where shares in companies are bought and sold. After the First World War, Wall Street became the world's major financial centre. However, the US stock market proved very unstable in the late 1920s. Although share prices seemed to be going up, many businesses and shareholders were irresponsible in their financial practices. In October 1929, share prices fell dramatically and investors lost large amounts of money. This collapse – known as the Wall Street Crash – caused a severe economic depression in the USA. As a result of this, the US was forced to end its loans to other countries. Germany was particularly affected by the Wall Street Crash, as it relied on US loans to pay the reparations (compensation) imposed on it by the Treaty of Versailles.

The Great Depression

Most countries were soon plunged into what became known as the Great Depression. This was a global economic event, resulting in widespread distress – high unemployment, inflation, industrial decline in production and trade, and poverty – in most capitalist countries in the 1930s. (The economic crisis that began in 2008 is regarded as the worst since then.) One impact of the Great Depression was to turn many of its victims towards supporting extremist political parties: this was especially marked in Italy and Germany. Another was that during the 1930s, some countries – notably those with fascist or militaristic regimes – increasingly resorted to an aggressive foreign policy to solve their economic problems.

Summary

By the time you have worked through this book, you should be able to:

- understand the main impacts of the First World War, and the problems faced in European countries after 1918
- understand and account for developments and policies in Weimar Germany between 1918 and 1933, including economic problems and the rise of political extremism

- show an understanding of developments in Italy after 1918, and explain the rise of Mussolini's Fascist Party
- understand the impact of the Great Depression on Germany, Italy, Spain and France
- understand and explain the main domestic policy decisions introduced by Hitler in Nazi Germany in the period 1933–39
- show an understanding of Mussolini's main economic and social policies in the years up to 1939
- understand the problems of Spain after 1918, and explain the causes and events of the Spanish Civil War, 1936–39
- show a broad understanding of the main developments in France during the interwar years.

2 | Germany

Unit 1: Weimar Germany, 1918–1929

Introduction

In October 1918, after four years of war, a series of spontaneous revolutionary uprisings ended the rule of the German kaiser, Wilhelm II. He fled, and a new German republic – known from January 1919 as the Weimar Republic – was proclaimed. A strongly democratic constitution was drawn up and it seemed as though Germany was about to develop into a modern and progressive state. However, the Weimar Republic faced both communist and nationalist political risings and became strongly reliant on the army. The situation was further complicated by an economy severely weakened by the war, the terms of the Treaty of Versailles, and a French invasion of the Ruhr in 1923. All these factors contributed to hyperinflation in 1923. The advent of Gustav Stresemann in 1924 brought an easing of the economic situation by the reorganisation of reparations payments (in 1924 and 1929).

More stable (and longer-serving) governments and an economic revival helped to make Berlin a vibrant cultural capital, but despite the positive image, very little had really changed. Coalition governments still ruled, extremist parties had not gone away, the revived economy was built on foreign and short-term loans and from April 1925, the republic had a right-wing, conservative president who openly expressed his dislike of democracy. Stresemann himself commented that Germany was 'dancing on a volcano', and it remains a matter of debate whether the country really enjoyed a 'golden age' at this time.

TIMELINE

1918 **3 Oct:** Prince Max appointed chancellor and asks US for peace terms

3 Nov: Kiel Mutiny; sailors' and soldiers' soviets established

9 Nov: General strike in Berlin; Kaiser Wilhelm II abdicates; Prince Max hands power to SPD leader Friedrich Ebert; republic declared

11 Nov: Armistice signed

30 Dec: German Communist Party (KPD) founded

1919 **11 Feb:** Ebert becomes president of Weimar Republic

29 Jun: Treaty of Versailles signed

1920 **Mar:** Right-wing Kapp putsch fails when Berlin workers call a general strike

1921 Aug: Centre Party leader Matthias Erzberger assassinated by right-wing extremists

1922 Jun: Jewish foreign minister Walther Rathenau assassinated by right-wing extremists

1923 Jan: French and Belgian troops invade Ruhr region

Aug: Gustav Stresemann becomes chancellor

Sep: Hyperinflation

Nov: Unsuccessful Munich putsch by Adolf Hitler and Nazi Party; Stresemann's government falls but he remains foreign minister

1924 Apr: Dawes Plan reorganises reparations

May: General election; 61% vote for republican parties

Dec: Moderate parties gain at expense of extremists in general election

1925 Feb: Friedrich Ebert dies

Apr: Paul von Hindenburg elected president

1927 Agricultural prices start to fall

1928 May: Moderate parties make gains in elections

1929 3 Oct: Gustav Stresemann dies

29 Oct: Wall Street Crash

KEY QUESTIONS

- How did the new government of Germany address the constitutional, political and social challenges it faced in 1918 and 1919?

- To what extent were the problems of Weimar Germany between 1918 and 1923 caused by the Treaty of Versailles?

- In what ways did economic, financial and social issues cause problems for the new state?

- What were the political consequences of the economic problems?

- To what extent were the Stresemann years between 1924 and 1929 a 'golden era' for Weimar Germany?

Overview

- The Weimar Republic arose from the political turmoil that accompanied Germany's defeat in the First World War.
- The republic faced an immediate threat from the left-wing Spartacist movement, which forced moderate left-wing politicians into a dependence on the right-wing élites and the army.
- The Treaty of Versailles created huge problems for the new republic, causing anger and psychological trauma among the German people, as well as territorial losses.
- Germany suffered severe economic problems and after it failed to meet its reparations payments, French and Belgian troops invaded the Ruhr in January 1923.
- The decline of industrial output in the Ruhr contributed to hyperinflation, which had profound political and social consequences.
- A series of uprisings broke out in late 1923, including the failed Munich putsch, led by Adolf Hitler, leader of the National Socialist German Workers' Party (the Nazis).
- With Gustav Stresemann's appointment as Chancellor, a new currency was introduced, reparations were reorganised, and foreign loans negotiated. Germany enjoyed a booming culture, particularly in the capital, Berlin, although some objected to the Americanisation of society.
- Between 1925 and 1929, there appeared to be greater political stability in Germany, despite continued government changes and the election of Paul von Hindenburg as president, although there were still underlying political and economic problems.
- Despite positive developments, by 1929 there were signs of renewed economic, social and political instability. However, there was no suggestion that the Weimar Republic was about to fall.

2.1 How did the new government of Germany address the constitutional, political and social challenges it faced in 1918–19?

The birth of the Weimar Republic

The abdication of Kaiser Wilhelm II, on 9 November 1918, marked the end of Imperial Germany. Although a relatively new European state – established in 1871 when 39 separate German states were united – prewar Germany was a proud, militaristic empire. It had an elected parliament (the Reichstag), but power really lay with the Kaiser and his chancellor. Imperial Germany enjoyed rapid economic growth in the period between 1890 and 1914, and this created an influential working class. This group favoured left-wing socialist policies and tended to vote for the Social Democratic Party (SPD, *Sozialdemokratische Partei Deutschlands*). However, although the SPD had become the largest single political party represented in the Reichstag by 1912, the Kaiser's ministers did everything they could to ignore or limit its influence. When war broke out in 1914, a wave of patriotism enabled the Army High Command to advance its own position, and by 1918 the military was running the government almost single-handedly.

Figure 2.1: Philipp Scheidemann proclaims the end of the monarchy and the establishment of the Weimar Republic from the window of the Reichstag building in Berlin on 9 November 1918

The first German revolution

The war proved disastrous for Imperial Germany, and by autumn 1918 all hopes of victory had been abandoned. In an effort to win favourable peace terms and avoid the blame for what seemed like certain defeat, the Army High Command passed power to the civilian authorities on 2 October. Germany was transformed from a regime headed by the Kaiser but dominated by the military 'warlords' (as they called themselves) **Paul von Hindenburg** and Erich von Ludendorff, into a parliamentary monarchy with Prince Max von Baden as chancellor.

> **Paul von Hindenburg (1847–1934):**
>
> He was an army general who was brought out of retirement to lead the German forces in the east in 1914. He was promoted to the rank of field marshal in 1914 and chief of staff of the armed forces in 1916. In this position, he and Ludendorff established a semi-military dictatorship in Germany in the last years of the war. Hindenburg returned to private life in 1918, but was called upon by the political right to run for president in the 1925 election, which he won. He was re-elected in 1932, and his consent was decisive in the appointment of Hitler as chancellor in January 1933. Hindenburg remained president until his death.

This is sometimes referred to as the 'first German revolution'. It was a revolution 'from above', designed to preserve the monarchy by creating a broad political base that allowed parliament to play a major role in government, as it did in other Western parliamentary democracies. However, this arrangement was unlikely to last long because the US president, Woodrow Wilson, refused to negotiate an armistice with a regime that was still headed by the Kaiser.

Conditions in Germany were desperate, and the German people needed peace. The economic disruption caused by the war effort and the British blockade of German ports (in place since 1916) had reduced industrial production to around two-fifths and grain production to about half of their prewar levels. The average German citizen existed on fewer than 1000 calories per day in the last months of 1918. Around 750 000 people died of starvation and malnutrition in the winter of 1918–19, when a flu epidemic added to the misery. Electricity supplies were cut off, public transport stopped operating and businesses were forced to close. The people felt demoralised. Around 2 million German soldiers had been killed and a further 5 million were left wounded or disabled – and it all seemed to have been for nothing.

The second German revolution

The worsening economic situation led to political upheaval. There was a naval mutiny in Kiel on 28 October 1918, when sailors refused to leave port for a final attack on the British navy. They took control of the harbour and raised the red (communist) flag on their ships.

This provoked what historian Geoff Layton has referred to as a 'genuinely revolutionary situation' in November 1918. Workers' and soldiers' councils (or soviets) were established in other ports and towns across Germany. These brought a series of strikes, mutinies and left-wing uprisings inspired by the recent Bolshevik Revolution in Russia. In Dresden and Leipzig, these councils promised to arm the workers and establish a socialist society. In Bavaria, an independent socialist republic was proclaimed on 7 November, and in Berlin the Revolutionary Shop Stewards' movement encouraged disillusioned workers to challenge the authorities. This began Germany's second revolution – the 'revolution from below'.

It should be noted that few of the German revolutionaries genuinely wanted a communist-style workers' state. Most were not communists, they simply sought some form of democracy. Many of the councils were influenced by members of the Independent Socialist Democratic Party of Germany (*Unabhängige Sozialdemokratische Partei Deutschlands*, USPD). This group had broken away from the mainstream socialists of the SPD in 1916 because it disapproved of the SPD's support for the war. For example, the leader of the Bavarian Republic, Kurt Eisner, was an independent socialist. According to William Carr, most councils were 'local ad hoc bodies formed by patriotic Germans aiming to maintain services in a time of national crisis'.

Nonetheless, Prince Max of Baden was unable to restore order. Afraid that the circumstances were being exploited by left-wing extremists, and that further uprisings would leave Germany vulnerable to invasion by its enemies, the SPD felt compelled to act. At first, its members tried to persuade Kaiser Wilhelm II (who had fled to Belgium) to abdicate in favour of one of his sons, but he refused. Therefore, on 9 November 1918, one of the SPD leaders, Philipp Scheidemann, simply went to a window of the Reichstag building and announced to the crowds gathered below that Germany had become a republic.

This decision was probably prompted by rumours that Karl Liebknecht, who led a group of extreme socialists known as Spartacists, was planning to proclaim a 'workers' republic' from a balcony at the Royal Palace in the centre of Berlin. Liebknecht actually did so two hours after Scheidemann's announcement, but – with few genuine revolutionaries among the masses – there was no Bolshevik-style uprising.

Prince Max announced Wilhelm's abdication (before the Kaiser had agreed to it) and transferred his political authority to one of the most

31

prominent members of the SPD, **Friedrich Ebert**. This made the new political regime seem more formal and legitimate. The Kaiser was angered by these events, but when the Army High Command agreed to support Ebert, Wilhelm realised he was powerless to change the situation. He formally abdicated and went into exile. At last the socialists had an opportunity to make a real difference in Germany.

Friedrich Ebert (1871–1925):

He was the son of a tailor and began his career as a left-wing journalist. He was elected to the Reichstag in 1912 and became president of the SPD in 1913. Ebert was briefly chancellor after Prince Max resigned in 1918, and was made president of the Council of People's Commissars during the November revolution that year. He negotiated the Ebert-Groener pact with the army to ensure the survival of the parliamentary government, and in doing so he marginalised the revolutionary left. Ebert was elected president of the Weimar Republic by the Reichstag in January 1919. He continued to defend parliamentary democracy until his death in 1925.

DISCUSSION POINT

Is it always possible to discover the cause of an event? Is it ever possible to conclude that an event does not have a cause?

ACTIVITY

Create a spider diagram to show how Germany emerged from its defeat in the First World War. Colour-code the political, economic, social and 'other' results of defeat.

The interim government

Ebert formed an interim government consisting of three SPD and three USPD members (the USPD members were led by Hugo Haase) in order to maintain control until elections could be held. This group was known as the Council of People's Commissars, to emphasise its left-wing beliefs and therefore win the support of the workers' and soldiers' councils. However, neither Ebert nor Scheidemann wanted to see a communist revolution in Germany, so Ebert reached an agreement with the right-wing army on 10 November 1918. By the terms of this pact, General Wilhelm Groener agreed to suppress the remaining revolutionary activity in return for a promise that the government would allow the army and its existing officers to maintain their authority.

Ebert has sometimes been accused of betraying his principles by signing a deal with the men who had ruled Germany under the Kaiser. However, the move reflected his determination to protect the new republic from illegal protests. Ebert and his colleagues believed in parliamentary democracy, not direct action and campaigns like those of the Spartacists. Ebert probably overestimated the threat posed by extreme left-wing violence, but he seems to have acted in good faith.

SOURCE 2.1

In the evening of 10th November, I telephoned the Reich Chancellery and told Ebert that the army put itself at the disposal of the government and that in return for this the Field Marshal, Hindenburg, and the officer corps expected the support of the government in the maintenance of order and discipline in the army. The officer corps expected the government to fight against bolshevism and was ready for the struggle. Ebert accepted my offer of an alliance. From then on we discussed the measures which were necessary every evening on a secret telephone line between the Reich Chancellery and the high command. The alliance proved successful.

General Wilhelm Groener, recalling the pact between the German government and the army. Quoted in McKichan, F. 1992. **Germany 1815–1939**. *Edinburgh, UK. Oliver and Boyd. p. 122.*

QUESTION

Consider the value and limitations of Source 2.1 for historians studying the Ebert-Groener pact.

While an armistice was being signed with the Allies on 11 November 1918, Ebert was negotiating with representatives of major industrial companies, led by Hugo Stinnes, and the trade unions, under Carl Legien. On 15 November, they signed the Stinnes-Legien agreement. By the terms of this agreement, the employers acknowledged that the unions were legal and agreed to introduce an eight-hour day. The unions promised to maintain production, end unofficial strikes and oppose the influence of the workers' councils, which were demanding the nationalisation of industry. An arbitration board was also set up to mediate in future conflicts.

Again, Ebert was accused by both the Spartacists and members of the USPD of compromising his socialist principles and siding with the industrialists who had supported the Kaiser's regime. However, Ebert feared that nationalising industries would only add to Germany's economic problems. He emphasised how significant it was that the employers now officially recognised the trade unions.

Ebert was also criticised for allowing several groups of people to keep their positions despite their often outspoken anti-republican views. These included many civil servants, military officers, judges, policemen, teachers and government officials. Some members of the USPD argued that the government needed to purge society completely before elections were held, but Ebert defended his policy decisions.

SOURCE 2.2

We had to make sure, once we had taken over power, that the Reich machine did not break down. We had to make sure the machine continued to operate so as to be able to maintain our food supplies and the economy. And that was not an easy task. The six of us could not do that alone; we needed the experienced cooperation of the experts. Had we removed the experienced heads of the Reich offices, had we replaced them with people who did not possess the necessary knowledge and experience, then we should have faced failure in a few days.

Extract from a speech given by Friedrich Ebert, 25 November 1925. Quoted in McKichan, F. 1992. **Germany 1815–1939**. *Edinburgh. Oliver and Boyd. p. 125.*

Do you agree with the view expressed in Source 2.2? Give a reason for your decision.

Historian A. J. Nicholls has supported Ebert, stating: 'It is certainly clear that socialist experiments could have seriously worsened Germany's already difficult economic situation and might well have led to civil war.' However, Jürgen Tampke has argued against this: 'The SPD should have remembered – in the light of the Empire's prewar and wartime policies, which aimed at establishing German leadership in Europe – that it would be necessary to crush, or at least severely curtail, the power of the reactionary army establishment and of sections of German industry.'

Keeping the support of the servants of the old empire was clearly more important to Ebert than retaining the loyalty of his USPD colleagues. On 23 December 1918, 1000 sailors broke into the government's headquarters, demanding overdue wages and a pay rise. They held Ebert captive until he gave in to their demands. This led to a fierce exchange between the USPD and SPD over the behaviour of the USPD police chief in Berlin, who had failed to stop the action. The USPD ministers resigned in protest.

Theory of Knowledge

Significance

To what extent do you think Ebert was the 'victim of circumstance'? 'Historical determinism' suggests that events are historically predetermined because of past developments. Do you think this is a helpful concept and how might you apply it, or question it, in relation to Friedrich Ebert's position?

The Spartacist uprising

Elections to a new National Assembly were announced for 19 January 1919. However, before the elections could take place, the government faced a violent challenge from the Spartacists, who were also known as the KPD (*Kommunistische Partei Deutschlands*), or German Communist Party. The Spartacists strongly opposed Ebert's moderate approach, and the Spartacist leaders Karl Liebknecht and Rosa Luxemburg wanted power to be given to the workers' councils (although some involved in the uprising, which included USPD members, were less extremist). The problems began when Ebert dismissed the USPD police chief. On 6 January, the Spartacists seized the SPD's newspaper office in Berlin in retaliation.

Fighting broke out on the streets of Berlin between the Spartacists and army units reinforced by the Freikorps, a group made up of recently demobilised soldiers of the former imperial army. These ex-soldiers were strongly opposed to communism, and Ebert called on them to put down the Spartacist rebels. On the orders of the new defence minister, General Noske, the Freikorps brutally crushed the uprising and killed Liebknecht and Luxemburg. By 15 January, the rebellion had ended.

Figure 2.2: Armed Spartacists in the streets of Berlin during the 1919 uprising; the violent suppression turned the communists into permanent opponents of the SPD, and prevented any future alliance between the two groups against the right-wing threats that later arose.

The Spartacist uprising caused a serious division among the socialists. The USPD could not forgive the SPD for allowing some of its members to be killed by the Freikorps. Furthermore, the two men arrested for the murders of Liebknecht and Luxemburg were treated leniently due to a sympathetic right-wing judge – one escaped unpunished and the other served only a few months in prison. Unsurprisingly, the government was accused by some of its own left-wing supporters of condoning violence. However, the uprising also demonstrated the lengths to which the SPD would go to preserve the republic. The high level of support the SPD received in the January elections suggests that most Germans supported Ebert's actions.

The elections resulted in a decisive victory for supporters of the republic, headed by the SPD. However, the new government could not meet in troubled Berlin. Instead, it settled on Weimar, a cultural city with a very different image from that of Berlin. Ebert was elected as the first president of the new 'Weimar Republic' on 11 February 1919 (for a comparison of election results, see 2.2, Source 2.3).

In March 1919, the remaining German communists attempted another takeover in Berlin, which was again crushed by the Freikorps and the army. There were also troubles in Bavaria. Here, the USPD-led republic established in November 1918 came to a sudden end when its leader, Kurt Eisner, was shot by a right-wing student in February 1919. In the chaos that followed, the communists established a 'Republic of Workers' Councils', led by Eugen Leviné, including a guard of armed workers. In response, Ebert ordered the army to besiege the Bavarian capital of Munich. With its food supplies running out, and 700 people killed, the city surrendered on 1 May 1919.

A failed revolution?

There has been some historical debate about whether the events of October 1918 to May 1919 can really be referred to as a 'German revolution'. Marxists have suggested that Germany came very close to a true revolution, but others question whether the situation in Germany was really revolutionary, because the transfer of political power in October and November 1918 took place peacefully and the workers' uprisings came to nothing.

Sebastian Haffner has argued that there was no revolution because Ebert was prepared to cooperate with the traditional German élites. However, A. J. Ryder and Rudolf Cooper have suggested a different reason, blaming the workers for not being revolutionary enough in their aims. Modern historians tend not to emphasise the existence of a revolutionary situation, but Tampke condemns Ebert for his failure to seize the opportunity to break fully with the old regime, and claims this made it easier for the Nazis to come to power in the 1930s.

The new constitution

A committee of the Reichstag, led by the liberal new secretary of state Hugo Preuss, drew up a new constitution for Germany. There was great debate over whether the country should have a strong central government, as it had in imperial times, or whether it should adopt a federal structure, which would mean power lay with the individual states (*Länder*) in Germany. Preuss preferred the centralised system, but a compromise was agreed. The *Länder* had control of their own police, schools and judges, but the central government controlled taxes and the military. Prussia and Bavaria also lost their monarchies.

The Constitution of Weimar Germany

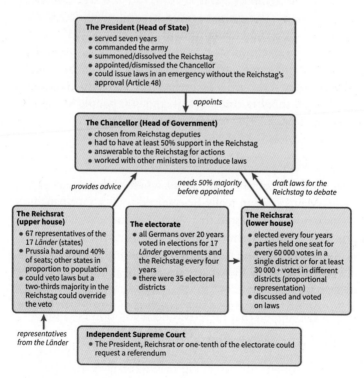

Figure 2.3: The system of government in Weimar Germany.

In what ways was the new constitution democratic and in what ways did it preserve elements of authoritarianism? Make a two-column chart showing the aspects that support each view.

The constitution also laid down the 'fundamental rights and duties of German citizens', outlining individual freedoms (for example, freedom of speech and the right to own property), and giving illegitimate children the same rights as legitimate ones. Other clauses promised the nationalisation of industry and the right of all Germans to 'earn a living through productive work' or to receive a state benefit.

Some historians regard this constitution as fundamentally flawed. Karl Bracher, for example, describes the presidential powers as 'a kind of substitute for the lost absolute monarchy'. Both Bracher and Gordon Craig also criticise proportional representation for several reasons, including the fact that it gave many different parties a place in the Reichstag, thus creating unstable coalition governments. Proportional representation also enhanced the power of the president and allowed extremist parties to win seats. Some historians claim that the division of power between president, chancellor, *Länder* and the Centre weakened authority, while Michael Burleigh questions the use of referendums for allowing minority opinions to gain publicity.

However, while Bracher believes that the constitution did not go far enough because it 'preserved powerful elements of the absolutist state including the continuation of anti-democratic forces', Burleigh asserts that the 'spirit' of the constitution was sound – it was simply the way it was put into practice that caused problems. Hans Mommsen also disagrees that proportional representation was a main cause of instability in the new Weimar government, blaming instead the political parties' 'reluctance to assume political responsibility'. The constitution certainly worked reasonably effectively in the early years, when Ebert used his powers wisely, and perhaps even the continuity of administrative personnel was justified by the need for stability. It was a bold experiment and, as a result, Germany had the most democratic constitution in Europe.

2.2 To what extent were the problems of Weimar Germany between 1918 and 1923 caused by the Treaty of Versailles?

The Treaty of Versailles, 1919

The armistice was signed in November 1918, and peace talks began at Versailles in Paris in January 1919. Germany and the other defeated powers were not invited to attend the Paris Peace Conferences, and this led the Allies to draw up a treaty that appeared to show little concern for its effects on Germany.

The Fourteen Points

Germany was presented with a draft of the Treaty of Versailles on 7 May 1919, and was given 15 days to respond (actually extended to 21 days). The terms of the treaty came as a shock to the Germans; the armistice had been signed as an agreement between equals, and Germany had fully expected to be treated leniently.

In part, this expectation was based on US president Woodrow Wilson's 'Fourteen Points' – his vision for a new, democratic and peaceful postwar world, drawn up in January 1918. The Fourteen Points held a promise of just treatment for Germany after the war and, having broken with the past and created a new democratic state, the Germans felt they deserved a fair settlement. Instead, the Allies laid all responsibility for the war on Germany and used this to justify harsh terms.

> **KEY CONCEPT ACTIVITY**
>
> **Causation:** Find out more about President Wilson's Fourteen Points. Why do you think that knowledge of the 14 points helped to exacerbate the German reaction to the Treaty of Versailles?

Land and military losses

The treaty terms included the loss of land, notably the regions of Alsace-Lorraine to France, North Schleswig to Denmark, Upper Silesia to Poland and Eupen-Malmédy to Belgium. Of even greater concern was the loss of the 'Polish Corridor', which cut Germany in two and left Eastern Prussia geographically isolated (see Figure 2.4). In addition, all Germany's overseas colonies were taken away.

The treaty also put severe restrictions on Germany's military (which became known as the *Reichswehr*). The army was limited to 100 000 troops and conscription was banned; only six battleships were permitted and Germany was allowed no submarines or air force. The Rhineland – an area of land along the border with France – had to be demilitarised. Germany also had to pay reparations (compensation) to the victorious powers for the cost of the war and postwar reconstruction.

The Germans demanded changes to the draft treaty, but only a few minor amendments were made. The final version was issued on 16 June 1919. Germany was told to accept within seven days or face renewed military action.

Consequences of the treaty

German ministers debated the treaty for days, and the chancellor, Scheidemann, resigned in protest at the terms. However, there was little the government could do. After the German naval commanders at Scapa Flow scuttled (deliberately sank) their own fleet so they would not have to surrender it to the Allies, the attitude of the victorious powers hardened even more. There was little chance of further negotiation. Hindenburg (see 2.1) urged the Germans to fight again, arguing that a heroic defeat was preferable to humiliation. However, this was not realistic – Germany could not afford to continue the war.

2 European States in the Interwar Years (1918–1939)

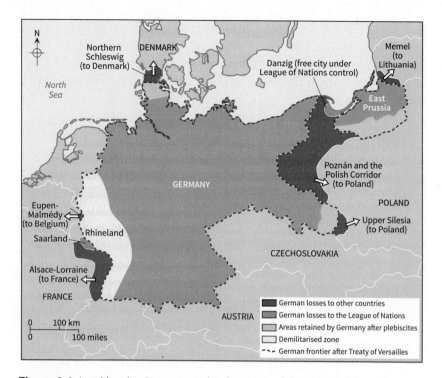

Figure 2.4: Land lost by Germany under the terms of the Treaty of Versailles.

On 22 June, the day the ultimatum expired, the Reichstag voted to accept the terms by 237 to 138. The news sent shock waves through the country. It seemed that Wilson's Fourteen Points did not apply to Germany. Germany was to be disarmed while Britain, France and Italy could maintain whatever forces they wished.

Furthermore, Germany was not allowed to join the newly formed League of Nations. 'National self-determination' was forbidden by the treaty. Germany was denied *Anschluss* (unification) with Austria and, as the map of Europe was redrawn in the months after the war, many ethnic Germans – former citizens of the Austro-Hungarian Empire – found themselves living outside Germany's national boundaries, notably in the new state of Czechoslovakia and the re-formed country of Poland. The loss of Germany's overseas colonies also conflicted with Wilson's view that there should be 'impartial adjustment of all colonial claims' (Point 5 of the Fourteen Points).

German reactions to the treaty

In Germany, the Versailles treaty was regarded as a diktat (dictated peace) and it added to the Germans' sense of humiliation and isolation. According to Anthony Wood, 'the fundamental significance of Versailles was emotional rather than rational'. Hostility towards Article 231 of the treaty, the 'War Guilt' clause that blamed Germany for the war, united the enemies of the Weimar Republic.

Hindenburg's 'stab-in-the-back' myth – claiming that Germany had been betrayed by the socialist politicians who had first agreed to the armistice, and then to the treaty – proved an effective slogan. Even moderates who had previously supported the republic began to take notice of nationalist and communist propaganda. In addition, the burden of reparations payments had a longer-term impact on Germany, leading to an economic crisis in 1923.

Although the Germans felt that the Treaty of Versailles was harsh, in fact its terms were more lenient than those Germany itself had imposed on Russia in the Treaty of Brest-Litovsk (the peace deal between Germany and Russia, agreed in March 1918). Indeed, German historian Eberhard Kolb has argued that the Treaty of Versailles was too lenient because it failed to destroy Germany as a great power. Despite its losses, Germany still had significant industrial assets. Its position in Europe was also potentially stronger in 1919 than it had been in 1914, because of the break-up of the Turkish, Austro-Hungarian and Russian empires. However, as Nicholls has written: 'The one thing the new republic brought the Germans – peace – had been transformed by a settlement which their newspapers and political leaders all agreed was a form of prolonged slavery. It was not an encouraging start.'

KEY CONCEPT ACTIVITY

Perspective: Use the internet to find out the terms of the Treaty of Brest-Litovsk. Does this make you view the Treaty of Versailles from a different perspective?

The context of the elections of June 1920

The signing of the Treaty of Versailles led to the establishment of the *Vaterländische Verbände* (Patriotic Associations) – a group of right-wing patriotic organisations that used intimidation and violence to persecute public figures.

These groups had their own paramilitary forces made up of former soldiers, and they carried out 354 politically motivated assassinations between 1918 and 1922. One victim was USPD politician Hugo Haase, who was shot in front of the Reichstag building in October 1919.

A potentially dangerous right-wing rebellion occurred when the government started disbanding some Freikorps units – in accordance with the treaty – in January 1920. General Walther von Lüttwitz refused to cooperate, and he was supported by the right-wing civil servant, journalist and politician Wolfgang Kapp. On 12 March, they led 12 000 troops into Berlin and, there, declared a new government. The Weimar government was forced to withdraw to Dresden. When Ebert called on the army to crush the putsch (uprising), the army commander Hans von Seekt replied that 'troops do not fire on troops'.

The uprising was not very coordinated. Bankers and civil servants, traditionally on the right in politics and who therefore might have been expected to support it, chose not to get involved, and some were even hostile towards the rebels. To restore order, the Weimar government called on the workers to begin a strike. This cut off transport, as well as power and water supplies in Berlin, bringing the city to a standstill. The putsch collapsed within four days, and the government returned to the capital. However, the episode highlighted the weakness of government authority. The rebels were treated leniently in court – almost all of them went unpunished, and General Lüttwitz was allowed to retire with a full pension.

Later that month, encouraged by the success of the workers' strike in Berlin, communists in the Ruhr region established a 'Red Army' of 50 000 workers. They fought the Freikorps for several weeks before order was restored. Other left-wing rebellions occurred in Halle, Dresden, Saxony and Thuringia.

The June 1920 elections

The first elections under the terms of the new constitution were held against the background of this political unrest. The German people were torn between fear of a communist revolution and hatred towards the politicians who had signed the Treaty of Versailles and who were associated with the violent actions of the Freikorps.

The results of the election showed a move away from the moderate centre-left parties that had dominated the first 18 months of the Weimar Republic. Extreme groups – both left- and right-wing – gained more support than they had previously. Although the pro-republican parties did not have a strong following among the powerful middle class (*Mittelstand*), they remained dominant. The results of the election meant that the SPD was forced to form a coalition government with the right-wing German People's Party (*Deutsche Volkspartei*, DVP) and the German Democratic Party (*Deutsche Demokratische Partei*, DDP). This showed acceptance of the republic by a centre-right party, but it also added to the political problems – making it difficult to reach decisions and provide the stability that Germany needed so badly. There were eight successive governments in the first four years of the republic. These constant changes made people lose confidence in the government, and left it vulnerable to attacks from the right and left extremes.

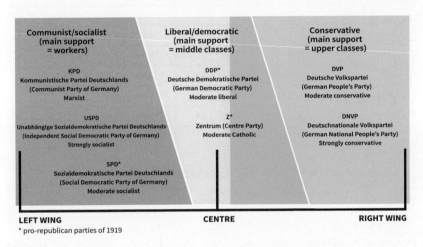

Figure 2.5: The main political parties in Germany in 1919 and 1920.

SOURCE 2.3

A table of statistics comparing the election results of June 1920 with those of January 1919. The old coalition parties of the SPD, DDP and Centre Party received only 43.5% of the vote (compared with 76.2% in 1919), while the right-wing DNVP [German National People's Party, *Deutschnationale Volkspartei*] increased its share of the vote to 14.9% and the left-wing USPD to 17.9%.

Party	January 1919 election			June 1920 election		
	Total votes	%	Seats	Total votes	%	Seats
SPD	11 509 100	37.9	165	6 104 400	21.6	102
USPD	2 317 300	7.6	22	5 046 800	17.9	84
KPD	–	–	–	589 500	2.1	4
Centre Party (Z)	5 980 200	19.7	91	3 845 000	13.6	64
BVP	–	–	–	1 238 600	4.4	21
DDP	5 641 800	18.6	75	2 333 700	8.3	39
DVP	1 345 600	4.4	19	3 919 400	13.9	65
Wirtschaftspartei	275 100	0.9	4	218 600	0.8	4
DNVP	3 121 500	10.3	44	4 249 100	14.9	71
Other parties	209 700	0.6	3	651 200	2.5	5

Adapted from McKichan, F. 1992. **Germany 1815–1939.** *Edinburgh, UK. Oliver and Boyd. p. 128.*

DISCUSSION POINT

Do you think that most people have a natural political inclination (for example to the left or right)? If so, where does this attitude come from?

Political instability, 1920–23

In December 1920, membership of the communist KPD increased dramatically when 400 000 former USPD supporters joined the party. This gave the KPD the confidence to start a new series of rebellions in the spring of 1921. Beginning in Merseburg in Saxony, these rebellions spread to Hamburg and the Ruhr. However, harsh action by the police and army in the Ruhr left 145 people dead.

There were 376 political assassinations between 1919 and 1923, 22 by the left wing and 354 by the right. The right-wing murders included that of the USPD leader, Karl Gareis, in September 1921. Philipp Scheidemann narrowly escaped death after acid was thrown in his eyes. Matthias Erzberger, a former finance minister from the Centre Party (*Zentrum*, Z), who had led the German delegation that signed the armistice and had been present at the signing of the Treaty of Versailles, was assassinated (on the second attempt) by members of a right-wing nationalist league called Organisation Consul.

On 24 June 1922, the Jewish industrialist and DDP foreign minister Walter Rathenau was shot by Organisation Consul. He, too, had participated in the signing of the armistice. Rathenau had also just negotiated the Treaty of Rapallo (setting up trade and secret military links) with communist Russia, despite following a policy of cooperation with the West at the same time.

Fears for the future of the republic led to new legislation, the Law for the Protection of the Republic, which increased the penalty for conspiracy to murder. However, many judges simply ignored it. Rathenau's four killers received an average of four years each in prison, and while 326 of the 354 right-wing assassins went unpunished, 10 of the 22 left-wing murderers were sentenced to death.

The last major series of political disturbances came in 1923. There were left-wing uprisings in Thuringia, Saxony and Hamburg in the autumn, and a right-wing putsch took place in northern Germany in October. In November, Adolf Hitler led another failed uprising in Munich, in Bavaria (see 2.4, The Munich putsch). Despite this unrest, the Weimar Republic survived, largely by relying on the army. However, the people – particularly the middle classes – lacked faith in their government; it seemed all too often that their republican rulers were barely in control.

2.3 In what ways did economic, financial and social issues cause problems for the new state?

Economic instability, 1918–21

Germany emerged from the war in considerable debt. The kaiser's government had financed the war effort by borrowing from other countries, assuming that it would be able to pay back its debts by seizing land and taking reparations from defeated nations after Germany won the war. Germany had also abandoned the link between paper money and its gold reserves in order to put more money into circulation.

The government did not want to raise taxes, so printing more money was simply a way of paying the army and armaments manufacturers. However, the more paper money there was in circulation, the more worthless it became, and this caused serious inflation. By 1919, there were 45 000 million paper marks in circulation compared with 2 000 million in 1913. In the same period, the national debt rose from 5 000 million to 144 000 million marks. There was no corresponding increase in productivity, so goods were in short supply and this raised prices. By 1919, the mark was worth less than 20% of its prewar value.

The financial situation in Germany worsened as the terms of the Treaty of Versailles were carried out. Germany lost land in Europe and its colonies overseas, and with them the income this land generated. The coal mines of the Saar were passed to the League of Nations, to be run for the benefit of the French for 15 years, and Germany had to supply free coal to France, Belgium and Italy. In addition, 90% of the German merchant fleet was surrendered to the Allies, which severely limited trading opportunities. Russia had been paying Germany reparations since the Treaty of Brest-Litovsk in 1918, but these now ceased. Instead, in 1921 Germany itself was presented with a huge reparations bill.

Reparations

The issue of how much Germany should pay in reparations caused some disagreement among the Allies at the Paris Peace Conferences. Britain, France and Belgium were anxious to gain money to rebuild their own countries and repay their war loans to the USA.

Furthermore, under considerable pressure from their electorates, both Britain and France argued that Germany should be made to pay for starting the war. France was determined to ensure that Germany should not become a strong and threatening neighbour again. However, some delegates argued that a strong German economy could benefit Europe. While the USA favoured some reparations, the attitude of the US and British representatives was less vengeful than that of the French. Initially, a sum of 20 billion gold marks was demanded. However, discussions continued and in April 1921 a final bill of 132 billion gold marks (£6.6 billion) was decided. Germany had to pay 2 billion marks a year and 26% of the value of any goods it exported.

Historians debate whether Germany's economic problems and the hyperinflation that developed in 1923 were mainly caused by unrealistic reparations demands. Historians such as Louis Snyder believe that reparations were a main reason for Germany's economic crisis. Others, including Geoff Layton, claim that the crisis was caused by long-term inefficiencies in the German economy, which were simply made worse by reparations. The British economist John Maynard Keynes referred to a 'policy of reducing Germany to servitude for a generation', while Detlev Peukert, writing in 1991, argued that the reparations – which represented only 2% of Germany's national output – were actually quite manageable.

Germany made its first reparations payment at the end of May 1921. However, by January 1922 the country was in such economic difficulties that the Reparations Commission – the organisation set up to oversee reparations payments – granted a moratorium (postponement) on the January and February instalments. In July, the German government asked for a further suspension of payments, and in November it requested a four-year non-payment period to allow the German currency to stabilise. The Weimar government also asked for a loan of 500 million gold marks. The French were very suspicious of this request, particularly as the Germans had just negotiated the Treaty of Rapallo with Russia, which outlined the basis of economic cooperation between the two countries.

ACTIVITY

Were the French right to be suspicious of Germany's request for a loan? Could Germany afford the reparations payments? Using books and the internet, find some more information and statistics on the state of the German economy in 1919 and 1922. Present your views to the rest of your group.

The invasion of the Ruhr, 1923

At a conference in Paris on 9 January 1923, the Reparations Commission concluded that Germany had deliberately defaulted on the coal deliveries it was required to make to France and Belgium.

Two days later, French and Belgian troops moved into the Ruhr to seize German coal, steel and manufactured goods as payment.

Historian Ruth Henig states that, as far as the French were concerned, 'if the invasion triggered off an economic crisis or fanned the flames of separatism in the Rhineland or in Bavaria, so much the better. Anything that weakened Germany and thereby contributed to French security in the future was seen as a positive outcome.' By the end of 1923, there were 100 000 French and Belgian troops in the Ruhr area – controlling mines, factories, steelworks and railways. They set up machine-gun posts in the streets and demanded food from local shopkeepers without paying for it.

With a greatly reduced army, Germany was in no position to fight back. Instead, the chancellor ordered a policy of passive resistance. The Germans refused to cooperate with the French authorities in the Ruhr. The Weimar government promised the workers strike payments if they stayed away from the mines, and paramilitaries (civilian soldiers) were sent to the area to blow up railways, sink barges and destroy bridges.

The French forces reacted harshly – shooting people, taking hostages and conducting aggressive house searches. Around 150 000 Germans were forced out of the Ruhr, and 132 were killed in clashes with the French police. The French brought in their own workers, but by May 1923 the mines were producing only one-third of their 1922 levels and overall industrial output in the Ruhr had fallen by 20%.

Hyperinflation

The loss of income from taxes and exports in the Ruhr added to the strain on the Weimar Republic's finances. Further shortages of goods pushed up prices, and the government met the demand for strike pay by printing more money. International confidence in the value of the mark collapsed, leaving Germany to pay for coal imports with its declining reserves of foreign currency.

In January 1922, 1 US dollar bought 80 marks; a year later, after the occupation of the Ruhr, a dollar was worth 18 000 marks. By the middle of 1923, 4420 billion marks were required in exchange for 1 dollar. A new chancellor, Gustav Stresemann (see 2.5), was appointed in August 1923 and passive resistance in the Ruhr was called off the following month, but hyperinflation continued.

The printing presses could hardly keep up with demand for paper money, which was issued in increasingly large denominations. Workers had to be paid daily – or even twice daily – to keep pace with inflation. Due to the shortage of goods and the worthlessness of paper money, Germans began to trade by bartering (exchanging one type of product or service for another) rather than by using money.

They would get hold of any goods they could find, in the hope that they could exchange them for items that they needed. Some people from the towns and cities went to the countryside to get what they could from the fields. Many employers began to pay their workers 'in kind' (in goods rather than cash).

People who were in debt, had large mortgages or long-term fixed rents, or who were able to negotiate short-term loans, benefited from hyperinflation because they could pay back what they owed in worthless marks. Those with reserves of foreign currencies also did well, while farmers, some shopkeepers and skilled workers could benefit from the high demand for their goods.

However, people with savings, investments, fixed incomes or pensions, and those who relied on welfare benefits, suffered badly. Young people could not find jobs, while elderly pensioners and war widows struggled to survive financially. Those who had bought war bonds (fixed interest-rate loans to the government in wartime) and landlords who relied on rent from their tenants were also badly affected. Unskilled workers fared worst of all. Conditions varied around the country, but everywhere in Germany the economic crisis fuelled resentment and caused uncertainty about the future.

2.4 What were the political consequences of the economic problems?

Hyperinflation provoked further political uprisings. This led Ebert to use his emergency powers and issue laws without the approval of the Reichstag. In September 1923, he transferred power from local governments to regional military commanders. He also appointed a new Reich commissioner, forcing out the democratically elected SPD prime minister in Saxony.

The Munich putsch

The most notorious of the uprisings that occurred towards the end of 1923 was the attempted putsch in Munich, Bavaria, in November. Since the failure of the attempted communist takeover in May 1919, Bavaria had been ruled by a right-wing government, and paramilitary groups with strong nationalist feelings continued to flourish in the region. These groups were outraged by the ending of passive resistance in the Ruhr in September 1923. The state governor, Gustav von Kahr, and commander-in-chief of the Bavarian army, Otto von Lossow, considered marching on Berlin to overthrow the federal government. The attitude of the Bavarian authorities and paramilitary groups encouraged

Adolf Hitler, the leader of a small right-wing party, to plan a national uprising starting in Bavaria.

Adolf Hitler (1889–1945):

He was born in Branau, Austria, and was the son of a customs official. He left school in 1905 and moved to Vienna where, having twice failed to gain a place at the Academy of Arts, he lived as a vagrant. Hitler moved to Bavaria to avoid Austrian military service in 1913, but volunteered for the Bavarian regiment shortly before the outbreak of war in 1914. He was wounded twice during the war and was awarded the Iron Cross for bravery.

In 1919, Hitler was given a post in the army political department in Munich, and shortly afterwards he joined the right-wing German Workers' Party (*Deutsche Arbeiterpartei*, DAP). The DAP disliked the wealth of the upper classes and was strongly anti-Semitic. It aimed to create a 'classless socialist organisation led only by German leaders'. Hitler helped to re-form the DAP as the National Socialist German Workers' Party (*Nationalsozialistische Deutsche Arbeiterpartei*, NSDAP, or Nazi Party) and became its chairman in July 1921. Hitler led the unsuccessful putsch in Munich in November 1923, but served only a brief term of imprisonment, during which he wrote his book *Mein Kampf* ('*My Struggle*'). After his release in 1924, he re-launched the Nazi Party.

Hitler tried to win the support of the middle classes, but despite large gains in the 1930 and 1932 elections it was not until January 1933 that he was appointed chancellor, at the head of a minority right-wing coalition. However, the Enabling Act of March 1933 gave his cabinet authority to act without approval of the Reichstag, and this effectively gave Hitler unlimited powers. After the death of Paul von Hindenburg in 1934, Hitler styled himself Führer (leader) of the German Reich and began his dictatorship. His invasion of Poland triggered the Second World War in 1939. Six years later, when it became clear that Germany would not win the war, Hitler committed suicide.

Figure 2.6: Hitler greets the crowds with a Nazi salute as he arrives at an NSDAP conference in Nuremberg in 1927.

Background to the putsch

Hitler's single-mindedness and his skills as a public speaker had already helped him turn the small German Workers' Party, formed in September 1919 by Anton Drexler, into the more influential Nazi Party which had 55 000 members by November 1923. Nazis were anti-democratic and authoritarian in their views, and were united by a sense of loyalty to Germany based on a belief in the superiority of the German race. The Nazis blamed communists and Jews for Germany's problems, and communists were regularly attacked by Nazi paramilitaries (the *Stürmabteilung*, SA, also known as stormtroopers).

The Nazis won support through carefully organised mass public meetings, with giant posters, banners, flags and the 'Heil Hitler' salute. The Nazis' policies and beliefs were outlined in a 25-point programme in February 1920, which combined nationalist and socialist ideas. Key themes of the 25-point programme included:

- the abolition of the Treaty of Versailles and the union of Germany and Austria (which was forbidden by the treaty)

- German citizenship only to be granted to those of German blood (Jews were to be excluded)
- *Lebensraum* (more living space for Germans)
- a strong, central German government
- the nationalisation of large industries and businesses
- war profiteering to be made illegal
- large department stores to be divided up and leased to small traders
- a generous provision for old-age pensions.

This wide-ranging message appealed to many Bavarians. It was especially attractive to the lower middle class – merchants and low-ranking civil servants – and unskilled workers, as the Nazis promised to end unemployment.

QUESTION

Which of the themes in the 25-point programme represent nationalist ideas, and which socialist? Why do you think the Nazis adopted a mix of left- and right-wing policies?

Events of the putsch

On 8 November 1923, Hitler and the SA broke into a meeting being held at a beer hall in Munich. The meeting was attended by 2000 right-wing sympathisers, and was being addressed by Lossow, von Kahr and Colonel Hans Ritter von Seisser, the head of the Bavarian state police. Hitler interrupted Kahr's speech and announced the start of a national revolution. He proclaimed the formation of a new government with General Ludendorff as the commander-in-chief. Hitler hoped that the three leaders at the meeting would take action, but he had to force them into a side room and hold them at gunpoint before they agreed to support his putsch.

On 9 November, 2000 members of the SA marched through Munich, copying Mussolini's fascist March on Rome the previous year (see 3.4, The March on Rome, October 1922). By this time, Lossow (under orders from General von Seeckt) and von Kahr had publicly denounced Hitler's attempt to seize control. The march was halted by armed police. Fourteen Nazis were shot dead, Ludendorff was arrested and Hitler fled. He was captured and arrested two days later, and the army was sent from Berlin to re-establish control of Bavaria.

Hitler's putsch had been badly planned and executed. Afterwards, the Nazi Party was banned. Hitler was sentenced to five years in prison (although he served only nine months). The failed uprising ended the Nazis' hopes of bringing down the republic by force. However, it did bring Nazi ideology to national attention and, despite his time in prison, the episode did nothing to weaken Hitler's resolve.

SOURCE 2.4

During his trial for high treason at Munich in April 1924, Hitler was allowed by nationally minded Bavarian judges to launch a fierce attack on the whole Republican system. He did not attempt to excuse his role in the Munich putsch. On the contrary he glorified it. Hitler appeared as a fearless, honest leader willing to take the consequences for his actions. Hitler was incarcerated at Landsberg. His treatment was generous in the extreme. It was in prison that Hitler dictated *Mein Kampf*, a book which became one of Hitler's main sources of income in the lean years which followed the putsch. The right of the strong to dominate the weak, his violent racism, his fascination with the techniques of mass manipulation and his contempt for the masses themselves all found expression here.

Nicholls, A. J. 2000. **Weimar and the Rise of Hitler.** *Basingstoke. Palgrave Macmillan. pp. 144–5.*

2.5 To what extent were the Stresemann years between 1924 and 1929, a 'golden era' for Weimar Germany?

The initial impact of Stresemann's chancellorship

The appointment of **Gustav Stresemann** as chancellor on 13 August 1923 was a turning point in the development of the Weimar Republic, both politically and economically. Stresemann was the leader of the right-wing German People's Party (DVP) – a group that was bitterly opposed to the Treaty of Versailles and the payment of reparations.

Gustav Stresemann (1878–1929):

He was born into a lower-middle-class family in Berlin. He studied economics and became a successful businessman and industrial legal advisor. He was a member of the Liberal Party before and during the First World War, entering the Reichstag in 1907 as its youngest deputy. Stresemann became the leader of the Liberal Party in 1917, but he was also a member of the ultra-nationalist Pan-German League. When the Liberals split, Stresemann became co-founder of the conservative DVP in 1918. He was made chancellor in August 1923, at the height of the inflation crisis, and left in November of that year. He was foreign minister of Germany from August 1923 until his death in 1929.

Alarmed by the hyperinflation crisis of 1923, Stresemann agreed to serve as chancellor, a position he held for just 100 days – until his coalition of the Centre Party, SPD and DVP collapsed in November. During this short time Stresemann not only set the Weimar Republic on the path to economic recovery, he also showed that middle-class parties such as the DVP could be more effective serving the republic than opposing it. This established greater political stability.

Stresemann called off the passive resistance in the Ruhr, reduced government expenditure – dismissing many civil servants – and promised to start making reparations payments again. He also appointed the banker-politician **Hjalmar Schacht** as currency commissioner and head of the Reichsbank, the German central bank. In November 1923, Schacht introduced the rentenmark (one rentenmark was worth a trillion old marks) as a temporary new currency. This currency was guaranteed by land and resources rather than by gold, and it was believed to be secure because its supply was limited.

> **Hjalmar Schacht (1877–1970):**
>
> He grew up in the USA, but returned to Germany to study economics before beginning a career in banking. From 1916, he was director of the German National Bank, and in 1923 he was appointed Reich currency commissioner. His introduction of the rentenmark halted hyperinflation. Schacht played an important part in the negotiations over the Dawes and Young plans. The Nazis appointed him head of the Reichsbank in 1933 and economics minister in 1934. However, the establishment of Göring's four-year plan in 1936 led to Schacht's removal as economics minister and president of the Reichsbank. He was imprisoned after the July Bomb Plot in 1944, but was cleared at the Nuremberg trials and resumed his banking career.

Schacht also controlled lending rates and introduced new taxes to keep inflation and the exchange rate at reasonable levels. The government stopped offering credit to industry, as this had encouraged speculation and inflation, and gradually stability was re-established. A number of companies went bankrupt in the process (233 in 1923 and more than 6000 in 1924), but this made the economy more efficient and resulted in greater confidence both within Germany and overseas.

The Dawes Plan and economic recovery

Stresemann also wanted to revise the reparations agreement. He was supported in this by the USA, which had a vested interest in Germany's ability to meet these payments. The US had made wartime loans to the Allies, and without reparations these countries – particularly France – were struggling to repay the debts. An American banker, Charles Dawes, led a committee that drew up the Dawes Plan in April 1924.

Although the original reparations sum of 132 billion gold marks (£6.6 billion) stayed the same, the Dawes Plan outlined a sliding scale of payments that Germany would find more manageable. The plan also stated that no action would be taken in the event of non-payment without joint consultation. In order to help Germany begin making payments again, the committee recommended a large US loan worth 800 million marks. In return, the Reichsbank was to be reorganised under Allied supervision and the rentenmark would be replaced by the reichsmark, which was backed by the German gold reserve.

The Dawes Plan was bitterly opposed by right-wing groups, including the DNVP and the Nazi Party, which wanted Germany to stop paying reparations altogether. However, the plan was formally agreed in July 1924, and in August the new reichsmark came into circulation. As a result of these steps, the French withdrew from the Ruhr in 1924 and 1925, and better relations with France were established as Germany began payments once again.

Effects on industry

The plan contributed significantly to the recovery of the German economy. Industrial output had already reached its prewar level by 1923 (despite the fact that the country was smaller), but from 1924 the economy grew rapidly and exports increased by 40% between 1925 and 1929. Germany received 25.5 billion marks in US loans and other substantial foreign investments between 1924 and 1930, and these were used to boost industry and improve the country's infrastructure.

German manufacturers replaced old machinery (some of which had been handed over as reparations) with new machines. This enabled them to adopt modern production methods and to increase efficiency. New management styles were introduced to German industry, and large manufacturers used American money to buy out smaller firms. Some of them merged assets to form cartels (unions of independent businesses) that could benefit from economies of scale. By 1925, there were around 3000 cartel arrangements, including one covering 90% of Germany's coal and steel production.

The old industrial giants — coal, iron and steel — flourished alongside newer industries such as electricals, chemicals and synthetic materials. The Leuna works near Merseburg began the large-scale production of artificial fertilisers, and the aircraft industry expanded. Although cars were still a luxury item, Daimler and Benz went into partnership in 1926, and two years later BMW began production.

As the inflation rate dropped to almost zero from 1924, and industrial disputes were resolved by a new system of arbitration introduced in October 1923, real wages began to increase and living standards improved. New roads, schools, hospitals and municipal buildings were built with the help of foreign capital, and the gas and electricity services were taken into public ownership and extended. There was also a massive housebuilding programme using state funds and self-build housing initiatives.

Social improvements

In keeping with the second part of the Weimar Constitution, new welfare schemes were developed and social benefits increased. A new National Insurance Code was launched in 1923, and a single agency was set up to administer social insurance for miners.

The Public Assistance Programme was introduced in 1924, and in 1925 the Accident Insurance Programme was reformed. This was followed by the National Unemployment Insurance Programme in 1927, which extended social insurance to provide relief payments to 17 million workers. Such measures helped raise the standard of living for many factory and industrial workers. The Weimar Republic finally seemed to be bringing prosperity to Germany.

Was there greater economic and social stability?

Although the German economy showed a strong recovery after 1924, its rate of growth was unsteady and by the late 1920s there were signs that the economy was slowing down. For example, in 1926, Germany's balance of trade moved into deficit (the country was importing more than it was exporting). Global economic conditions caused problems for Germany, which relied on exporting goods at a time when world trade was declining. Nonetheless, many other countries experienced greater economic growth rates than Germany (see Source 2.1).

The German historian Kurt Borchhardt has suggested that Germany was living beyond its means. Social welfare benefits, pensions and attempts to compensate those who had lost savings through hyperinflation placed a severe burden on state finances and kept taxes high. The resulting lack of capital, made worse by the controls on the circulation of money, prevented the government from funding industry. Internal investment in the late 1920s was actually below that of the prewar years, and wages – pushed upwards by powerful trade unions – rose considerably faster than productivity.

SOURCE 2.5

A table of economic performance (where 1913 = 100), comparing Germany with the rest of the world.

	1920	1925
World	93	121
USA	122	148
Germany	59	95
UK	93	86
France	70	114
USSR	13	70
Italy	95	157
Japan	176	222
Sweden	97	113

From Waller, Sally. 2009. **The Development of Germany, 1871–1925.** Cheltenham. Nelson Thornes. p. 139.

Borchhardt blames working-class greed for this 'sick economy'. However, Carl-Ludwig Holtfrerich believes that much of the responsibility lay with the industrialists, whose cartels reduced healthy competition and who relied on government subsidies rather than reinvesting their profits. Whatever the reason, this lack of internal capital made Germany overdependent on its foreign loans and investments, many of which offered risky terms over a short-term period. Germany was therefore vulnerable to any recession in the world markets and, as Stresemann himself recognised, was living on 'borrowed prosperity'.

Furthermore, the new prosperity did not extend to everyone. The farming community only recovered slowly after 1918, and living standards in rural areas remained well below those of many towns. Although the Reich Resettlement Law of 1919 redistributed large estates among smaller farmers, by 1928 only 3% of small-scale farmers had benefited from the law. As landowners struggled to maintain their traditional lifestyle while prices fell due to worldwide overproduction, they put more pressure on their tenants. By 1927 and 1928, farmers were seeing little return on the cost of running their farms, but they still faced high tax demands, rents or interest payments on mortgages.

The wealthy middle- and upper-class industrialists were also taxed heavily, as the Weimar government needed the income to support its extensive welfare system. These industrialists were angry at the state for favouring the workers. Some employers tried to get the working day increased from eight to ten hours. The cartels that they formed were used to monopolise production, limit competition and keep prices high. Some employers cut wages, and in 1928 employers in the Ruhr locked out 250 000 workers. Although the government resolved the dispute, the event highlighted the extent of the social divide.

ACTIVITY

What factors do you think should be taken into account when assessing a country's economic stability? Carry out some additional research and find some statistics to support your own judgement as to whether the Weimar Republic achieved economic stability in the period 1924–29.

Was there a golden age of culture?

Throughout the 1920s, there was a wave of new cultural achievements in Germany. Cultural experimentation was not, of course, exclusive to Germany. Helped by improved methods of communication and a breaking-down of traditional controls, new forms of expression spread across Europe and the USA in the aftermath of the First World War. However, in Germany after 1924, 'modernism' became linked with 'liberty' and the new republican values.

Figure 2.7: A painting by Otto Dix, entitled *The Big City*, which shows some aspects of the freer atmosphere of postwar Berlin.

The arts

New media such as radio, gramophones and film made the arts more accessible to the general population, and the government subsidised art exhibitions and sponsored cultural works that often reflected a strong left-wing bias. In the visual arts, George Grosz and Otto Dix used the Expressionist style to depict life in Weimar Germany. The writers Thomas Mann and Hermann Hesse conveyed blunt messages about the decadence of Western society. Readers and audiences were invited to challenge established ideas. Erich Maria Remarque's novel *All Quiet on the Western Front*, for example, questioned whether war was the heroic enterprise it had previously been depicted as.

Bertolt Brecht wrote plays such as *Mother Courage*, which encouraged sympathy for ordinary people. With the musician Kurt Weil, Brecht also produced *The Threepenny Opera* – a satirical look at contemporary Weimar society. Paul Hindemith introduced new musical forms, while Arnold Schoenberg and his pupils Anton von Webern and Alban Berg challenged musical convention. In architecture, the Bauhaus movement developed by Walter Gropius made use of ordinary geometric designs and emphasised the functionality of buildings.

ACTIVITY

Undertake some research into an aspect of Weimar culture that interests you – art, architecture, music or literature – reflecting on what was new about it.

Popular culture

A new youth culture reflected the Americanisation of society, with its chewing gum, cigarettes, fashions and cropped hairstyles for women. Spectator sports, dance halls and Hollywood films, with stars such as Marlene Dietrich, became popular. Berlin was filled with nightclubs and cabarets with a more accepting climate for same-sex couples, naked dancing and women's boxing.

Reactions to the new society

For some, this tide of cultural experimentation was exciting and liberating. For others, it was a sign of the decline of a once-great nation. The Centre Party and right-wing nationalist groups campaigned against 'tides of filth', and in 1926 the Reichstag passed a law to 'protect youth from pulp fiction and pornography'. George Grosz was fined for 'defaming the military' and state governments imposed their own forms of censorship.

Groups were formed to campaign against female emancipation, nudism, same-sex relationships and Americanisation. The Nazis, exploiting Jewish involvement in the arts, argued against 'un-German' behaviour, and disrupted theatre performances and exhibitions. The views of the pessimists were reinforced by books such as Oswald Spengler's *The Decline of the West* (first published in 1918 and reissued in 1923), which depicted democracy as the type of government of a failing civilisation. Spengler argued that only an 'élite of heroes' could save nations from decline.

DISCUSSION POINT

How much can we learn about the way the Germans viewed themselves in this period by studying their culture? Do people turn to the arts to be challenged or comforted?

What was Stresemann's contribution as foreign minister in this period?

The Locarno Treaty 1925

One of Stresemann's greatest triumphs was persuading the Western European Allies to meet with Germany at Locarno in Switzerland in October 1925, in an effort to improve relations. Stresemann wanted to prevent France and Britain from forming an anti-German alliance, since the French were beginning to feel threatened by Germany's industrial recovery. The USA also attended the Locarno conference, although the USSR did not. The outcome of the meeting was the Rhineland Pact and a number of arbitration treaties (often known collectively as the Locarno Treaty or Pact) which were finally signed in London on 1 December 1925.

The Rhineland Pact confirmed Germany's acceptance of its western border, as agreed at Versailles, with the loss of Alsace-Lorraine to France and Eupen-Malmédy to Belgium. These borders were 'internationally guaranteed' by Britain, Italy, Belgium and France, which meant that Britain would come to France's aid if Germany attacked. It also meant that Germany would never face another Ruhr invasion. In addition, the French promised to withdraw troops from the Rhineland, which had been stationed there to enforce the Versailles treaty terms. (In fact, full withdrawal from the Rhineland was not completed for another five years.)

The arbitration treaties included Poland and Czechoslovakia, and gave some guarantees that any disputes in the east would be settled by committee. However, the eastern borders were not guaranteed in the same way as the western ones. The treaties were a triumph of diplomacy by Stresemann, but they left the new Eastern European states feeling very vulnerable.

At Locarno, Stresemann established Germany's position as an equal partner with France and Britain, with very little loss to Germany itself. He impressed the European Allies with his emphasis on European cooperation, and his reputation soared.

THE CLASP OF FRIENDSHIP (FRENCH VERSION).

Figure 2.8: A cartoon commenting on the Locarno Treaty (or Pact), published in the British newspaper *The Star* in 1925.

SOURCE 2.6

I should like to express my deep gratitude for what you said about the necessity of cooperation of all peoples – and especially of those peoples who have suffered so much in the past. This Europe of ours has made such vast sacrifices in the Great War, and yet it is faced with losing, through the effects of the Great War, the position to which it is entitled by tradition and development. We are bound to one another by a single and common fate. If we go down, we go down together; if we are to reach the heights, we do so, not by conflict, but by common effort. For this reason, if we believe at all in the future of our peoples, we ought not to live in disunity and enmity, we must join hands in common labour.

Gustav Stresemann to the French foreign minister, Pierre Laval. Quoted in McKichan, F. 1992. **Germany 1815–1939**. *Edinburgh. Oliver and Boyd. p. 140.*

QUESTION
Assess the value and limitations of Source 2.6 for a historian studying the influences of Stresemann's foreign policy?

Further diplomatic successes

In recognition of Stresemann's work towards international peace, Germany was admitted to the League of Nations and made a permanent member of the Council in September 1926. Stresemann himself was awarded the Nobel Peace Prize the same year for his contribution to the 'Spirit of Locarno'. However, Stresemann used the League of Nations as a platform from which to air Germany's grievances – for example, the ethnic Germans who were living under foreign rule and the failure of other nations to match German disarmament.

In 1926, Stresemann also renewed Germany's ties with USSR, first forged by Walther Rathenau in the 1922 Treaty of Rapallo (see 2.2, Political instability, 1920–23). The benefits of developing trade and military links with the USSR were obvious, and Stresemann did not want to risk losing these by making the Soviets feel that the Locarno Treaty was directed against them. In April 1926, therefore, he negotiated the Treaty of Berlin to reassure the USSR that Germany remained committed to good relations. This treaty also helped Stresemann win the trust of the German army, which had avoided the disarmament clauses of the Treaty of Versailles by conducting military training on Russian soil.

Under Stresemann, Germany took on a far more influential international role. A further example of this is the 1928 Kellogg–Briand Pact (see 5.3, Policies to safeguard French security), which condemned military action as a way of solving international disputes. Stresemann signed this pact on Germany's behalf, along with 64 other states.

The Young Plan

In February 1929, Stresemann achieved another success when he persuaded the USA to re-examine the reparations issue. The Young Plan – named after Owen Young, chairman of the committee that investigated the issue – of August 1929 reduced the total reparations sum from 132 billion marks to 37 billion. This meant much-reduced annual payments. The plan also included a 59-year payback period, the end of Allied supervision of German banking, and provision for any disputes to be settled at the International Court of Justice at The Hague.

The right wing objected to Germany paying any reparations at all, and opposed even the reduced sum agreed by the Young Plan. Nationalist groups led by Alfred Hugenburg of the DNVP forced a referendum on the issue, losing with only 14% of the votes. Hitler – whose Nazi Party had been re-formed and reorganised after his release from prison – made passionate speeches against the Young Plan, and became a household name.

ACTIVITY

Carry out some additional research into the Dawes and Young plans, which provided loans to the German government and industries – largely from private banks and financial institutions. In what ways were these plans a gamble for Germany?

Stresemann: an assessment

Stresemann died in October 1929, at the age of just 51. Almost immediately his achievements, strategies and plans began to be questioned. Although Stresemann encouraged European cooperation, his long-term aim was for the Treaty of Versailles to be revised. Even while he was negotiating the Locarno Treaty in September 1925, he wrote a letter to the ex-crown prince of Germany, in which he spoke of the 'three great tasks' that confronted the country: a solution to the reparations problem; the 'protection' of the 10–12 million Germans living under a 'foreign yoke'; and the 'readjustment' of Germany's eastern frontiers. Indeed, the aims Stresemann outlined in this letter are not very different from those that Hitler openly expressed.

Some historians, such as Jonathan Wright, regard Stresemann as a hypocrite who secured European trust, US money and protection from

French invasion, in order to leave open the opportunity for a revision of Germany's eastern borders. However, not all historians see Stresemann's actions as hypocritical. A. J. Nicholls, for example, has written: 'It is unlikely that the French or British politicians really imagined Stresemann had changed [from his nationalist views]. They knew the German foreign minister was a tough negotiator, well able to defend the interests of his country.'

DISCUSSION POINT

Stresemann's motivation and actions are the subject of continuing historical debate. Is it possible for historians to discover the truth about individuals' motivations?

How stable was the Weimar Republic in the years 1924–29?

Political developments

There appeared to be much greater political stability from 1924 to 1929. More than 50% of people voted for the republican parties (SPD, DDP, DVP/BVP and Centre Party) in May 1924, and that percentage rose to nearly 60% in a second election in December 1924.

The extremist vote declined – in May, the Nazis polled 6.5% of the vote; but in December their vote fell to just 3%. The communist KPD saw its percentage of votes fall from 12.6% to 9% in the same few months.

Furthermore, from 1925 the nationalist DNVP chose to work with the republicans rather than against them, which meant that in the elections of May 1928 there was a 72.6% vote for pro-republican parties. Although there continued to be a high turnover of governments, with six different coalitions between November 1923 and June 1928, the state appeared to be working as the authors of the constitution had hoped.

SOURCE 2.7

A table of statistics comparing the election results of May and December 1924 and May 1928.

Party	May 1924 election			December 1924 election			May 1928 election		
	Total votes	%	Seats	Total votes	%	Seats	Total votes	%	Seats
SPD	6 008 900	20.5	100	7 881 000	26.0	131	9 153 000	29.8	153
KPD	3693 300	12.6	62	2 709 100	9.0	45	3 264 800	10.6	54
Centre Party (Z)	3914 400	13.4	65	4 118 900	13.6	69	3 712 200	12.1	62
BVP	946 700	3.2	16	1 134 000	3.7	19	945 600	3.0	16
DDP	1 655 100	5.7	28	1 919 800	6.3	32	1 505 700	4.9	25
DVP	2 964 400	9.2	45	3 049 100	10.1	51	2 679 700	8.7	45
Wirtschaftspartei	692 600	2.4	10	1 005 400	3.3	17	1 397 100	4.5	23
DNVP	5 696 500	19.5	95	6 205 800	20.5	103	4 381 600	14.2	73
NSDAP	1 918 300	6.5	32	907 300	3.0	14	810 100	2.6	12
Other parties	2 059 700	7.0	19	1 389 700	4.5	12	2 903 500	9.6	28

Adapted from Eddy, S. and Lancaster, T. 2004. **Germany 1866–1945.** *London, UK. Causeway Press. p. 89.*

KEY CONCEPT ACTIVITY

Change and continuity: Draw a diagram to show different ways in which the Weimar Republic recovered after 1923. Under each heading, give at least one reason why that recovery was incomplete.

Further evidence of growing support for the republic came from the success of the Reichsbanner, a state defence force established in 1924. Its rallies honouring the flag and the constitution helped to spread a sense of national pride. Some of those from the old right-wing military associations joined, and within a year of its formation the Reichsbanner had over 1 million members.

Widespread revulsion at Walter Rathenau's murder (see 2.2, Political instability, 1920–23), along with economic improvements, resulted in less political rioting. After 1924, there were no more attempted coups or assassinations and the number of right-wing paramilitaries declined. Prussia felt secure enough to lift the speaking ban that it had placed on Hitler in 1928, and the same year even the DNVP voted to review a 1922 law that banned the former kaiser from ever returning to Germany.

Also in 1928, a 'Grand Coalition' was formed under the SPD leader **Hermann Müller**, bringing together the SPD, Centre Party, DVP, BVP and DDP. These parties seemed to have found something in common, and Müller's cabinet remained in office for nearly two years – longer than almost any other government in the Weimar period.

Hermann Müller (1876–1931):

He joined the SPD in 1893. He was elected to the party leadership in 1906 and to the Reichstag in 1916. He was on the right of the party, and cooperated with the kaiser's government during the First World War. Müller was appointed foreign minister in 1919 and was one of the men who signed the Treaty of Versailles. He remained the chairman of the SPD throughout 1919 to 1927 and was chancellor twice (March to June 1920 and 1928 to 1930). Müller faced internal divisions in his later ministry, and his government eventually fell after disagreements about the unemployment benefit system during the economic crisis.

Significantly, after Friedrich Ebert died in February 1925, there was a smooth transition to a new president. The constitution stated that unless a candidate received more than 50% of the vote in the first round of presidential elections then a second ballot had to be held. After the first vote, on 29 March, no clear winner emerged, so a second vote was taken on 26 April. At this point, Field Marshal Paul von Hindenburg chose to stand for the right. Wilhelm Marx (Centre Party) and Ernst Thälmann (KPD) stood against him, but because the left-wing vote was split between these two, Hindenburg won with 48.3% of the vote (Marx took 45.3% and Thälmann just 6.4%).

Figure 2.9: A poster for Paul von Hindenburg during the second round of the presidential election in 1925. It reads 'You won't find better.'

Hindenburg was a widely respected conservative monarchist, and in many ways his election encouraged the political right to accept the republic. Hindenburg has been described as an *Ersatzkaiser* (kaiser substitute), who helped give the republic respectability and was, according to Geoff Layton, 'absolutely loyal to his constitutional responsibilities and carried out his presidential duties with absolute correctness'. However, Hindenburg had little understanding of economic matters, and he did not like the cultural innovations of the Weimar years. According to Sebastian Haffner, those on the right regarded Hindenburg's presidency 'not as the stabiliser of the republic, but as the transition to monarchy'.

In fact, the situation in Germany was not as politically stable as it appeared to be, and the coalitions of 1924 to 1929 were fragile. This was partly caused by a drop in support for liberal or centre parties, such as the DDP and the DVP, and a rise in 'sectional interest' parties that split the moderate centre vote. An example of a sectional interest group was the Reich Party for People's Rights and Revaluation, which represented people who sought compensation after the hyperinflation crisis.

Without central support, the majority SPD remained in opposition until 1928. Gordon Craig believes that the SPD leadership acted foolishly and John Hiden considers their choice to remain out of government 'a serious mistake'. The result was a series of coalitions that struggled to work together. Those made up of the right-of-centre parties agreed on domestic issues but not on foreign affairs, while those of the centre-left shared a common foreign policy but had different domestic agenda. Detlev Peukert argues that this loss of a centre seriously weakened the republican administrations.

The Centre Party, which might have been a stabilising force, was weakened by a split between its left and right wings, while the DDP, DVP and DNVP all adopted a more right-wing position in the second half of the 1920s. According to William Carr, 'it was little short of tragic that precisely when the more moderate German nationalists [of the DNVP] were starting to play a constructive political role, the forces of reaction should have triumphed in the party'. Cabinets fell on quite minor issues, such as a heated debate over the new German flag. Few parties were willing to compromise, and even when the Grand Coalition was formed in 1928, there was still disagreement between the SPD and right-wing liberals.

Although extremist groups did not do well in the elections, they remained a presence on the political stage. The Nazi Party began to expand into a national organisation, with local branches, youth and other groups in addition to a well-trained SA (see 2.9, Society, 1933–39). Most importantly, the Nazis worked to increase support in the countryside, among farmers who had grown disillusioned with Weimar democracy.

The communists also kept a relatively strong following in working-class areas. Violence occasionally broke out between these extremist groups: the communist Red Fighting League was created in July 1924 and clashed in the streets with the Nazi SA.

The Nazi Party after the Munich putsch

The Organisation of the Party	Leadership and Growth
• Although officially banned, the Nazi Party was unofficially led by Alfred Rosenberg while Hitler was in prison.	• Hitler established his supreme power over the party – the *Führerprinzip*.
• The Nazis fought their first elections in May 1924 and won 32 seats, but in the December elections they only took 14 seats.	• In 1924, the SA (stormtroopers led by Ernst Röhm) adopted the 'brownshirt' uniform with a swastika armband. They used passive aggression to provoke communist opponents and then posed as authority figures restoring order. Numbers grew steadily.
• When Hitler was released in December 1924, the party was in disarray.	• Hitler designed the Nazi flag (a swastika on a red and white background) and insisted on the Nazi salute.
• Hitler was banned from political activity and not allowed to make public speeches (March 1925 to March 1927). He could only speak at party gatherings.	• On 14 February 1926, Hitler called the Bamburg Conference to rewrite the Nazi programme and reassert his authority. He spoke for five hours, ending previous attempts to develop the party along socialist lines. **Joseph Goebbels** supported Hitler.
• The ban on the Nazi Party was lifted in January 1925.	
• On 26 February 1925, the NSDAP was officially re-founded.	• From November 1927, the party worked hard to win support from the lower middle class.

Joseph Goebbels (1897–1945):

After graduating from university with a doctorate in 1921, he joined the Nazis in 1924. He edited a Nazi newspaper and, at first, was part of the more radical wing of the party. He was appointed Gauleiter of Berlin in 1926, in return for his loyalty, and in 1929 he became director of Nazi propaganda. Goebbels was elected to the Reichstag in 1933 and was appointed minister for popular enlightenment and propaganda. He exercised huge control over Germany's mass media, which increased during the Second World War. Goebbels committed suicide in 1945.

Reorganisation	Preparing for office
• A new party structure was established, controlled by Hitler from Munich. Germany was divided into *Gaue* (regions) – each Gau had a *Gauleiter*, or leader. • In 1928, the *Gaue* were reorganised to match the Reichstag electoral districts. These regions were divided into units. • Associated organisations for young people, women, students and different professions were established; a Welfare Organisation set up soup kitchens for the needy. • Activists were recruited to carry out door-to-door campaigns, issue pamphlets, posters and leaflets, and address meetings.	• Annual rallies (in Weimar in 1926 and in Nuremberg from 1927 onwards) were stage-managed to impress spectators. • Funds were gained from members through meetings and donations, and from some industrialists, notably the Thyssen family. • The Nazis had a disappointing result in the 1928 election (12 seats), while Hitler was still re-establishing his control. • In 1929, the Nazis backed Alfred Hugenberg's Anti-Young campaign, which enabled them to exploit his media empire for publicity. Goebbels was made responsible for Nazi propaganda. • **Heinrich Himmler** was given responsibility for developing an élite bodyguard for Hitler – the SS (*Schutzstaffel*).

Heinrich Himmler (1900–45):

He joined the Nazi Party in 1923 and took part in the Munich Putsch. In 1929, Himmler was chosen to develop a unit to act as Hitler's personal bodyguard – the SS. He became a Reichstag deputy in 1930 and he built up the SS and his own political authority so that by the end of 1933, he was commander of the political police in all states except Prussia. Himmler helped organise the Night of the Long Knives in 1934, and later took control of the Gestapo and Prussian police. In 1936, he became Reichsführer SS, and his SS Death's Head Units ran the concentration and extermination camps. Himmler committed suicide at the end of the war.

Theory of Knowledge

History, causation and bias

When studying history, you are often asked your thoughts about the causes or consequences of an issue or event. Where do your thoughts come from? Can they ever be free from prejudice?

Paper 3 exam practice

Question

To what extent is it true to say that, **by 1923**, the **weaknesses** of the Weimar Republic **vastly outweighed** its **strengths**? [15 marks]

Skill

Understanding the wording of a question

Examiner's tips

Although it seems almost too obvious to state, the first step in producing a high-scoring essay is to look *closely* at the wording of the question. Every year, students throw away marks by not paying sufficient attention to the demands of the question.

It is therefore important to start by identifying the argument that the question requires you to address, and the **key or 'command' words** in the question. Here, you are being asked to evaluate the strengths and weaknesses of the Weimar Republic by 1923. The argument centres on whether or not the republic would be able to survive. The key words are as follows:

- to what extent...?
- by 1923
- weaknesses
- vastly outweighed
- strengths.

Key words are intended to give you clear instructions about what you need to cover in your essay. If you ignore them you will not score high marks, no matter how precise and accurate your knowledge of the period.

For this question, you will need to take a balanced look at the following aspects of the Weimar Republic:

- **its establishment:** did it have a strong foundation?
- **the constitution:** did this contain more strengths or weaknesses?

- **the attitude of the political parties, the position of the army and the old élites:** did these strengthen or weaken the republic?
- **the Treaty of Versailles:** how significant was this for the Weimar Republic?
- **the reparations issue and the 1923 economic crisis:** was this handled well and what was its legacy?

You will need to decide how each issue – or combination of issues – shows the republic's strengths and weaknesses. It is up to you to decide whether to address the strengths first and weaknesses afterwards in the final essay, or whether to look at themes, analysing the strengths and weaknesses of different aspects of the republic in turn.

Try to consider whether there were more strengths or more weaknesses, and decide whether it is fair to say that the weaknesses 'vastly outweighed' the strengths by 1923. This will form your 'thesis', or view, which you should maintain throughout your answer. However, your essay needs to be structured to show that you understand both sides of the question, and that you can introduce relevant evidence for a variety of possible interpretations, while still showing that your view is the most convincing.

Common mistakes

Under exam pressure, a particularly common mistake is to start at the beginning, describing the history of the Weimar Republic and perhaps making a few links to the question, but without explicitly addressing strengths and weaknesses or answering the question 'to what extent...?'

Another common mistake is to write a one-sided essay – for example, to put forward a strong case for the republic's weaknesses, but ignore any strengths it might have shown.

You should also pay particular attention to the dates in the question. Some candidates ignore these and include information that goes far beyond the end date given, which in this case is 1923.

Remember to refer to the simplified Paper 3 mark scheme in Chapter 6.

Activity

In this unit, the focus is on understanding the wording of questions. Look at the questions given below and the simplified mark scheme in Chapter 6. Note the key words of each question and give a brief indication of how you would respond in each case. Exchange your views with those of a partner and see if you can jointly draw up a list of ideas that would ensure a full consideration of all aspects of the questions.

Paper 3 practice questions

1 To what extent is it appropriate to refer to a 'revolution in German government' in the period 1919–23?

2 Compare and contrast the challenge posed by the right wing with that posed by the left wing, in the years 1919 to 1923.

3 Compare and contrast the Weimar Republic's economic and political problems in the years 1919 to 1929.

4 Evaluate the political and economic developments of the years 1924 to 1929.

5 Discuss the reasons for the survival of the Weimar Republic in the years 1919 to 1929.

6 To what extent do the years between 1924 and 1929 deserve to be called the 'golden age' of the Weimar Republic?

2

Germany

Unit 2: Germany and Hitler

Introduction

The Great Depression in Germany after 1929 helped the Nazi party to increase its support to such an extent that, in January 1933, President Hindenburg was persuaded to appoint Hitler as chancellor of Germany. Hitler immediately began to create a Nazi dictatorship, destroying other parties and organisations that stood in his way and creating a one-party authoritarian regime. However, although his political, economic, financial and social policies were driven by National Socialist ideology, pragmatic choices and overlapping responsibilities within the state meant that the regime was not as 'totalitarian' in practice as it was in theory. There was some resistance to the regime, but overall, Hitler commanded a good deal of support in the years 1933 to 1939.

TIMELINE

1929 **Oct:** Wall Street Crash

1930 **Mar:** Müller's coalition government resigns; Brüning becomes chancellor

Sep: General election brings gains for Nazis and Communist Party

1932 **Feb:** Unemployment exceeds 6 million

Apr: Presidential election: Hindenburg returned

Jun: Papen becomes chancellor

Jul: General election; Nazis become largest party in Reichstag

Nov: General election sees support for Nazis decline

Dec: Schleicher succeeds Papen as chancellor

1933 **Jan:** Secret deal between Hitler and Papen; Schleicher resigns

30 Jan: Hindenburg appoints Hitler as chancellor

Feb: Reichstag fire; communist KPD banned

Mar: New elections; Enabling Act passed

May: Trade unions banned

Jun: SPD banned; other parties disbanded

Jul: Germany becomes one-party state

1934 **Jun:** Night of the Long Knives

Aug: Hitler becomes Führer; army swears oath of loyalty to him

1935 **Mar:** Rearmament announced

Sep: Nuremberg race laws passed

Nov: Kristallnacht

1939 Sep: Start of Second World War

KEY QUESTIONS

- How did Hitler come to power in the 'crisis years' of 1929 to 1933?
- How did Hitler consolidate his dictatorship in the years 1933 to 1934?
- What political policies did Hitler use to build the National Socialist state before 1939?
- What were Hitler's main economic and social policies in the years 1933 to 1939?
- What was the nature of the Nazi state?
- What was the extent of resistance to the Nazi state?

Overview

- The withdrawal of US loans to Germany following the Wall Street Crash led to the closure of factories and businesses, a drastic decline in industrial output, large-scale unemployment and the collapse of the banking system.
- A succession of weak coalition governments failed to provide effective solutions to the economic problems, resulting in a loss of confidence in democracy, and growing support for authoritarian measures to solve the crisis.
- This situation provided Hitler and the Nazi Party with the opportunity to increase their support and present themselves as the only viable solution to Germany's problems.
- In January 1933, Hitler was appointed chancellor of a coalition government. He immediately began moves to increase his power and create a Nazi dictatorship.
- After the Reichstag fire and the March 1933 elections, Hitler pushed through the Enabling Act, which gave him emergency powers for four years. By July 1933, trade unions had been banned and Germany had become a one-party state.

- In June 1934, Hitler carried out the Night of the Long Knives, which established his power over the Nazi Party.
- The Nazis followed policies designed to fulfil their ideology, establish their political control, overcome the problems arising from the Great Depression and enforce a *Volksgemeinschaft* ('people's community'). These policies achieved mixed results.
- The Nazi state was characterised by overlapping competencies, rivalry and, at times, confusion.
- There was some resistance to this state, particularly among socialists and communists, some young people, churchmen and army officers.

Figure 2.10: By 1932, over 6 million Germans were unemployed. This Nazi election poster proclaims 'Our Last Hope: Hitler'.

ACTIVITY

Analyse the appeal of the Nazi poster in Figure 2.10.

2.6 How did Hitler come to power in the 'crisis years' of 1929 to 1933?

In October 1929, the US stock exchange collapsed. Following the 1920s 'boom years' of lucrative investment in America's expanding industries and infrastructure, share prices fell dramatically as the market became saturated. Investors were bankrupted, banks failed and a severe economic depression set in which affected the rest of the world, and above all, Germany which had benefited from large-scale US investment following the 1924 Dawes Plan (see 2.5, The Dawes Plan and economic recovery). The recall of US loans, combined with the loss of trade as the USA and other nations tried to protect their own industries with heavy import tariffs, plunged Germany into severe depression, bringing widespread unemployment. This, in turn, created political instability, ending the 'Golden Era' of the Weimar Republic. Hermann Müller's 'Grand Coalition' government, formed in 1928, collapsed in March 1930 after failing to agree on how to deal with the crisis. The dilemma over whether to cut expenditure (notably unemployment benefits) in order to balance the budget, or increase spending power (by maintaining benefits) in order to stimulate the economy proved divisive. Müller's reluctant decision to cut unemployment benefits alienated the Socialists and created a political impasse. For the next three years, the president, Paul von Hindenburg, appointed a series of chancellors who were unable to command a majority in the Reichstag and propped them up by using his authority, granted by Article 48 of the Weimar Constitution, to issue decrees without Reichstag consent. Confidence in democracy was thus undermined and conservative opposition to the Republic grew, providing fresh opportunities for Hitler and the Nazi Party.

The Nazis and the Great Depression

The Nazis took full advantage of the economic crisis and the breakdown of parliamentary democracy. Although their economic policies were not well developed, they promised solutions to unemployment at mass rallies and through a constant flood of propaganda. The Nazis focused their appeal on the middle and lower-middle class – the *Mittelstand* of small businessmen, independent artisans, small shopkeepers, office workers and farmers.

They played on the memories these groups had of the economic catastrophe of 1923, and on their panic as bankruptcies increased and unemployment levels soared. Many voters deserted the moderate and conservative parties to vote for the Nazis. Young people also flocked to join the Nazis. In 1931, nearly 40% of Nazi membership was made up of people between the ages of 18 and 30. Source 2.8 explains the appeal of the Nazis to many German voters.

SOURCE 2.8

Disgusted with the floundering of the Weimar government, which could not restore sanity to an economy gone crazy for the second time in ten years, these voters saw a striking contrast in Nazi dynamism. They also expected Nazi force to restore law and order to a turbulent political scene. Eighty-two people had been killed and hundreds wounded in six weeks of street fighting in one German state alone. If the price of an end to chaos was the establishment of a dictatorship, many were prepared to pay it – indeed looked forward to it.

Findley, C. V. and Rothney, J. A. M. 1986. Twentieth Century World. *Boston. Houghton Mifflin. p. 143.*

Violence on the streets, coordinated by the SA, as well as intimidation of voters, also played a role in the dramatic increase in support for the Nazis.

Brüning's chancellorship, March 1930 to May 1932

Hindenburg appointed **Heinrich Brüning**, as chancellor in 1930. **Brüning** tried to solve the economic crisis by using presidential decrees to cut prices, wages and state spending, but his strict measures failed to stop the economic downturn, and unemployment soared. Mistakenly believing that he could gain a parliamentary majority of centre-right parties, he persuaded Hindenburg to call for new elections in September 1930. However, the working class, the unemployed and the lower-middle classes that were worst hit by Brüning's unpopular policies demonstrated their anger and frustration by turning towards the more extreme parties – the Communists and the Nazis. The Nazis made significant gains, jumping from 12 to 107 seats in the Reichstag.

> ### Heinrich Brüning (1885–1970):
>
> He was a teacher who served in the German army during the First World War. He entered politics and became leader of the Centre Party in 1929. As chancellor, the austerity measures he adopted to meet the economic crisis made him very unpopular with voters and resulted in a rise in support for more extreme parties. Brüning left Germany in 1934 and settled in the United States.

This made the Nazis the second-largest party after the Social Democrats and, encouraged by this success, they made a huge effort over the next two years, using posters, public meetings and eight Nazi-owned newspapers to increase their support still further. In April 1932, Hitler even felt confident enough to stand against Hindenburg in the presidential election. Hitler only gained 26.8% of the vote, as opposed to Hindenburg's 53%, but the publicity the campaign brought was a huge bonus to the Nazis.

Brüning, in desperation, tried to ban marches of the SA stormtroopers, but by May 1932 he had lost Hindenburg's support and General Kurt von Schleicher persuaded the President to appoint **Franz Von Papen**.

> ### Franz von Papen (1879–1969):
>
> He was a right-wing politician and friend of Hindenburg who served briefly as chancellor despite limited political experience. He negotiated the Nazi-Conservative alliance that brought Hitler to power in January 1933. Under the Nazi regime, Papen served as German ambassador to Austria and then Turkey. Although he was tried and acquitted at the war-crimes trials at Nuremberg, he was later imprisoned for three years by a German court.

Figure 2.11: SA stormtroopers on the streets of Berlin in 1932.

Franz von Papen's chancellorship, June to November 1932

Papen tried to ease the financial crisis by imposing exchange controls, which gave the government strict rule over the import and export of currency. However, the controls had a negative effect on foreign trade. In an unsuccessful bid to increase his support, Papen called for new elections in July 1932. The results showed a dramatic increase in support for the Nazi Party. With 230 seats, and 37.3% of the vote, it became the largest party in the Reichstag, making its support critical for any government to succeed. However, when Hitler was offered the position of vice-chancellor, he declined and instead demanded to be made chancellor, which Hindenburg refused. Papen hoped to strengthen his own position by holding further elections in November 1932. Although the Nazis did well, their overall support fell – they won 196 seats and 33.1% of the votes, creating panic in the party, whose finances were at a low ebb after the demands of the constant election campaigns. Papen, however, failed to gain enough support to govern effectively and Hindenburg dismissed him and replaced him with Schleicher.

SOURCE 2.9

A table of statistics showing the election results in Germany from September 1928 to March 1933.

Party	Seats				
	September 1928	July 1930	July 1932	November 1932	March 1933
KPD	54	77	89	100	81
SPD	153	143	133	121	120
BVP	78	87	97	90	93
DVNP	73	41	37	52	52
NSDAP	12	107	230	196	288
Other parties	121	122	22	35	23

Adapted from www.atschool.eduweb.co.uk/.../Germany%201919.../

ACTIVITY

Between them, the two left-wing parties – the Communists (KPD) and the Social Democrats (SPD) – won nearly 40% of the seats in the Reichstag between 1928 and 1932. Reflect on what you learned about the Weimar Republic in Part 1, Unit 1. Why do you think the parties failed to cooperate to form a united front against Hitler?

The chancellorship of Kurt von Schleicher, December 1932 to January 1933

Kurt von Schleicher was appointed because he convinced Hindenburg that he could divide the Nazi Party by winning over some of its leaders, but his plan failed. The main result of his political manoeuvring was to antagonise Papen, who consequently entered into negotiations with Hitler. Having arranged a deal, Papen approached Hindenburg with his plan. Hitler was to be appointed as chancellor of a coalition government, whose 11 members included only three Nazis and in which Papen would be deputy chancellor.

> **Kurt von Schleicher (1892–1934):**
>
> He was an army officer who had held various posts linking the army and the government between 1919 and 1932. As a close and influential advisor to Hindenburg, he was responsible for the appointments of Brüning and Papen as chancellor, and reluctantly accepted the post himself. Schleicher was concerned about the growing power of the Nazis and hoped to control their influence by including them in government. He was murdered by the Nazis during the Night of the Long Knives in 1934.

The conservative advisors surrounding Hindenburg believed that Nazi extremism would be held in check by the conservative majority in the government. They were also influenced by evidence of growing support for the Communist Party in the November 1932 election. As a result, on 30 January 1933, Hitler was appointed chancellor.

It is ironic that by late 1932 the German economy was actually starting to improve. This was due in part to some public works programmes set up by Brüning and the allocation of some unused land to dispossessed farmers and workers by Papen. However, the improvements were too limited to influence the voters. It was the Nazis who later won credit for Germany's economic recovery.

Theory of Knowledge

History and economics
How do events in Weimar Germany between 1929 and 1933 demonstrate that historians need to examine the link between economics and politics in order to understand historical events?

What other factors contributed to Hitler's rise to power?

Apart from the fundamental weaknesses in the Weimar Republic and the direct results of the Depression, other factors played a role in Hitler's rise to power.

The rise of extremism

During the depression, the German electorate turned to parties that offered extreme solutions. The Communists blamed the economic collapse on the failure of the capitalist system, while the Nazis blamed the Weimar system, the Treaty of Versailles, the Communists and the Jews and promised strong, decisive leadership as a solution.

Fears of communism

As support for the communists grew, the Nazis used propaganda to play on middle-class fears of the 'communist threat'. Increased support for the Communist Party in the elections frightened the conservative élite into backing the Nazis. One of the Nazis' aims was to win the support of leading industrialists, who willingly financed them to prevent a communist takeover. This was partly due to the efforts of a powerful ally, Alfred Hugenberg – a nationalist leader and owner of a chain of right-wing newspapers. In October 1930, Hugenberg and other influential business leaders joined the Nazis to form the Harzburg Front, an alliance that was determined to keep the Communists out of power.

The use of propaganda and technology

The Nazis made skilful, cynical and extremely effective use of propaganda to undermine their opponents and spread the appeal of Nazism. Above all, they promised work to the unemployed, stability to the middle classes, and a revival of pride to German nationalists. They were the first party to demonstrate the effectiveness of the new medium of radio as a means of mass political communication. In the presidential election of 1932, the Nazis chartered planes to fly Hitler all over Germany to speak at Nazi rallies. Even though Hitler did not succeed in defeating Hindenburg, the Nazi message was spread. Mass rallies, parades, uniforms and marches reinforced the message that the Nazis were a party of action, organisation and teamwork.

Divisions among the opposition

The system of proportional representation in the Weimar Constitution gave rise to numerous parties, none of which could gain a workable majority in the Reichstag. There were too many divisions between the parties for them to unite against the threat posed by the Nazis. The main left-wing parties, the Social Democrats and the Communists, refused to work together. Some of the conservative parties saw the

Nazis as a preferable alternative to the left-wing parties. All of them underestimated the Nazis.

The collapse of democracy and 'backstairs' political intrigue

The use of presidential decree in place of parliamentary rule, which had started under Brüning, hastened the collapse of democracy. By 1932, Germany had effectively become an authoritarian state in which a handful of individuals held political power. Their intrigues, largely motivated by self-interest, provided Hitler with the opportunity he wanted. He did not need to risk seizing power in an unpredictable putsch (which the SA had been urging); he was offered it by self-serving politicians. The 'backstairs' intrigue between Papen and Hindenburg allowed Hitler to come to power legally. They mistakenly believed that, while the Nazis were strong enough to keep the Communists out of power, they were too weak to threaten the position of the traditional political élite, which they thought could retain control in Germany. Their error soon became clear.

KEY CONCEPT QUESTION

Causation and consequence: To what extent was democracy in Germany destroyed by the Depression? Look at the material from Part 2 and discuss the relative importance of different factors.

2.7 How did Hitler consolidate his dictatorship in the years 1933 to 1934?

With only two other Nazis in his 12-strong coalition cabinet, Hitler's position as chancellor was far from secure. However, one of these Nazis was minister of the interior, which gave him control over the police; within weeks, therefore, the Nazi Party took control of Germany.

Figure 2.12: Hitler addresses a crowd of thousands of uniformed men during a Nazi rally in Dortmund in 1933.

The road to dictatorship, 1933–34

Initially, Hitler and the Nazis set about destroying the Weimar Republic and establishing their dictatorship mainly through legal means.

The March election, 1933

Hitler's Nazi-Nationalist coalition lacked a majority in the Reichstag, so Hitler immediately called another election for March 1933. He obtained presidential decrees to ban meetings of any opposition parties and to close down their newspapers so they could not influence public opinion. At the same time, **Hermann Göring** was given sweeping powers to act against the socialist SPD and the communist KPD when Hitler dissolved the provincial parliament. The Nazi election campaign was also helped by large donations from business leaders.

Hermann Göring (1893–1946):

He joined the Nazi Party in 1923, and by 1933 he had become one Hitler's most trusted senior advisors. Göring helped establish the first concentration camps, arranged (with Himmler) the Night of the Long Knives, and supervised the Four-Year Plan. In 1935, Göring became head of the Luftwaffe and, in 1938, he took control of all the German armed forces. In 1939, he was appointed Hitler's deputy. Göring was convicted of war crimes after the Second World War, but he committed suicide before he could be executed.

The Reichstag fire, February 1933

On 27 February, a week before the elections were due to be held, the Reichstag building was set on fire. Hitler immediately claimed that this was the start of a communist revolution. The following day he issued the Decree for the Protection of the People and State, which banned the KPD and gave the government the power to suspend most of the civil and political liberties guaranteed by the Weimar Constitution. Thousands of opponents (especially communists and socialists) were arrested. Although the Nazis only won 43.9% of the vote in the election, they quickly seized control of several state governments where their opponents were in power.

The Enabling Act, March 1933

The support of the 52 nationalists of the DNVP gave the Nazis a majority in parliament, but they still lacked the two-thirds majority needed to overthrow the Weimar Constitution. Hitler therefore demanded an Enabling Act, giving him full emergency powers for four years. In addition, to win the support of other centre-right parties, Hitler claimed that the Nazis shared the values of Imperial Germany, and in the first session of the Reichstag, Hitler excluded all communist deputies. By promising to respect the rights of the Catholic Church and Christian principles, Hitler persuaded the Centre Party to support his demands. As a result of these political manoeuvrings, Hitler eliminated all opposition except the SPD deputies – and thus won the Nazis a two-thirds majority.

Gleichschaltung – creating a one-party state

From this point, the Nazis began to establish a one-party totalitarian dictatorship under Hitler's leadership. This was achieved mainly through a process of *Gleichschaltung*, aimed at 'coordinating' German political, social and cultural life with Nazi ideology and values. The first targets were local government, trade unions and other political parties.

SOURCE 2.10

The Enabling Act was the constitutional foundation-stone of the Third Reich. In purely legal terms the Weimar constitution was never formally dissolved, but in practice the Enabling Act provided the basis for creating the arbitrary dictatorship which evolved in the course of 1933. The intolerance and violence exhibited by the Nazis along the road to power could now be converted into a tool of government, thus legally sanctioning the creation of a personal and party dictatorship under Hitler and the Nazis. The destruction of Weimar's remaining hallmarks of an open, liberal and pluralist society into the Nazi state system is usually referred to as Gleichschaltung – literally 'bringing into line' or, more commonly, 'coordination' ...Gleichschaltung was a deliberate attempt to Nazify the life of Germany... However, in the spring and summer of 1933 it was the 'coordination' of Germany's political system which was the real focus of attention, for the continued existence of the federal states, the political parties and a labour movement were totally at odds with Nazi political aspirations.

Layton, G. 1992. **Germany: The Third Reich 1933–45.** *London. Hodder & Stoughton. pp. 50–1.*

QUESTION

Why was the Enabling Act such an important step in establishing the Nazi dictatorship?

The provinces

Since February 1933, Nazis in the provinces (*Länder*) had been intimidating their opponents and undermining local governments in order to establish control. In April, Nazi-dominated state governments were granted the authority to make laws without having to obtain the approval of the provincial parliaments (*Landtage*). Hitler then appointed ten Nazi Reich governors (*Reichsstatthälter*), who had almost total control. In January 1934, the Law for the Reconstruction of the Reich abolished the *Landtage*, and all federal governments were placed under the control of the Ministry of the Interior.

The trade unions

Although the trade unions in Germany had a large membership, the effects of mass unemployment eroded their potential power. In addition, many trade union leaders believed that Hitler's government would soon fall, so they tried to avoid provoking the Nazis. Nonetheless, on 2 May, the SA occupied trade union buildings, and most leaders and the more militant activists were arrested. Trade unions were then abolished, and all workers were ordered to join the Nazis' German Labour Front, the *Deutsche Arbeitsfront* (DAF), which had no power to negotiate wages or working conditions.

The political parties

The elimination of opposition parties was carried out through a range of actions over a short period of time. The communist KPD was banned after the Reichstag fire. On 22 June 1933, the SPD was also abolished.

In the following weeks, the remaining political parties either merged with the Nazis or disbanded. On 14 July, Hitler imposed the Law Against the Formation of New Parties, which made the NSADP the only legal political party in Germany. Thus, within six months of being appointed chancellor, Hitler had turned Germany into a one-party dictatorship, known as the Third Reich – a great empire intended to last 1000 years.

"In these three years I have restored honor and freedom to the German people!"

Figure 2.13: A cartoon published in the US periodical *The Nation* in 1936.

The Night of the Long Knives, June 1934

Although *Gleichschaltung* had gone a long way towards establishing a Nazi dictatorship, Hitler's position was not fully consolidated. The German army had not been 'coordinated' and still had the power to overthrow him. Hitler's position was also increasingly threatened by the more militant lower sections of the NSDAP, who wanted a 'second revolution' based on the socialist sections of the party's programme.

Ernst Röhm – leader of the 2.5-million strong SA – demanded that the regular army be merged with the SA to form a new People's Army under his command.

Hitler did not want to upset the army commanders, partly because he needed their support for his foreign policy objectives, and partly because he feared that Röhm's activities might provoke the army into taking action against the new Nazi regime. He therefore needed to eliminate the threat from Röhm and the SA, and to establish his total control of the NSDAP.

On 30 June 1934, the SS (*Schutzstaffel*), the élite troops which formed Hitler's own bodyguard and were distinguished from the SA by their blackshirts and high level of discipline, arrested and shot many of the SA leaders, including Röhm. This became known as the 'Night of the Long Knives', and over the next few days more than 400 people were murdered. This action secured Hitler's popularity with the army, and when Hindenburg died on 1 August the army supported Hitler's takeover of the post of president and that position's merger with the role of chancellor. On 2 August, the army swore an oath of loyalty to the new Führer and 'supreme commander of the armed forces'.

2.8 What political policies did Hitler use to build the National Socialist state before 1939?

Terror and propaganda both played an important part in allowing the Nazis to consolidate their domination of German politics, and in enhancing Hitler's own power.

Terror and the police state

The cornerstone of the Nazi police state was the SS. By 1939, the SS and the Gestapo (the secret police) had complete power to arrest, torture and execute all 'enemies of the state'. Concentration (detention) camps were set up almost as soon as Hitler became chancellor. The first one was established at Dachau; its inmates were the communists who had been arrested after the Reichstag fire. Nazi officials called *Blockleiters* ('block leaders') supervised urban neighbourhoods, and reported to the police anyone who showed signs of not fully supporting Hitler. Many Germans, therefore, lived in constant fear of being arrested and interned in one of these camps. Documents released after 1945 show that thousands of ordinary Germans denounced their neighbours, work colleagues and even family members to the authorities.

KEY CONCEPT ACTIVITY

Perspectives: Historian Daniel Goldhagen has commented that many Germans were Hitler's 'willing executioners', and there is some evidence that there were Germans who were active participants in support of Nazi policies. Carry out some further research on this. Do your findings suggest that Goldhagen's comments are valid?

The Nazis also pushed through a 'legal revolution', which ended most of the legal rights established by the Weimar Constitution. Only judges who were considered loyal and who were trained in the ideological foundations of Nazism were appointed. As early as March 1933, a parallel Nazi legal system was also created; special courts were set up – with no juries – to administer Nazi justice more swiftly.

Theory of Knowledge

History – past and present

According to historian Bettany Hughes, *'History's job is not just to catalogue the world, but to try to comprehend it. History, can, and should, act as a moral agent.'* While history helps us understand why something happened, can it ever teach us any moral lessons that can be applied to the present? In what ways can history act as a 'moral agent'?

Propaganda, censorship and the spread of the 'Hitler myth'

The Nazi propaganda machine was run by Joseph Goebbels (see 2.5, The Nazi Party after the Munich putsch), who quickly established

Nazi control of the mass media and spread Nazi propaganda in order to unite all Germans behind their Führer. One of Goebbels' first acts as minister was to set up the Reich Radio Company which centralised all broadcasting in Germany. Fewer than 25% of German households had a radio in 1933, so the Nazis mass-produced cheap radios. By 1939, over 70% of German households owned one of these *Volksempfänger* ('people's receivers'). Radios and loudspeakers were also set up in all the main public spaces across Germany to ensure that as many people as possible heard the Nazi message.

Goebbels' first step was to ban all newspapers owned by the SPD and the KPD. Control of the press extended to the NSDAP's own publishing house, Eher Verlag, which bought many of the other remaining newspapers. By 1939, the Nazis owned more than 60% of all German newspapers. Newspapers were only allowed to print news and pictures that had been officially approved. Finally, in October 1933, the Editors' Law made editors responsible for ensuring that their newspapers' content met with the approval of Goebbels' ministry.

Nazi ideals were also publicised through literature, cinema, music and art – all of which came under the control of Goebbels' Reich Chamber of Culture, established in 1933. Under the Nazis, literature and art had to serve the Nazi state and promote values intended to bind Germans together in the new 'people's community'. Goebbels also organised mass gatherings (for example, the Nuremberg rallies) and various public celebrations to widen support for Hitler and the Third Reich. Cinemas showed newsreels covering Hitler's speeches, Nazi rallies and all important announcements.

Historians including David Schoenbaum have argued that these methods allowed the Nazis to change the values and beliefs of the German people after 1933. However, this view has been criticised by other historians such as Dick Geary, who point out that – given the fear and terror, and the lack of any alternatives – it is extremely difficult to identify what was genuine support for Nazi aims and values and what was merely passive assent.

Nazi attitudes towards the élites

Until 1938, Hitler avoided antagonising influential élite groups such as the army, the civil service, big business and landowners. The Nazis did not completely take over existing institutions – instead, they either attached themselves to established administrative organisations, or created new groups that worked in parallel with them. The army, in particular, was one organisation that avoided Nazi control throughout most of the Third Reich's rule. However, in 1938, Hitler removed some of the army's top officers and made himself supreme commander.

Personnel changes were not imposed immediately: three key ministries (War, Foreign Affairs and Economics) remained under the leadership of the traditional élites until the late 1930s. It was not until February 1938 that every ministry was headed by a high-ranking Nazi. The German civil service remained largely staffed by conservatives and nationalists, although in 1939 Nazi Party membership was made compulsory for all new recruits.

Hitler as Führer

Historians disagree over exactly how power was distributed in the Nazi state and, especially, the extent to which Hitler was the sole dictator of the Third Reich. The nature of the Nazi state was highly complex, and historians such as Jeremy Noakes regard the different organisations within Nazi Germany as semi-independent empires, acting in competition with one another. For example, although Hjalmar Schacht was minister of economics from 1934 to 1937, after 1936 he often came into conflict with the growing economic 'empire' built up by Göring under his Four-Year Plan – see 2.9, The Four-Year Plan and the development of the *Wehrwirtschaft* ('war economy'). The most powerful of these Nazi empires was the SS: its leader, Himmler, was answerable only to Hitler. Confusion has also arisen because Hitler himself never clearly stated what the relationship between the party and the state should be.

Debate about the nature and distribution of power in the Nazi state mainly concerns Hitler's supremacy and style of rule. According to Franz Neumann, although there were four power blocs in Nazi Germany (the party, the army, the bureaucracy and big business), Hitler remained in charge of them all. The importance of the personal oath of loyalty to Hitler, and the *Führerprinzip* ('leadership principle') that prevailed at all levels of party and state, ensured he remained in overall control.

However, historians are divided over whether Hitler was a strong or weak dictator. Although some have argued that he played little part in the development of economic or social policy, most agree that Hitler did play a decisive role in foreign policy, and in decisions involving war and race. Historians in the intentionalist school (such as Alan Bullock, Klaus Hildebrand and K. D. Bracher) stress that, although there was administrative confusion and rivalry, Hitler was the overall Führer or 'master of the Third Reich' and no important steps were taken without his approval. Sebastian Haffner refers to this as 'controlled chaos'.

Structuralists such as Martin Broszat and Hans Mommsen, on the other hand, believe that Hitler was lazy and weak, and often failed to give clear and consistent directions. The result of this was a chaotic 'polycratic' system. Where many intentionalists see this as a deliberate attempt by Hitler to 'divide and rule', structuralists argue that it resulted in Hitler's role being mainly to approve policies pushed by the various power blocs.

ACTIVITY

Using the internet, carry out some additional research into the historical debates about whether Hitler was a strong or weak dictator. Then write two to three paragraphs evaluating the different arguments.

2.9 What were Hitler's main economic and social policies in the years 1933 to 1939?

Nazi promises to create a new order and a classless national society led many Germans to expect a 'second revolution' as soon as power had been established. However, Hitler (like Mussolini in Italy) became ruler of Germany by cooperating with the traditional ruling élites rather than by overthrowing them. Nazi economic and social policies were therefore cautious and conservative.

The economy, 1933–39

Hitler had little interest in economic policy, but he wanted the economy to be strong enough for Germany to undertake military conquest. As early as February 1933, he began talking of the need to create a 'military economy'. The Nazis had two broad economic aims: to overcome the effects of the depression and restart the economy; and to create a *Wehrwirtschaft*, or war economy, in part by achieving German autarchy (economic self-sufficiency).

Dealing with the depression

An early indication that Nazi economic policy would not follow a revolutionary path was Hitler's appointment of Hjalmar Schacht (see 2.5) to oversee economic policy. Schacht was a conservative banker with close ties to Germany's industrialists and bankers. Although he was not a Nazi, he was president of the Reichsbank from 1933 to 1939, and from 1934 to 1937 he was also minister of economics. Schacht's appointment reassured the élites that the Nazis had no intention of harming the interests of big business.

In January 1933, unemployment stood at over 6 million – more than 30% of the labour force. By 1936, this had dropped to 1.7 million and it continued to decline, partly due to government spending on public works schemes. Subsidies and tax concessions were also given to private companies to encourage them to employ more workers. After 1935, conscription and the expansion of the armed forces also helped reduce unemployment. However, it should be noted that some credit for the rise in employment levels lies with programmes that had been set up by the last Weimar governments; in addition, the Nazis benefited from a general improvement in the world economy after 1933.

Figure 2.14: Previously unemployed men march to begin work on the first Autobahn (motorway) in September 1933.

For all his efforts, Schacht's policies led to inflation and, more seriously, a balance of payments deficit (that is, imports were costing Germany more than its exports earned). To overcome these problems, Schacht was given wide powers to deal with the economy. In September 1934, he introduced the New Plan, based on total government control of trade and currency exchange, to prioritise imports for heavy industry in general and the armaments industry in particular. He also suspended all interest payments on Germany's foreign debts. These policies had some success, and by the end of 1935 Germany had achieved a trade surplus, while industrial production was up by almost 50% from 1933.

However, there was no significant increase in exports or efficiency. Schacht's policy of printing secret government bonds (known as 'mefo' bills) to conceal the true expenditure on armaments also contributed to inflation. In addition, despite efforts to achieve self-sufficiency, Germany still needed to import raw materials for its rearmament programme. In 1936, a new economic crisis developed over the balance of payments – Schacht argued this could only be solved by reducing spending on rearmament. This ran counter to the Nazis' plans, and was opposed by the armed forces.

The Four-Year Plan and the development of the *Wehrwirtschaft* ('war economy')

Hitler's response, in September 1936, was to put Göring in charge of a plan designed to make Germany's economy and military forces ready for war in four years' time. The plan outlined the need to control all imports and exports, increase agricultural production, and make Germany self-sufficient in all important raw materials. Göring's plan was supposed to operate alongside Schacht's, but in practice Nazi control over industry increased. Schacht found his position and policies increasingly undermined, and his warnings about the balance of payments problem were ignored. He resigned in November 1937.

Large companies benefited most from Nazi rule during 1933 to 1936. However, the Four-Year Plan reduced the amount of influence big business had after 1936. The massive amounts of state money poured into research and development, and into armaments production, gave the Nazi regime increasing control over several sectors of the economy. There were also some compulsory mergers in order to create monopoly firms which, it was hoped, would be more efficient. In 1933, about 40% of German production was under monopoly control; by 1937, this had risen to over 70%.

Economic success and failure

Schacht's and Göring's plans did result in big increases in production in some key industries, and by the end of 1938 Germany's total industrial production had increased by just over 100% from its 1933 levels. During the same period, the official number of unemployed dropped to 300 000. However, the Nazis had not carried out an economic miracle, and there were several crucial failures. Firstly, the aim to be self-sufficient in raw materials failed: over 30% of Germany's main raw materials and 20% of its food still had to be imported. At the same time, rearmament also failed to reach the set targets. By 1939, therefore, Germany was not in a position to fight a long-lasting war.

As Schacht had feared, the cost of rearmament created huge problems regarding exports, gold reserves and foreign currency earnings. By 1939, with the German economy close to collapse, there was therefore a strong temptation to take advantage of weaker states. Göring believed that expansion into new territories was the only way to 'stay afloat' by obtaining extra resources.

Society, 1933–39

Just as the Nazis' economic policies tended to confirm the existing state of affairs, so too did their social interventions. Despite talk of creating a *Volksgemeinschaft* ('people's community') in many ways the Third Reich remained very similar socially to the Weimar Republic. The concept of *Volksgemeinschaft* put forward in the Nazi propaganda suggested a society in which class divides would be forgotten as all members of the state contributed productively to a national purpose. *Volksgemeinschaft* was based on blood and race. The German 'Volk' was made up of racially pure Aryans, who were to be encouraged to think of themselves as part of a master race, in which the state was superior to the individuals that comprised it. Nationalism and a common world view (*Weltanschauung*) was to bind the people together. The *Volksgenossen* ('members of this community') would be Aryan and politically and socially committed, and every member would strive towards the goals of the state, which were driven by the need for expansion and world domination. In contrast, the Nazis sought the eradication of social outsiders, and in particular racial outsiders. Aryan Germans were to be united around common nationalist and anti-Semitic goals and, for the most part, policy decisions were subordinate to this aim.

Nazism and class

Since there were significant variations in the material benefits received by different social classes in the Third Reich, social division was, in practice, perpetuated. Overall, the real benefits of the economic recovery after 1933 tended to go to the wealthy élites, and there was a clear redistribution in wealth *away* from the working classes to the upper classes.

The *Mittelstand* (middle classes) had increasingly turned to the Nazis after the depression began, and following the Nazi victory in 1933 they expected to benefit. However, few of the earlier Nazi promises to help small businesses were carried out. The Law for the Protection of the Retail Trade, which was passed in 1933, placed some general restrictions on further expansion of large department stores. Significantly, however, these were not closed down and, in fact, the five main department store chains experienced a 10% growth in the years 1936 to 1939. Then, in 1937, the Nazis placed restrictions on setting up small businesses.

The farming community had been attracted by Nazi promises of financial support and propaganda which suggested that the German peasant farmer, whose very life was dependent on the German soil and whose background was rooted in German tradition, was the ideal German citizen. The smaller peasant farmers did gain in some ways. For example, a significant number had their farm debts written off. There was also an increase in food prices of about 20%, following the introduction of the Reich Entailed Farm Law of 1933. Walther Darré, as Minister of Food and Agriculture, ensured strict controls over food production and sales; targets, output quotas and prices were all laid down by the government. Darré's work brought some improvements in the years 1933 to 1937. However, the main beneficiaries of Nazi economic policy were the owners of the larger estates and commercial farms and there was a continued flight from the land to the cities where standards of living were higher.

Once trade unions were banned in May 1933, industrial workers had no way of obtaining pay increases or of resisting any decline in working conditions. Although their material situation improved in the period 1933 to 1939 as a result of the reduction in unemployment, national and regional wage rates were abolished and were replaced by individual piece-rates – by which each person's wage depended on how much they produced, rather than the number of hours they worked. The Nazi DAF, which replaced independent trade unions, prevented workers from asking for increased wages; instead, DAF trustees set wage levels that were acceptable to the employers. As a result, industrial workers did not regain the level of real wages that they had enjoyed before the depression until 1938. Workers did benefit from rent controls, as well as the recreational opportunities provided by the *Kraft durch Freude* ('strength through joy', KDF) scheme. However, even here the benefits were limited, as these tended to go to white-collar workers and the better-off skilled manual workers.

Policies towards young people

The Nazis believed that the long-term future of their *Volksgemeinschaft* lay with the young, and they adopted several different approaches to impress Nazi ideology on young people across Germany.

In 1934, Hitler's government created a centrally controlled system under the Reich Ministry of Education and Science, and changed the school curriculum. In German and history lessons, nationalism, militarism, the different roles of men and women, and the greatness of Hitler and the NSDAP were all emphasised. In biology classes, 'race science' indoctrinated children with the Nazis' racist ideas. The Nazis also purged the teaching professions of any politically unreliable or 'racially unsuitable' members, while others were sent on special 'reconditioning' courses. The universities were also 'Nazified' – in all, over 3000 lecturers and professors were sacked for political or racial reasons.

Central to creating the new *Volksgemeinschaft* generation were the various Nazi youth organisations. These included the *Deutsches Jungvolk* (German Young People, DJ) and the *Hitler Jugend* (Hitler Youth, HJ) for boys aged 10 to 14 and 14 to 18 respectively. For girls, the corresponding organisations were the *Jungmädelbund* (League of Young Girls, JM) and the *Bund Deutscher Mädel* (League of German Girls, BDM). At the end of the 1930s, membership of these groups was made compulsory; however, recent research suggests that many young Germans were not won over by the Nazis, and tried to avoid membership.

Policies towards women

Nazi ideology and *Volksgemeinschaft* plans were utterly opposed to social and economic equality for women, and thus to the educational and employment rights that women had gained during the period of the Weimar Republic. The Nazis' attitude to women was summed up in the 'three Ks' slogan: *Kinder, Küche, Kirche* ('children, kitchen, church'). The Nazis believed that women should not be involved in politics or paid employment – the home was their domain, and they should confine themselves to the role of mother and homemaker.

Although women retained the right to vote, they were no longer allowed to be political representatives, and were barred from being judges. The new Nazi government implemented several policies to drive women out of the workplace and back into the home. Between 1933 and 1936, married women were excluded from employment in various professions, and legislation was introduced to dramatically reduce the number of female teachers and university students.

In June 1933, interest-free loans were given to all young women who gave up employment in order to get married. Employers and labour exchanges were told to favour men rather than women.

SOURCE 2.11

The slogan 'Emancipation of Women' was invented by Jewish intellectuals and its content was formed by the same spirit. In the really good times of German life, the German woman had no need to emancipate herself...

If the man's world is said to be the State, his struggle, his readiness to devote his powers to the service of the community, then it may perhaps be said that the woman's is a smaller world. For her world is her husband, her family, her children and her home... The two worlds... complement each other... We do not consider it correct for the woman to interfere in the world of the man, in his main sphere. We consider it natural if these two worlds remain distinct.

Extracts from Hitler's 'Address to Women' at the Nuremberg Party Rally, 8 September 1934. Quoted in Laver, J. 1991. **Nazi Germany 1933–1945.** *London. Hodder & Stoughton. pp. 63–4.*

QUESTION

Assess the value and limitations of Source 2.11 in understanding the Nazis' attitude towards women and the role played by women in the Nazi state?

The Nazis then tried to increase Germany's birth rate. Laws against abortion were enforced, birth-control clinics were closed and contraception was increasingly restricted. At the same time, maternity benefits and family allowances were increased. Newlyweds were offered loans, and women who had large families were awarded the Honour Cross of the German Mother.

The results of these Nazi policies were mixed. Although the percentage of women in paid employment in the period 1932 to 1937 dropped from 37% to 31%, the actual numbers increased from about 5 million to 6 million. Then, from 1937 to 1939, both the percentage and the numbers increased – from 31% to 33%, and from 6 million to just over 7 million. In part, this was the result of labour shortages caused by conscription and rearmament after 1935. Women who were well-qualified, however, never regained the position and status they had enjoyed under the Weimar Republic.

Policies towards 'outsiders'

While membership of the Nazis' *Volksgemeinschaft* was open to all 'good Aryans', several categories were seen as outsiders or 'a-socials', and were specifically excluded from the Nazi community.

Minority groups increasingly persecuted by the Nazis included people with hereditary physical disabilities or mental problems, Roma and Sinti, gay men and lesbians, and homeless people. More than 300 000 of these people were forcibly sterilised under the 1933 Law for the Prevention of Offspring with Hereditary Disease. Members of 'a-social' groups also later became Holocaust victims in the concentration and death camps.

DISCUSSION POINT

Form four groups. Each group should carry out some research into the ways in which one of the non-Jewish minorities identified in this section was persecuted by the Nazis in the years 1933 to 1939. Each group should prepare a presentation for the others.

Right from the start, Jews were specifically excluded from the Nazi community. Anti-Semitism was the central policy of the Nazis' *Volksgemeinschaft*, based on their belief in the 'superiority' of the Aryan race. Hitler's appointment as chancellor allowed him to take action against the Jewish community – although in 1933, there were fewer than 500 000 Jewish people in Germany (about 1% of the population).

From 1933 to 1938, the Nazis moved cautiously, mainly restricting themselves to legislative measures. In April 1933, Hitler announced an official boycott of all Jewish shops and professional services. Although this was not widely supported – and was quickly dropped because of opposition and ineffectiveness – it was almost immediately followed by the Law for the Restoration of the Professional Civil Service, which removed all Jewish people from government posts. Jews were also officially classified as 'non–Aryans'. Further laws in 1934 banned them from other professions and from the media.

The Nuremberg race laws of 1935 took anti-Semitic policies even further. The Reich Citizenship Act deprived German Jews of all civil rights, while another law banned sexual relations or marriage between Jews and other German citizens. In 1937, measures were taken to remove Jewish people from the professions and from business – this was known as 'Aryanisation'. Propaganda depicting Jewish people as the 'polluters' of the Aryan race increased, and Jewish children were humiliated in front of their classmates in schools.

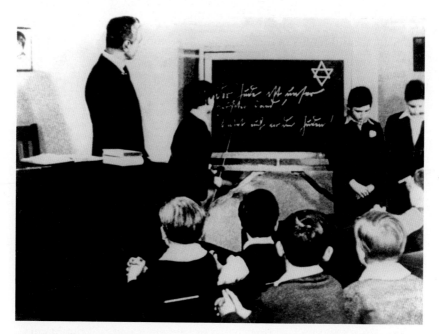

Figure 2.15: A scene from a US documentary showing two German Jewish boys next to a blackboard which reads 'The Jews are our greatest enemy! Beware of the Jews!'

QUESTION

What can you learn from Figure 2.15 about Nazi policies towards Jewish people and how other Germans responded to such policies?

From 1938, the Nazi campaign became more violent. First, over
15 000 Polish Jews living in Germany were expelled and, in July, Jewish
people were banned from all commerce. At the same time, all Jews were
forced to have 'Jewish' forenames such as Israel or Sarah, to register all
the wealth or property they possessed, and to carry identity cards and
internal passports.

In November 1938, the Nazis led an attack on the Jews that became
known as Kristallnacht ('Night of the Broken Glass'), after all the
smashed windows. Thousands of Jewish homes, shops and synagogues
were destroyed and more than 100 Jews were killed; 25 000 more were
sent to concentration camps. Later that month, all Jewish pupils were
expelled from state schools. In December, Jewish businesses were closed
and sold off, and all Jews in skilled jobs were sacked.

By 1938, almost 150 000 Jewish people had emigrated; yet around
300 000 stayed on, in the hope that the persecution might eventually
lessen. When all Jewish valuables were confiscated in April 1939, leaving
the country became much more difficult as Jews could no longer buy or
bribe their way out. In addition, few countries were prepared to accept
any significant number of impoverished immigrants. By 1939, Jewish
people had been 'eliminated' from economic, political, social, cultural
and legal life in Germany. After the outbreak of the Second World War
in 1939, Nazi treatment of Jewish people worsened. As early as January
1939, Hitler threatened that any outbreak of war in Europe would result
in the 'annihilation of the Jewish race'. Ultimately, almost 6 million Jews
and 5 million others (including Roma and Sinti, gay men and lesbians)
were slaughtered in the Holocaust under the Nazi regime.

ACTIVITY

Carry out some further research into Nazi anti-Semitic policies in
the years 1933 to 1939. Draw up a timeline, giving details of the
dates, main laws and events, and the terms of those laws.

Policies towards the Churches

Germany was an overwhelmingly Christian country with Protestants
forming 58% of the population and Catholics, 32%. Hitler's
determination to set up an Aryanised social community left little room
for religion, but he appreciated that religion could be 'used' to reinforce

National Socialism – with which the Christian Churches shared a good deal of common ideological ground in their dislike of Marxism, their conservatism, their belief in family values and their underlying anti-Semitism (even if in principle they spoke out against it).

The Protestant Church

In May 1933, Hitler set up a new national people's church' – the 'Reich Church'. **Ludwig Müller** was appointed as the Reich bishop and given the task of coordinating the Protestant churches under his authority. This move was supported by a pro-Nazi group which styled itself the 'German Christians', who were given senior posts. They became the SA of the Church, wearing swastika armbands and adopting the motto 'the swastika on our breasts and the cross in our hearts'.

Ludwig Müller (1883–1946):

He held strongly nationalist and anti-Semitic views and was a staunch Nazi supporter. He became influential in the association of German Christians and in 1933 was appointed as the country's Reich bishop of the Protestant Church. However, he was increasingly marginalised and committed suicide in 1946.

However, not all German protestants approved of this move and in September 1933, a group of 100 pastors headed by **Martin Niemöller** set up the Pastors' Emergency League to defend traditional Lutheranism. This became the Confessional Church in 1934. Despite some initial Nazi attempts to arrest those who resisted their Reich Church, for the most part, the Confessional Church was allowed to continue in its spiritual role and, despite some harassment from the state authorities, gained strong support in some areas.

Martin Niemöller (1892–1984):

He was a co-founder of the Confessional Church. In 1933, he was working as a Protestant pastor in Berlin where he initially welcomed Hitler as chancellor. However, he opposed Hitler's efforts to politicise the Church. He was arrested in 1937 for his outspokenness and sent to Sachsenhausen concentration camp. During his time in prison he repudiated his earlier anti-Semitism. He was released by the Allies in 1945.

Overall the Protestant Church suffered less from direct persecution than from attempts to curb its activities. Church schools were abolished and religious teaching downgraded in schools, but direct attacks on the Church were only sporadic and uncoordinated, with some Gauleiters being far more anti-religious than others.

The Catholic Church

The Catholic Church came to terms with the Nazis in July 1933, signing a concordat, by which the Pope recognised the Nazi regime and promised not to interfere in politics (accepting the dissolution of the Centre Party), while the Nazis promised not to interfere in the spiritual role of the Catholic Church, which was to keep control over its educational, youth and communal organisations.

However, between 1933 and 1939, the Nazis went back on their promises. Propaganda was used to encourage anti-Catholic feeling, Catholic organisations and societies were closed down and from 1936 all youth organisations disbanded, while Catholic schools were removed and had almost disappeared by 1939.

In 1937, Pope Pius XI issued the encyclical *With Burning Anxiety* (*Mit Brennender Sorge*), attacking Nazi beliefs. This was smuggled into Germany and read out in Catholic churches. However, his successor in 1939, Pius XII, failed to condemn Nazism outright and has been criticised for his tolerance of the regime.

Bishop Galen's protest against euthanasia in 1941 was the most outspoken criticism to come from a Catholic prelate but, although between a third and a half of Catholic clergy were harassed by the regime, only one Catholic bishop was expelled and one imprisoned for any length of time, suggesting that protest against the Nazis was limited.

The German Faith Movement

In the mid-1930s, a Nazi 'Church Secession' campaign deliberately encouraged Germans to turn away from Christianity and some Nazis, although not Hitler himself, encouraged a pagan 'German Faith Movement'. Members rejected Christian ethics and returned to pagan practices. They believed in the *Blut und Boden* (blood and soil) ideology of the Nazis and enjoyed ceremonies such as sun-worship at the solstice. This small sect attracted only about 200000 supporters, but it was particularly strong among the SS.

Although some individuals opposed Nazism, for the most part both the Protestant and Catholic Churches accepted Nazi political leadership. However, Christianity as a faith was little affected. Church attendance remained steady, and Christian belief can be seen as a limitation to a fully National Socialist state.

2.10 What was the nature of the Nazi state?

The National Socialist state was an authoritarian one-party regime. At the top Hitler possessed unlimited power as Führer and, in theory, through his Reich cabinet, state governors and Nazi party organisations, could ensure that, under his direction, party and state worked together to fulfil his ideological principles. However, Hitler's control and the influence of National Socialism was not as pervasive as might have been expected.

Some historians, notably the German Martin Broszat, have referred to the Nazi regime as a confused, 'polycratic' system, because Hitler superimposed his party structure on to the state that he took over and deliberately generated competition between individuals and groups within it. For example, ministers had ill-defined responsibilities leading, for example to the rivalry between Hermann Göring and Albert Speer over the management of the economy. There was also considerable overlap between the duties of civil servants and party officials and Hitler deliberately encouraged competition. Policy decisions were often little more than a matter of guesswork on the part of ministers and officials who sought to 'work towards the Führer', and carry through measures they believed he would approve of.

Having no clearly organised pattern to government was partly the result of Hitler's fundamental laziness and lack of interest in bureaucratic detail, but it also fitted his ideological belief in the survival of the fittest and provided an opt-out if things went wrong. Hitler only intervened when it suited him. According to structuralist historians such as Theodor Mommsen, Ian Kershaw, Jeremy Noakes and Martin Broszat, this produced a chaotic governmental structure and a confusion of authority. They describe Hitler as a 'weak dictator'.

However, members of an alternative historical school of intentionalist historians, such as Karl Dietrich Bracher and Hugh Trevor-Roper, have suggested that the overlapping of interests was deliberate and that the internal rivalries reinforced Hitler's powerful position, since he was able to take the praise for effective policies and blame others for ineffective ones. As a powerful integrating figure at the centre of government, they have described him as a 'strong dictator'.

The Nazis never achieved the full 'totalitarian control' which they sought over politics, the economy – which largely remained in private hands – or society. The 'National Community' which they sought eluded them. Compromises were made and even though Nazi Germany was radicalised, through a mixture of ideology and Hitler's own personality, to create a state upheld by the SS–Police–SD system and capable of conducting the savage persecution of its enemies, it was never the masterful state that the propagandists tried to suggest.

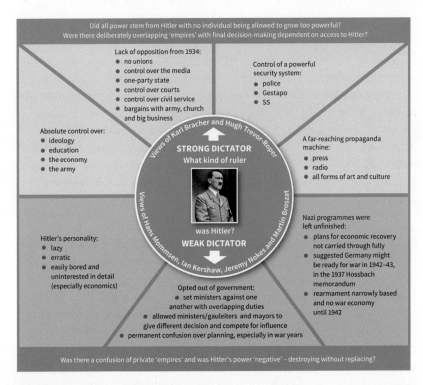

Figure 2.16: Hitler's strengths and weaknesses as a dictator.

2.11 What was the extent of resistance to the Nazi state?

In the years from 1934 to 1939, there was very little opposition to Nazi rule in Germany. This was partly the result of propaganda, repression and the general success of Hitler's policies both at home and abroad. After the initial rounding up of political dissidents, particularly Socialists and Communists, and the suppression of dissenting voices in the SA between 1933 and 1934, resistance was generally low-key and took place in private. Some simply grumbled or told anti-Nazi jokes, while others read banned literature, listened to foreign news broadcasts, protected Jews and other Nazi victims or refused to join Nazi organisations or contribute to national campaigns. Such behaviour was, nevertheless, quite daring as punishments could be severe.

Some young people also resisted Nazi dictates. Middle-class teenagers, for example, joined the Swing Movement, which perpetuated the freer moral values of the earlier Weimar Republic, seen by the Nazis as degenerate. Members listened to jazz music and dressed and behaved in an American/Western way. Those from working-class backgrounds were more attracted to the Edelweiss Pirates (a broad term for various groups set up in German cities). The 'pirates' similarly adopted 'freer' social attitudes and engaged in their own outdoor activities, such as hikes and camps, in opposition to the Hitler Youth. Neither group was strongly political but showed resentment of Nazi control and a desire to defy authority.

There was some more overt public opposition. Some brave Socialists, for example, continued to distribute anti-Nazi leaflets or wrote slogans in public places. The SPD continued to operate from a base in Prague, organising underground groups such as the Berlin Red Patrol and the Hanover Socialist Front within Germany. Resistance generally took the form of sporadic absenteeism, strikes and sabotage, but in November 1939, a socialist cabinet-maker, Georg Elser, came near to assassinating Hitler when he planted a bomb in a beer hall where the Führer was to speak. He only failed because Hitler left the hall early. The KPD also formed underground cells, particularly in Berlin, Mannheim, Hamburg and central Germany, from where they operated secret printing presses producing material attacking the regime. The Rote Kapelle (Red Orchestra), formed in 1935, was a particularly well-organised

Communist resistance network that gathered information to send to Russia.

There were also a number of churchmen, such as the Protestant Martin Niemöller and the Catholic Bishop Galen (see 2.8, Policies towards the Churches) who spoke out against Nazi policies. Another prominent Protestant resistor was Pastor Dietrich Bonhoeffer, an academic theologian and member of the Kreisau Circle, which started meeting at the home of Helmut von Moltke in the 1930s. This group comprised aristocrats, lawyers, SPD politicians and churchmen who sought ways to remove Hitler.

Resistance also festered within the army, where some generals resented the role of the SS (and even Hitler himself) and the pace of rearmament and plans for war against Russia, the traditional ally of the Prussian landed nobility (Junkers) which dominated the officer class. At the Hossbach Conference of November 1937, the Commander-in-Chief, Werner von Fritsch, and the War Minister, General Werner von Blomberg, directly opposed Hitler's strategies; both were dismissed on trumped-up charges as a result. Thereafter Hitler became his own war minister, and in an attempt to ensure obedience, 16 generals were forced to relinquish their positions and 44 others were transferred. This did not, however, end all resistance and many aristocratic officers remained suspicious of Hitler and were to join resistance movements in the war years.

It is difficult to give any reliable estimate of the extent of resistance to Nazism in the years of peace and as a percentage of the population. The numbers convicted of 'political crimes' were low, c. 225 000 with a further 162 000 in 'protective custody' or prison without trial between 1933 and 1939. Resistance was firmly dealt with by the security police but the limited evidence of resistance would suggest that most ordinary Germans were ready to accept or actively support the Nazi regime.

Summary activity

Copy the spider diagram below to show the policies adopted in Hitler's Germany during the period 1933–39. Then, using the information from this unit, and any other sources available to you, extend the diagram. Make sure you include, where relevant, brief comments about different historical debates/interpretations.

Paper 3 exam practice

Question

To what extent was Hitler successful in establishing a '*Volksgemeinschaft*' in Germany in the years 1933 to 1939? **[15 marks]**

Skill

Planning an essay

Examiner's tips

The first stage of planning an answer is to think carefully about the wording of the question, so that you know what is required and what you need to focus on. Once you have done this, you can start your planning.

This question clearly invites you to make a judgement about the success and extent of Hitler's policy of *Volkgemeinschaft*, weighing up its positive and successful aspects against its failures and limitations. You will obviously need to demonstrate your understanding of the concept of Volksgemeinschaft and you will probably want to consider its impact on the different German classes, young people, women, outsiders and the Churches. The question will also require some assessment of resistance.

Your essay will need to be in three parts: an introductory paragraph, a developed argument across a number of paragraphs (in which you present a case supported by precise evidence) and a concluding paragraph. You should begin by planning the body of the essay – your argument.

Create a plan by drawing up three columns headed topic: positive and negative, respectively. In the first column, on the left, make a list of the topic areas you want to address. You may wish to subdivide these – for example you will want to consider different groups within your section on classes. Use the other columns to record evidence to support success (positive points) and failure or limitations (negative points).

Reflect on what you have written and decide what argument (or 'thesis') you will adopt. You may wish to note this down, as it will be the basis for your introduction and conclusion and you must ensure that these are consistent.

There are a few further points to remember for a well-planned essay:

- Your essay needs to **convey a single view** but should show **balance** – in other words you need to look at both positives and negatives but comment on which side is the stronger. Your plan should enable you to keep your essay balanced.
- You should try to **link** the points you make in your paragraphs, both to the question and to the preceding paragraph, so that there is a clear thread that develops naturally, leading to your conclusion. Linking words and ideas help to ensure that your essay is not just a series of unconnected paragraphs.
- You should not spend too long on any one aspect and must avoid wandering off into narrative description.

Common mistakes

It is very easy to adopt an overly one-sided view – 'No, Hitler did not succeed in creating a *Volkgemeninschaft*…' A more sophisticated answer might suggest that he was more successful in some areas than in others. Linking different arguments can be difficult, but it is a good way of achieving the highest marks. Always consider the **full demands** of a question before you begin, and remember – constant reference to your plan will help you to keep focused.

Sample planning suggestions

There are many ways of planning essays, and which to use depends on the wording of the question.

'To what extent' questions can generally be planned using the two-column approach, but in 'analyse' questions, you may find that a spider diagram is more appropriate. Write the topic you have been asked to analyse in the centre and break it down into elements, recording a few examples on each 'leg'. In 'compare and contrast' questions, a two-table plan will be needed. Use one table to record differences, and the other for similarities. However, you will only need one table for questions beginning 'compare' (assessing similarities) *or* 'contrast' (assessing differences), in which you think of suitable common aspects and note specific examples.

Questions beginning 'discuss' or 'evaluate' can be more problematic. The crucial requirement in these is for you to think thematically, and after jotting down your initial ideas, you should create a plan that groups your thoughts so that you can present these in a logical way.

Activity

In this unit, the focus is on planning answers. Using the information from this unit, and any other sources of information available to you, produce some different essay plans – with all the necessary headings (and brief details) for well-focused and clearly structured responses – to **at least two** of the following Paper 3 practice questions.

Remember to refer to the simplified Paper 3 mark scheme in Chapter 6.

Paper 3 practice questions

1 Examine the impact of the Great Depression on the rise of the Nazi party between 1929 and 1933.

2 Discuss the importance of terror in maintaining Nazi control in Germany under the Third Reich between 1933 and 1939.

3 Evaluate the success of Hitler's economic policies between 1933 and 1939.

4 To what extent is it appropriate to describe Hitler as a 'strong dictator'?

5 Compare aspects of the resistance to the Nazi regime in the years 1933 to 1939.

6 Compare and contrast the rise to power of Hitler and Mussolini. (You will not be able to attempt this question until you have studied Chapter 3, Unit 1.)

3 | Italy

Unit 1: From Liberalism to Fascism, 1918–24

Introduction

In 1918, Italy was a monarchy with a liberal political system. Yet, only four years after the end of the First World War, Italy became the first European state in the interwar period to see the coming to power of a fascist movement. Many of the long-term factors behind the emergence of **Benito Mussolini** as fascist dictator of Italy can be found in Italy's weaknesses before 1918.

> ### Benito Mussolini (1883–1945):
>
> He followed an inconsistent political path in his early years. Initially more influenced by his father (a blacksmith with revolutionary socialist views) than by his mother (a school teacher and a devout Catholic), Mussolini drifted into socialist politics and journalism. Between 1904 and 1910, he developed a reputation as a militant as a result of articles in which he expressed traditional socialist views. However, when the First World War began, he rapidly abandoned his early 'beliefs' and instead supported Italy's involvement in the war. This resulted in his expulsion from the Socialist Party – soon, his political leanings moved towards a far-right ultra-nationalism that was violently opposed to socialism and communism. From 1919 to 1921, Mussolini formed Europe's first Fascist Party and, from 1922, began to establish a Fascist dictatorship in Italy. He was overthrown in 1943. In 1945, towards the end of the Second World War, he was captured and executed.

Italy – as a unified and independent state – was only formed in the period 1861–70, after many decades of struggle against the Austrian Empire. However, the people of the new kingdom were far from united.

TIMELINE

1861 Formation of an independent Italy

1870 Papal states incorporated into Italian kingdom

1915 **May:** Italy signs Treaty of London and enters First World War

1919 **Jan:** Start of *biennio rosso*; first Arditi Association set up in Rome

   Mar: Formation of Fasci di Combattimento

1920 Sep: Wave of factory occupations and electoral victories for socialists

1921 May: Mussolini forms National Bloc electoral alliance with Giolitti; 35 fascists elected, including Mussolini

Aug: Pact of Pacification between fascists and socialists

Oct: Formation of National Fascist Party (PNF)

Nov: Mussolini elected leader of PNF

1922 Jul–Aug: General strike broken up by fascist violence

Oct: March on Rome; Mussolini appointed prime minister

Nov: Mussolini given emergency powers for one year

Dec: Formation of Fascist Grand Council

1923 Jan: Formation of National Fascist Militia (MVSN)

Jul: Acerbo Law

Aug: Corfu Incident

1924 Mar: Fascist violence against opposition

Apr: Fascists and allies win a large majority in election

Jun: Matteotti murdered

Aug: Aventine Secession

KEY QUESTIONS
- What was the condition of Italy before 1918?
- What were the main problems affecting Italy in the years 1918–22?
- What political factors aided the rise of Mussolini's Fascist Party, 1919–20?
- How did Mussolini become prime minister in 1922?
- What were Mussolini's main actions, 1922–24?

Overview

- Italy's various political and economic problems before 1914 were worsened by entry into the First World War. The war led to high casualties and inflation. After the war, there was disappointment at Italy's limited territorial gains from the peace treaties, as well as higher unemployment.

- Between 1919 and 1922, many socialist-led strikes and factory occupations took place. Right-wing groups such as the *Arditi* and the *Fasci di Combattimento* used increasing violence against the left.
- In 1921, Mussolini established the National Fascist Party (*Partito Nazionale Fascista*, PNF) and then made an electoral pact with the liberals. A new wave of fascist violence was often ignored by the élites and the authorities.
- In 1922, local fascist leaders began to take over various towns and regions and, in October, their 'March on Rome' resulted in Mussolini being appointed prime minister of a coalition government in Italy.
- Mussolini was still not head of a Fascist government. So he began to take steps to increase his power over both the state and his own party.
- Securing the support of the Catholic Church and industrialists, in 1923 Mussolini pushed through a reform of the electoral system.
- In the 1924 election, using a variety of methods, the PNF became the largest party.
- However, the murder of Giacomo Matteotti by a fascist gang after that election, almost led to Mussolini losing power.

3.1 What was the condition of Italy before 1918?

Before the First World War, Italy experienced many problems. These included a severely restricted franchise (right to vote): it was only in 1912 that all men were given the right to vote. In addition, the system known as *trasformismo*, by which liberal groups dominated the political system, undermined support for parliamentary politics. At the same time, economic and social divisions – especially between the more prosperous industrial north and the poorer agricultural south – resulted in significant disunity. One result of these problems was increasing opposition from a growing socialist movement.

Italian politics and the impact of *trasformismo*

After unification, Italian politics were dominated by the liberals, who hoped to modernise Italy through social reforms such as state education (to break the conservative influence of the Catholic Church), and by stimulating economic development and progress. However, although the liberals were split into progressives and conservatives – or 'left-liberals' and 'conservative-liberals' – they were united in distrusting the masses, who had played little part in the struggle for unification.

The liberals also particularly feared the influence of socialists, anarchists and republicans on the left and the Catholic Church on the right. All of these groups were opposed to the new Italian state. Consequently, the liberals were determined to keep politics firmly under their control until the old internal divisions and rivalries were overcome and the new state was secure. The electorate was thus restricted at first, with only about 2% of the adult population allowed to vote.

The resentment many Italians felt at this restricted franchise was increased by the corrupt politics it encouraged. With no mass parties, and no real party discipline among the liberals, leading politicians formed factions that made deals with one another to alternate political control. This process became known as *trasformismo*, and was in part intended to 'transform' Italy's political life and bring about widespread national support for Italy's recent unification. Even though the franchise was gradually extended, and all adult males were allowed to vote by 1912, the practice of *trasformismo* continued.

> **QUESTION**
>
> How did the practice of *trasformismo* undermine support for parliamentary democracy in Italy before 1922?

Political disunity in Italy was intensified by the hostility of the papacy to the new Italian state. Papal opposition to the liberal regime was moderated during the 1890s out of fear that it might give way to socialism, and in 1904, the pope permitted Catholics to vote in constituencies where abstaining might result in a socialist victory. However, there was no real harmony between the liberal and Catholic powers.

Regional divisions

In addition to these political problems, many Italians felt more loyalty towards their own town or region than towards the national government. The mountain ranges and islands that dominate Italy's geography made communication difficult, hindering the development of a truly national identity among the country's 38 million people. This was especially true in the south, where earlier rulers had deliberately neglected road and railway development in an attempt to stop the spread of liberal and revolutionary ideas from the north.

The problems of communication and transport also contributed to economic divisions in Italy. The south was very poor in comparison with northern and central areas. Land suitable for farming in the south was restricted by geography and climate, and most of the fertile lands were part of large estates known as *latifundia*, which were owned by a small minority of wealthy landowners. The vast majority of the population was extremely poor.

Figure 3.1: Subsistence farmers in rural southern Italy, c.1900.

In northern and central Italy agriculture was more developed, and more modern farming methods and machinery were used. Even here, however, productivity was much lower than in the countries of northern Europe. There were also significant social divisions in even the more advanced agricultural areas. Most of the land was owned by wealthy landowners known as the *agrari*, who rented out land to poorer farmers and peasant sharecroppers. At the bottom of the social scale was a large class of rural labourers. As in the south, poverty and discontent in rural areas often led to conflict between the classes. The biggest economic difference between north and south, however, was in industry.

The Fiat car company was established in 1899, and by 1913 it was exporting over 4000 cars a year. Towns and cities in the north grew rapidly. This led to the creation of a large industrial working class, a sizeable lower-middle class, and a powerful class of rich industrialists and bankers. While industry expanded in the north, however, there was no real investment in the south.

As with agriculture, the social and economic inequalities in the industrial towns led to frequent clashes between employers and employees. Many workers joined the socialists or the anarchists, and in 1904 a general strike took place. The dissatisfaction felt by many Italians led them to emigrate – the majority going to the USA.

The problems of *terra irredenta* and the desire for empire

After 1870 – when the Roman Catholic Church finally recognised the new kingdom of Italy – many Italians felt that Italy was still not complete. Firstly, there were the lands in Europe known as *terra irredenta*, ('unredeemed land') which many Italians wanted Italy to have. This term originally referred to the areas inhabited by many Italian speakers but still ruled by Austria-Hungary in the early 20th century. The most important of these were Trentino and Trieste, in the northern Adriatic. Later, this term would also designate other surrounding foreign territories to which Italy believed that it had a rightful claim. Those who advocated this policy of territory reclamation were called 'irredentists'.

In addition, many Italians hoped that unification would enable Italy to join the top rank of European powers by establishing its own empire. They looked to the example set by Germany – newly created in 1871 – which had started to obtain colonies in Africa and Asia. The first step in Italian empire-building was taken in 1885, with the acquisition of the port of Massawa on the Red Sea. By 1890, this had become the centre of the Italian colony of Eritrea. At the same time, Italy began the conquest of what became Italian Somaliland. However, tensions grew between Italy and the independent African state of Abyssinia (now Ethiopia), which bordered both of these regions.

In 1911, Italy invaded the Turkish colony of Libya in an attempt to increase the size of the Italian empire and to block growing French influence in North Africa. In 1912, Turkey formally accepted its loss. Many Italian nationalists, still angry at their defeat by Abyssinia in 1896, continued to press for a more aggressive imperial policy.

3.2 What were the main problems affecting Italy in the years 1918–22?

Italy's problems were made worse by its entry into the First World War in 1915. The high casualties resulting from the war, the subsequent inflation, and Italy's limited territorial gains from the peace settlements of 1919 and 1920, led to increased tensions after 1919.

For these reasons, the postwar liberal government in Italy experienced several challenges. In addition to the increasingly dissatisfied nationalists, the liberals faced political opposition from other groups, including the Catholic Church. Previously, the papacy had banned any Catholic political party in Italy, but in January 1919 this ban was lifted, leading to the foundation of the Italian Popular Party (*Partito Popolare Italiano*, PPI). More serious threats to the liberals came from both the political left and, especially, the right.

Although Italy was a member of the Triple Alliance (the military alliance formed in 1882 between Germany, Austria and Italy), it did not join in when the First World War began in 1914. Instead, it decided to stay neutral.

Italy's involvement in the First World War

While most Italians (especially the socialists) were in favour of neutrality, nationalists felt that intervention in the war would offer Italy an opportunity to gain more land and expand its empire. In view of its ambition to reclaim the country's *terra irredenta*, the liberal government decided to see which side would offer the best terms in exchange for Italy's support. Negotiations with the other two Triple Alliance nations in the period 1914–15 revealed that Austria would never concede Trentino or Trieste. However, the nations of the Triple Entente (the military alliance between Britain, France and Russia) promised that in the event of their victory, these territories would be granted to Italy, along with similarly contested Austrian territory in the South Tyrol, and Istria and northern Dalmatia on the Adriatic coast.

The Treaty of London

While the Italian parliament debated the issues, interventionists organised street demonstrations demanding Italian involvement in the war. Many were members of the *fasci*, a mixture of anarcho-syndicalists (see Mussolini and the *Fasci di Combattimento* below) and national socialists who believed war would hasten revolution. They were joined by the right-wing nationalists of the *Associazione Nazionalista Italiana* (ANI) – the Italian Nationalist Association – which had been formed in 1910, and which had previously pushed for the conquest of Libya. The ANI (which soon grew close to Mussolini's Fascist Party, and merged with it in 1923) saw war against Austria as a way of gaining the *terra irredenta*. However, the leading liberal politicians had already decided on Italy's participation in the war. Consequently, in May 1915, Italy signed the Treaty of London and promised to join the war on the side of the Triple Entente.

Italy's performance in the First World War

Despite the interventionists' hopes, the war did not go well for Italy. Over 5 million Italians were conscripted and, though most fought bravely, they were ill-equipped and ill-supplied. In particular, military leadership was often poor and the Italian army found itself fighting a costly war of attrition.

In November 1917, the Italians suffered a terrible defeat at the hands of the Austrians at the Battle of Caporetto. Over 40 000 Italian soldiers were killed and about 300 000 were taken prisoner. The nationalists blamed the government for its inefficiency and for failing to supply the troops with enough equipment. Although the Italians won a costly victory at Vittorio Veneto in October 1918, this was overshadowed by previous defeats and the high casualties suffered. In all, over 600 000

Italians were killed, about 450 000 were permanently disabled, and a further 500 000 were seriously wounded. In addition, with the socialists maintaining strong opposition throughout, the war had clearly failed to unite Italians.

The 'mutilated victory': the terms of the peace treaties

When the war ended in November 1918, many Italians thought that their sacrifices should be repaid by substantial territorial rewards. **Vittorio Orlando**, the Italian prime minister, went to the Paris Peace Conferences in January 1919 expecting to receive all that had been promised by the Treaty of London. Under pressure from the nationalists, he also demanded the port of Fiume on the border of Istria as it contained a large Italian-speaking population. Finally, Orlando wanted Italy to gain a share of the former German colonies in Africa.

> **Vittorio Orlando (1860–1952):**
>
> He was appointed prime minister a few days after the Italian defeat at Caporetto in October 1917. At the Paris Peace Conferences, Italy had expected to be granted control of the Adriatic coastline. Orlando's failure to win this territory prompted his resignation in June 1919. His inability to secure all of Italy's territorial expectations at Versailles was used by Mussolini and the fascists in their campaign to demonstrate the weakness of the Italian government. Orlando initially backed Mussolini in 1922, but he withdrew his support in 1924.

Although most of Italy's postwar demands were eventually met, there were some important exceptions. The country gained no African territory, and Britain and the US refused to grant Italy Fiume and northern Dalmatia, arguing that these were vital for the development of the new state of Yugoslavia.

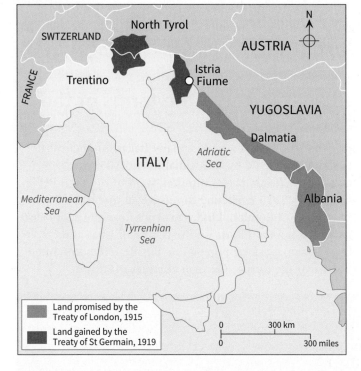

Figure 3.2: The land promised by the Treaty of London in 1915 and land actually gained by Italy in the 1919 peace treaties.

Italy's long-term opponent, Austria-Hungary, had been defeated and its empire dismantled, leaving Italy the dominant power in the Adriatic. Yet Italian nationalists were disgusted once the likely terms of the peace agreements became clear, and accused the liberal government of allowing Italy to be both humiliated and cheated. The popular nationalist Gabriele D'Annunzio spoke for many Italians – especially war veterans – when he called it a 'mutilated victory'.

QUESTION

What do you understand by the term 'mutilated victory'? What areas were claimed by Italian nationalists after 1919?

The economic impact of the First World War

The First World War had a significant impact on the relatively weak Italian economy. In order to finance its involvement, the liberal government had borrowed heavily from Britain and the US, and the national debt had risen from 16 billion lire to 85 billion. Even this proved inadequate, so the government printed more banknotes, causing rapid inflation – prices increased by over 400% between 1915 and 1918. This inflation destroyed much of the middle class's savings, reduced rental incomes for many landowners, and caused a drop of more than 25% in the real wages of many workers. At the end of the war the situation was worsened by high unemployment as war industries closed down and more than 2.5 million soldiers were demobilised.

The war also deepened the economic divisions between north and south Italy. Those industries in the north linked to war production (especially steel, chemicals, motor vehicles, and the rubber and woollen industries) did extremely well before 1918, as they were guaranteed large state contracts. When inflation began to rise, industrialists simply passed on the price increases to the government.

The south, still predominantly agricultural, did not share in this prosperity. Farming was badly affected by the conscription of large numbers of peasants and farm labourers. However, during the final years of the war – in an attempt to limit the attraction of socialism and the ideology of the Russian Bolsheviks (communists) – the government promised a programme of land reform after the war.

Art and culture before 1922

Italian art – and especially its applied graphic art – reflected much of the political and cultural revolutions of the interwar period, and was of European significance. In the second half of the 19th century, Italian artists had been influenced by French trends, such as Post-Impressionism and Art Nouveau – their version was known as Stile Liberty. Then, in the early 20th century, Italian artists developed a style much influenced by trends in France's Belle Epoch, along with additional influences from Germany, Austria and Britain. However, unlike these other countries – where the writers and artists of such artistic and cultural movements (such as the German Bauhaus, Dada and the Constructivists in Russia) tended to have left-wing and even revolutionary political tendencies –

the new cultural movements in Italy tended to be more nationalist and even ultra-right.

The 'Novecento' movement

This artistic movement began after the end of the war, and was greatly influenced by the poet and adventurer **Gabriele D'Annunzio**.

Gabriele D'Annunzio (1863–1938):

He was a poet and writer. As an ultra-nationalist, he supported Italy's entry into the First World War on the side of the Triple Entente. He joined up as a pilot and became something of a war hero after dropping propaganda leaflets over Vienna. He was an irredentist, and was angered when Fiume (now Rijeka in Croatia) was handed over to the new state of Yugoslavia after the First World War.

The movement took inspiration from ancient Rome, which was reflected in literature, painting, graphic art and architecture. One of the features of Novecento was its tendency to mythologise Italian history and to promote aspects of Italian nationalism. However, Stile Liberty and Novecento were soon overshadowed by a new movement known as Art Deco (or Art Moderne). Though this, too, harked back to the ancient civilisations of Rome, Greece and Egypt, it was also influenced by Cubist painting and especially the symbols of the 'Machine Age' of the early 20th century. However, arguably the biggest influences of Italian Art Deco were on the styles of the artistic movement known as Futurism, and on the politics of emerging fascism in Italy.

The Futurists

The most significant cultural development in Italy in the immediate postwar period was that associated with Futurism. Like the earlier movements mentioned previously, this had been much influenced by economic changes in Italy which saw – at least in the north – the move from an essentially agrarian economy to an industrial one. Many important graphic artists had already developed poster techniques which were widely used to advertise the new industrial products being produced – such as Pirelli tyres. The Futurists, however, used these techniques to sell ideas – their own ideas, but also fascist beliefs.

Futurism had first emerged before the war, and is particularly associated with the artist **Filippo Tommaso Marinetti**, its founder in 1909.

Filippo Tommaso Marinetti (1876–1944):

A writer and artist, he believed that art 'can be nothing but violence, cruelty and injustice', and proclaimed the unity of art and life. The artistic movement he founded, Futurism, incorporated elements of both anarchism and fascism. Marinetti was an early supporter of Mussolini and, like the early fascists, attacked the monarchy and the wealthy political and industrial élites which – like the nationalists – he saw as having sold out Italy at the peace conferences. He later distanced himself from what he saw as the more conservative aspects of Mussolini's fascism, but he remained an important influence on fascist ideology.

Futurism appealed in particular to young people, eager to throw off the past, destroy existing culture and modernise Italy – Marinetti's stated aim was to 'challenge inertia' by continually disrupting the status quo. He admired the 'Machine', and so worshipped modern industrial technology – including the machinery of war. Such sentiments – and his praise of war and conflict – soon led many Futurists to support Mussolini's fascist movement. Futurists involved in graphic art and advertising, literature and theatre, then used their techniques to sell 'modernism', industrialisation, war and fascism.

SOURCE 3.1

Futurism... became the house style of Italian fascism in the years after Mussolini's March on Rome. Marinetti provided Mussolini with his platform style, a rhetoric of newness, youth, anti-feminism, violence, war fever, and, uniting all these social virtues, the familiar central myth of dynamism. Futurist artists provided gratifyingly amenable to Il Duce's desire for self-commemoration, and for a time the Mussolinian chin bid fair to rival the Cubist guitar as one of the clichés of advanced-looking Italian art at the Venice Biennales. The desirable thing about modern art, from the Fascist point of view, was its modernity: it signaled the renewal of history on the cultural plane, as fascism promised it on the political.

Hughes, R. 1981. **The Shock of the New**. London. BBC. p. 97.

Initially, Futurism and the fascists worked well together, as they seemed to share the same objectives, while Mussolini saw the advantage of their ability to create an effective 'modern' image for his Fascist Party. This was important as, in 1921, 30% of Italians were illiterate – so the use of posters and architecture which combined Roman classicism with modernism was just what Mussolini wanted in order to increase the appeal of his fascist movement, and to promote the idea that fascism was exactly what Italians – and especially young Italians – needed in the modern world.

Figure 3.3: Continuous Profile: Head of Mussolini, by R. A. Bertelli, 1933. © Imperial War Museums: (Art.IWM ART LD 5975). Archive Renato Bertelli c/o George Bertelli,: "Renato Bertelli volume, sculptor" by Marco Moretti, Masso delle Fate Editions, Signa (Florence) in 2007

3.3 What political factors aided the rise of Mussolini's Fascist Party, 1919–20?

By 1919, it was clear that the liberal regime would face many problems in postwar Italy. In particular, the economic problems resulting from the First World War caused much social dislocation and suffering – and this led to various political threats to Italy's liberal political system.

The threat from the right

After the First World War, the various militant and disillusioned right-wing groups were joined by another force that was also in search of change. This was made up of demobilised and unemployed soldiers, who found it difficult to accept many aspects of postwar Italian society. One notable group was the *Arditi* ('Daring Ones'). The first *Arditi* association was set up in Rome in January 1919, while Filippo Tommaso Marinetti established another in Milan. From February, *Arditi* groups were established across Italy. As they grew in size, these groups increasingly used weapons to attack socialists and trade unionists, whom they regarded as enemies of the Italian nation.

Mussolini and the *Fasci di Combattimento*

In March 1919, Mussolini – himself a member of the *Arditi* – tried to bring together all these separate right-wing groups by forming the *Fasci di Combattimento* ('Fighting' or 'Battle' Group). On 6 June, the Fascist Programme was published, which combined various left- and right-wing demands. However, the main feature that held these nationalists and former servicemen together was a strong hatred of the liberal state.

D'Annunzio and Fiume

Although *Fasci di Combattimento* were established in about 70 other towns, Mussolini's tiny network of militant agitators was soon overshadowed by the actions of Gabriele D'Annunzio who, in September 1919, led 2000 armed men to the city of Fiume – one of the areas Italy had sought but not won in the peace treaties.

D'Annunzio's force quickly took control and, in open defiance of the liberal Italian government and the Allies, they ruled the city for the next 15 months. This bold action made D'Annunzio a hero to Italian nationalists, and proved an inspiration to Mussolini. In particular, Mussolini decided to adopt the theatrical trappings used by D'Annunzio, especially the black shirts of the *Arditi*, the ancient Roman salute they used, and the many parades and balcony speeches they performed.

ACTIVITY

Carry out some further research on the ways in which D'Annunzio and the *Arditi* influenced Mussolini as he began to build his fascist movement.

Politics and the Catholic Church

In addition to the growing dissatisfaction of the nationalists, the liberals also faced increased political opposition from other right-of-centre movements. In January 1919, the papacy finally lifted its ban on the formation of a Catholic political party, leading to the foundation of the Italian Popular Party (*Partito Popolare Italiano*, PPI) – often known simply as the Popolari. This party was a coalition of conservative and liberal Catholics who wanted to defend Catholic interests and improve life for the peasants. It was led by the priest Luigi Sturzo, and was backed by Pope Benedict XV in order to oppose the Italian Socialist Party (*Partito Socialista Italiano*, PSI). In 1919, the Popolari won 20% of the vote, and from 1919 to 1921 it was the second-largest party in Italy after the PSI. The Popolari was generally suspicious of liberalism because of the latter's history of anti-clericalism. Some members later became ministers of Mussolini's 1922 Fascist government.

The Italian Socialist Party and the 'threat' from the left

A threat to the liberal regime seemingly more serious than that of the fascists was posed by the Italian Socialist Party (*Partito Socialista Italiano*, PSI). The economic problems and hardship resulting from the First World War caused great discontent among industrial and rural workers in Italy. As a consequence, the PSI began moving towards an increasingly revolutionary position. In 1917, inspired by the Bolshevik Revolution in Russia, the PSI had called for the overthrow of the liberal state and the establishment of a socialist republic. In 1914, the PSI had had only 50000 members. By 1919, this had increased to more than 200000. However, in reality many socialist leaders were stronger on rhetoric than on action.

The *bienno rosso*, 1919–20

As unemployment in Italy rose to over 2 million in 1919, industrial workers began a wave of militant action that lasted from early 1919 to the end of 1920. This period became known as the *biennio rosso* (the 'two red years'). A series of strikes, factory occupations and land occupations – organised by trade unions and peasant leagues, and involving over 1 million workers – swept across Italy. By the end of 1919, socialist trade unions had over 2 million members, compared with about 250000 at the beginning of the year.

In many areas, especially in the north, socialists seized control of local government. To many industrialists and landowners, and to the middle classes in general, it seemed that a communist revolution was about to begin. Yet the government, headed by **Giovanni Giolitti**, did little to prevent this.

> **Giovanni Giolitti (1842–1928):**
>
> He was prime minister of Italy five times between 1892 and 1921. Bowing to nationalist pressure, he agreed to the Italo-Turkish war of 1911 to 1912. In 1915, Giolitti opposed Italy's involvement in the First World War, believing the country was unprepared. His last period as prime minister was 1920 to 1921. He was supported by the fascist *squadristi*, and did not oppose their violent takeover of towns and regions. Like Orlando, Giolitti backed Mussolini at first, but he withdrew his support in 1924.

Believing that the workers were less dangerous inside the factories than on the streets, and that militancy would soon decline, Giolitti urged employers and landowners to make some concessions. In response to riots against the high price of food, the government set up food committees to control distribution and prices. This lack of forceful action led many members of the middle and upper classes to view the government as dangerously incompetent.

SOURCE 3.2

The threat of Bolshevism was exploited cunningly by Mussolini and it is difficult to overestimate its importance in bringing Fascism to power. Yet in truth, the threat in Italy was almost entirely illusory. No master plan of revolution existed; peasants and workers acted without premeditation and on a local basis only... By the last quarter of 1921, the worst of the post-war depression was past; so was the worst of proletarian unrest. By the time, a year later, that Mussolini arrived in office to save Italy from Bolshevism, the threat, if it ever existed, was over.

Cassels, A. 1969. Fascist Italy. *London. Routledge & Keegan Paul. pp. 24–5.*

The November 1919 elections

However, the relative weakness of Mussolini's *Fasci di Combattimento* was underlined by the results of the November 1919 elections. These were for the Chamber of Deputies – the lower house of the Italian parliament (the upper house was the Senate). For the first time, the elections were held using a system of proportional representation. Each local *fascio* was allowed to decide its own election manifesto but, despite this, not a single fascist candidate was elected. Mussolini himself won only 5000 votes out of 270000 in Milan. So great was his disappointment at this result that he considered emigrating to the US. In all, there were probably only about 4000 committed fascist supporters throughout the entire country in 1919.

The economic élites and emerging fascism

However, the unrest of the *biennio rosso* gave a boost to Mussolini's organisation. In an attempt to end the factory and land occupations, he offered to send in *squadre d'azione* (action squads) to help the factory owners in the north and landowners in the Po valley and Tuscany. These industrialists and landowners, frustrated and angered by the liberal government's concessions and inaction, were only too pleased to give money to Mussolini's groups in return for the *squadristi's* violent actions against the left's strikes and occupations.

Figure 3.4: Fascist Blackshirts from a *Fasci di Combattimento* (Battle Group).

This growing alliance with industrialists, bankers and landowners began to finance the building of a mass base for Mussolini's *Fasci di Combattimento* among the middle and lower-middle classes, which feared socialist revolution. However, the more radical elements (such as Marinetti and the syndicalists) were increasingly alienated from this base.

The action squads were controlled by local fascist leaders, known as *ras* (an Abyssinian word, meaning 'chieftain'), who often had a large degree of independence. They included Italo Balbo (Ferrara), Dino Grandi (Bologna), Roberto Farinacci (Cremona) and Filippo Turati (Brescia).

As well as attacking strikers, the *squadristi* burned down offices and newspaper printing works belonging to the socialists and trade unions in many parts of northern and central Italy. As time went by, the *squadristi* came to be mainly composed of disaffected and demobilised army officers and non-commissioned officers (NCOs), and middle-class students. These supporters were united by a hatred of socialists and a belief in violent action, rather than by any coherent political ideology.

The practical appeal of the fascist *squadristi* grew after September 1920, when a new wave of factory occupations involving over 400 000 workers hit the industrial areas of the north. At the same time, agrarian strikes and land occupations continued to spread in central Italy. Then, in the local elections, the socialists won control of 26 out of 69 provinces, mostly in northern and central parts of Italy. This greatly increased the fears of the upper and middle classes, and encouraged the use of the action squads. As the *squadristi* proved effective in suppressing left-wing actions, their numbers were swelled by recruits from the ranks of small farmers, estate managers and sharecroppers.

SOURCE 3.3

In the Po valley, the towns were on the whole less red than the country, being full of landowners, garrison officers, university students, rentiers, professional men, and trades people. These were the classes from which Fascism drew its recruits and which offered the first armed squads.

Comments on the backgrounds of the fascist *squadristi* by Angelo Tasca, a member of the Italian Communist Party in the early 1920s:

Tasca, A. The Rise of Italian Fascism 1918–22. *Quoted in Macdonald, H. 1999.* **Mussolini and Italian Fascism**. *Cheltenham. Nelson Thornes. p. 17.*

3.4 How did Mussolini become prime minister in 1922?

By the end of 1920, the factory and land occupations had begun to decline – though *squadristi* violence had not. Mussolini had not initially ordered the attacks, which had been organised by powerful *ras* leaders such as **Italo Balbo** in Ferrara and Dino Grandi in Bologna.

Italo Balbo (1896–1940):

A right-wing republican, he joined the PNF in 1921. He became secretary of the fascist organisation in Ferrara, and soon the *ras* there. His fascist gangs – known as the Celbano – broke strikes for landowners and industrialists, and attacked socialists and communists. Balbo was one of the four main planners, known as the Quadrumirs, of Mussolini's March on Rome. In 1923, he became a member of the Fascist Grand Council.

Fascist violence, the *ras* and Mussolini

However, Mussolini soon realised the political – and financial –
opportunities offered by a more organised use of *squadristi*. Support for
Mussolini's *Fasci di Combattimento* increased when government military
action against D'Annunzio forced the latter to surrender control of
Fiume in January 1921. This removed a potentially powerful rival force
for Mussolini. Slowly, with much resistance at first, he began to assert
central control, arguing that without his leadership and newspaper (*Il
Popoli*), the various groups would fall apart. In particular, Mussolini
stressed the need to depict violence as necessary to prevent the success
of a Bolshevik-style revolution in Italy. In April 1921, Mussolini made a
speech (Source 3.4) in which he declared fascist violence to be part of
an anti-socialist crusade to 'break up the Bolshevist State'.

SOURCE 3.4

*Extracts from a speech about fascist violence by Mussolini to the fascists
of Bologna, April 1921.*

And, however much violence may be deplored, it is evident that we, in
order to make our ideas understood, must beat refractory skulls with
resounding blows... We are violent because it is necessary to be so...

Our punitive expeditions, all those acts of violence which figure in the
papers, must always have the character of the just retort and legitimate
reprisal; because we are the first to recognise that it is sad, after having
fought the external enemy, to have to fight the enemy within... and for
this reason that which we are causing today is a revolution to break up
the Bolshevist State, while waiting to settle our account with the Liberal
State which remains.

Robson, M. 1992. Italy: Liberalism and Fascism 1870–1945. *London.
Hodder & Stoughton. p. 51.*

The liberals and the Nationalist Bloc

While attacking the state in public, Mussolini privately reassured Giolitti
and other liberal politicians that talk of fascist revolution was not to
be taken seriously. As a result, Giolitti offered the Fascists an electoral
alliance – an anti-socialist National Bloc – for the national elections due

to be held in May 1921. During the election campaign, fascist squads continued their violence, and about 100 socialists were killed.

Nonetheless, the Socialists emerged, once again, as the largest party with 123 seats; the Popolari won 107 seats. Giolitti was disappointed by the results. Mussolini, however, was pleased with the outcome of the election – his group had won 7% of the vote and had taken 35 seats. Mussolini himself was now a deputy and, significantly, all 35 fascist deputies were from the right of the movement. More importantly, holding positions in parliament gave the fascists an image of respectability as well as a foothold in national politics. With this success achieved, Mussolini announced that the fascists would not support Giolitti's coalition government after all.

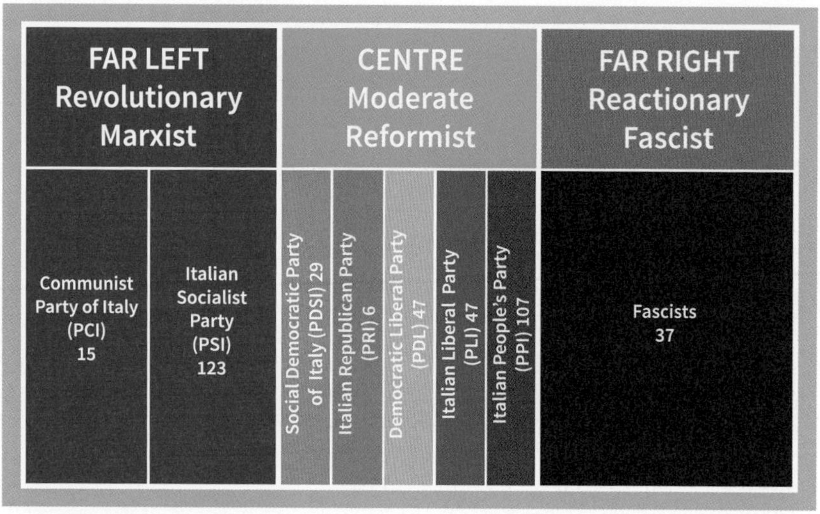

FAR LEFT Revolutionary Marxist		CENTRE Moderate Reformist					FAR RIGHT Reactionary Fascist
Communist Party of Italy (PCI) 15	Italian Socialist Party (PSI) 123	Social Democratic Party of Italy (PDSI) 29	Italian Republican Party (PRI) 6	Democratic Liberal Party (PDL) 47	Italian Liberal Party (PLI) 47	Italian People's Party (PPI) 107	Fascists 37

Figure 3.5: The results of the May 1921 elections in Italy.

After the May 1921 elections, and Mussolini's decision not to support Giolitti, Mussolini concentrated on gaining support from various quarters. From May 1921, Mussolini had hopes of achieving real power and he was determined to make full use of the opportunities to do so. He realised that he needed to convince the industrialists, landowners and the middle classes of three things: that the liberals were finished as an effective political force; that there was a real threat of socialist revolution; and that only the fascists were strong and determined enough to take the necessary action, and restore order and dignity to Italy.

Denied the support of the fascist deputies, Giolitti at first managed to form a coalition with the support of the Popolari, but this collapsed within a month.

The role of the élites

The unrest of the *biennio rosso*, 1919–20, had given a boost to Mussolini's organisation. From the spring of 1921, continued fascist violence – which was increasingly ignored by the police – resulted in a 'creeping insurrection' in northern and central Italy, which saw the fascists gaining control of many towns. When the socialists called a general strike at the end of July 1921 in protest against these actions, the fascists used violence to end the strike. The attitude of the élites now became increasingly crucial to the fascists' prospects of success. During the *biennio rosso*, the police and army leaders often turned a blind eye to fascist violence against socialists and industrial and agrarian militants. In fact, commanders in some areas even provided transport to take fascist squads to socialist demonstrations or congresses. In the first half of 1921, over 200 people were killed and more than 800 wounded by these action squads, and Emilia and Tuscany became fascist strongholds.

SOURCE 3.5

There were sectors who assisted Fascism indirectly: although they could not bring themselves to support Fascism openly they were at least prepared to tolerate it in a way which would have been out of the question with, for example, socialism. One of these groups was the political establishment… Another was the aristocratic class, who were appeased by Mussolini's willingness to end his attacks on the monarchy. In fact, the Queen Mother, Margherita, and the king's cousin, the Duke of Aosta, were admirers of Fascism. A third sector was the Catholic Church, taking its cue from Pope Pius XI who, from the time of his election in 1922, remained on good terms with Mussolini. The Church undoubtedly considered a Communist revolution to be the main threat.

Lee, S. 1987. **The European Dictatorships.** *1918–1945. London. Routledge. p. 95.*

As *squadristi* violence continued to disrupt law and order into the summer of 1921, Mussolini began to worry that it might alienate the conservative élites and unify anti-fascists. His concerns grew on 31 July, when 12 *carabinieri* (police officers) managed to disperse over 500 fascists at Saranza, in north-west Italy. This was hardly the sign of a party able to impose law and order.

The formation of the National Fascist Party

Between May 1921 and October 1922, three weak coalition governments ruled Italy. Mussolini used this time to strengthen his control of the fascist movement. On 2 August, Mussolini surprised the opposition – and angered the *ras* – by signing a peace deal, known as the Pact of Pacification, with moderate socialists and the main trade union organisation, the General Confederation of Workers (*Confederazione Generale del Lavoro*, or CGL).

He then resigned from the Fascist Central Committee in an attempt to outmanoeuvre the *ras*. In October 1921, he successfully persuaded members of the *Fasci di Combattimento* to re-form the organisation into a political party: the *Partito Nazionale Fascista* (National Fascist Party, PNF). Mussolini followed up this victory in November 1921 by persuading the Fascist National Congress to elect him as leader. In return, he agreed to end the truce with the socialists, and ordered all branches to organise action squads. Although the local *ras* still had considerable influence and some autonomy, Mussolini could now present himself as the clear and undisputed leader of an organised and united political party.

Mussolini's growing control of this new party allowed him to drop what remained of the more radical or 'left-wing' elements of the 1919 Fascist Programme, especially those that had been hostile to the Roman Catholic Church, and worried the upper and middle classes. In doing so, Mussolini hoped to increase fascist support among conservatives.

This was especially important as the new pope, Pius XI, did not support the leader of the Popolari and had previously – as archbishop of Milan – blessed the fascists' banners.

SOURCE 3.6

Mussolini alone has a proper understanding of what is necessary for his country in order to rid it of the anarchy to which it has been reduced by an impotent parliamentarianism and three years of war. You see that he has carried the nation with him. May he be able to regenerate Italy.

Comments made by Pope Pius XI to the French ambassador, shortly after Mussolini was appointed prime minister. Quoted in Hite, J. and Hinton, C. 1998. **Fascist Italy**. *London. Hodder Education. p. 75.*

Mussolini kept Fascist Policy policy statements deliberately vague, declaring his party to be against socialism and liberalism and for a strong and ordered Italy. By the end of 1921, the Fascist Party claimed to have over 200 000 members.

The fascists' 'creeping insurrection'

Despite Mussolini's growing control over the Fascist Party and its increasing appeal to conservatives, many of the local *ras* – including **Roberto Farinacci** and Italo Balbo – continued to endorse the violence of the action squads.

Roberto Farinacci (1892–1945):

He was originally a radical nationalist, but he soon became involved in the emerging fascist movement. He was the *ras* in Cremona, publishing his own newspaper (*Cremona Nuova*), and his action squads were among the most brutal in 1919. In 1922, Farinacci declared himself mayor of Cremona. Mussolini made him PNF secretary in 1925. Farinacci was anti-clerical and anti-Semitic, and after 1938, he strongly enforced anti-Jewish legislation.

Determined to avoid a split in his party, Mussolini followed a dual policy throughout 1922. He encouraged the *ras* to continue their violent activities, but he made it known to the conservatives that he had no intention of pushing for a violent seizure of power. In the spring of 1922, there was a concerted campaign of *squadristi* violence in northern and central Italy. By July, street fighting was common in most northern towns, and soon Cremona, Rimini and Ravenna were under fascist control. Once again, the police either stood by or intervened on the side of the fascists. In some areas, the police even offered the fascists weapons if it looked as though the socialists might win.

The socialists and their trade unions decided to call a general strike for 31 July, in an attempt to force the government to take action against the fascists' violence and their 'creeping insurrection', which was giving the movement control of an increasing number of towns and other areas of Italy. Mussolini used this as an opportunity to prove that the socialists were still a threat and, more importantly, a threat that only the fascists could stop. Fascists immediately began to break the strike, taking over public transport and the postal service, and attacking strikers. The socialists called off the strike on 3 August.

The fascist success impressed the conservative middle classes, and led to renewed contact between Mussolini and former liberal prime ministers – such as Antonio Salandra, Vittorio Orlando, Francesco Nitti and Giovanni Giolitti – to discuss the possibility of the fascists entering a coalition government. To increase fascist respectability, in September Mussolini declared he was no longer opposed to the monarchy.

According to historians such as Renzo De Felice, Mussolini's rise – and his ability to retain control until his overthrow in 1943 – had much to do with support from the élites. These, according to Martin Clark, were 'the Establishment men, the conservative trimmers and office-holders.' Different historians have tended to focus on other factors, such as the economic conditions in Italy, and the existence of popular support for fascism in Italy, as ways of explaining Mussolini's success.

The March on Rome, October 1922

Having obtained considerable control of northern and central Italy, the *ras* wanted to move from local to national power. Many of them had urged a coup after the collapse of the general strike, and Mussolini had struggled to restrain them. In early October 1922, the *ras* renewed their pressure. Balbo is said to have told Mussolini that the *ras* intended to march on Rome and seize power – with him or without him. To appease his more militant supporters, and to intimidate the liberal government into making concessions, Mussolini agreed to coordinate a 'March on Rome'.

Local squads were organised into a 40 000-strong 'national militia', under Balbo and Grandi, and a plan was drawn up by which four *ras* –

Balbo, Bianchi, Cesare De Vecchi and General De Bono – would seize control of major towns and cities in northern and central Italy. Once this had been achieved, the fascists would converge on Rome from three different cities.

On the night of 27 October, fascist squads took over town halls, railway stations and telephone exchanges across northern Italy. The following day, prime minister **Luigi Facta** persuaded the king, Victor Emmanuel III, as commander-in-chief of the army, to declare a state of emergency. This meant that the government could use the military as well as the police to stop the fascist columns assembling in Rome.

Luigi Facta (1861–1930):

A liberal, he held various ministerial posts before and immediately after the First World War. He initially favoured neutrality, but later supported the war effort. Facta became prime minister in February 1922. Dismissed in July, he was soon reappointed, as no one else could form a government. He was the last prime minister of Italy before Mussolini began his rule.

Initially, roads and railways were blocked, and army troops met little resistance as they began to take back control of some buildings seized by the fascists. Fascist commanders, including De Vecchi, began to waver. The prefect of Milan was instructed to arrest Mussolini, who was in the city as a precautionary measure (he planned to escape from Milan into Switzerland if things went wrong).

However, Mussolini was not arrested. The king changed his mind and refused to sign the papers authorising martial law. Facta resigned in protest. The king then asked the conservative Salandra to form a government, but Mussolini rejected the offer of four cabinet posts for the Fascist Party. He wanted the post of prime minister for himself. Salandra advised the king to appoint Mussolini – and the king agreed. Mussolini accepted on 29 October 1922.

DISCUSSION POINT

Working in pairs, develop arguments for a class presentation on the ways in which non-fascists might have been able to prevent Mussolini's rise. For each one, try to evaluate its likely success.

In fact, the March on Rome was more myth than reality. Mussolini himself did not march at the head of the fascist columns, but arrived in Rome by train, having already accepted the position of prime minister. The fascist militia did not reach the city until the following day, 30 October, when about 70 000 Blackshirts celebrated their victory in the streets of Rome.

ACTIVITY

Carry out some additional research on the different groups in Italy that supported Mussolini and the fascists before 1922.

Theory of Knowledge

History and the role of individuals

Does an examination of Mussolini in the period 1919 to 1922 provide adequate proof of the 'great person' theory of history? Or does a study of his rise during this period show the greater importance of economic factors – or even chance?

Victor Emmanuel III and fascism

Mussolini owed his success in October 1922 more to the king, **Victor Emmanuel III**, than to his fascist militia. The king himself claimed that he refused to sign the declaration of martial law because he could not depend on the army's loyalty. But he was assured that his soldiers were faithful, and that they could disperse the fascist marchers.

Victor Emmanuel III (1869–1947):

He was the last king of Italy, largely due to his role during the rise and rule of fascism. After 1922, the king made little comment on fascist violence, anti-Semitic laws or the destruction of democracy. In 1944, he handed most of his powers to his son, Umberto, and abdicated in his favour in May 1946. In June, 54% of Italians voted for a republic, and Victor Emmanuel went into exile in Egypt.

Figure 3.6: King Victor Emanuel shaking hands with Mussolini, just after appointing him as prime minister.

Historians are still undecided as to why the king acted as he did. Some argue that he was uncertain of the reaction of the military, that he had little faith in the liberal politicians, that he genuinely feared the outbreak of civil war, and that he was worried about being replaced by his cousin, the duke of Aosta, a known fascist supporter – the queen mother, Margherita, was also a fervent fascist. Other historians have pointed out how leading industrialists, landowners and senior churchmen favoured compromise with the Fascists and how the king himself regarded the fascists as a bulwark against the threat of communist revolution.

Causation and consequence: How did the attitudes of Italy's political élite help to cause the rise of Mussolini's Fascist Party?

3.5 What were Mussolini's main actions, 1922–24?

Although Mussolini was now prime minister, Italy was not yet a Fascist state. For that to happen, he needed to change the constitution and strengthen his own position – there were only four fascists in his cabinet, and the king still had the power to dismiss him as prime minister. The king and the other political leaders believed Mussolini could be tamed, transformed and used to their own advantage. However, Mussolini had no intention of being tamed, and soon began to increase his powers and, after 1924, to create a Fascist dictatorship.

The road to dictatorship, 1922–24

To establish a one-party Fascist state, with himself as dictator, Mussolini needed to win new political allies, widen the political appeal of fascism, and extend his powers. Such a move was crucial as Mussolini's government was essentially a Nationalist–Popolari–Liberal coalition that could fall at any time if one of the parties withdrew.

In his first speech to parliament on 16 November 1922, Mussolini made a veiled threat about the strength of the Fascist Party (he claimed 300 000 armed and obedient members). He also spoke of his desire to create a strong and united Italy, and asked for emergency powers to deal with Italy's economic and political problems. The deputies, including former prime ministers Giolitti, Salandra and Facta, gave Mussolini an enormous vote of confidence and granted him these powers for a one-year period.

The support of the élites

To increase his support among the conservative élites, Mussolini appointed the liberal Alberto de Stefani as his finance minister. Stefani's early economic policies (reducing government controls on industry and trade, and cutting taxation) pleased the industrialists. In March 1923, the small Nationalist Party – a member of the coalition with close links to big business and the army – merged with the fascists. This confirmed Mussolini's increasing shift towards the conservative élites, many of whom wanted an authoritarian government and a much-enlarged Italian empire.

However, many on the left of the Fascist Party were angered, as they wanted to see significant social reforms. Partly as an attempt to increase his control over the Fascist Party, in December Mussolini established a Fascist Grand Council. This was declared to be the supreme decision-making body within the Fascist Party. It could discuss proposals for government action, but Mussolini insisted on sole power over appointments to his council. In effect, he was attempting to establish total control over fascist policy-making.

In January 1923, Mussolini succeeded in persuading the Fascist Grand Council to agree that the regional fascist squads should be formed into a national militia, funded by the government. This militia, called the National Security Guards (*Milizia Volontaria per la Sicurezza Nazionale*, MVSN), swore an oath of loyalty to Mussolini, not the king. This gave Mussolini a paramilitary organisation of over 30 000 men, which he could deploy against anti-fascists. At the same time, it considerably reduced the power of the provincial *ras*.

The Fascist Grand Council also worked alongside the government's Council of Ministers – fascist ministers took important decisions, which were then passed on to the Council of Ministers for official approval. In addition to his role as prime minister, Mussolini also acted as interior and foreign minister.

SOURCE 3.7

What he did was to dissolve the squads and incorporate the squadristi into a new body, the Militia (*Milizia Volontaria per la Sicurezza Nazionale*, MVSN), organised by De Bono at the Interior. The Militia would 'defend the fascist revolution', would protect the fascist regime from its enemies, would give the *squadristi* status, pay and some local power, and would also discipline them: the ordinary ex-squadristi would supposedly find themselves serving under the command of ex-army officers. It was, therefore, an ambiguous body, part reward, part constraint; it was also part Fascist, part state, and it had ambiguous functions, part military, part police. However, it soon became clear that neither the army nor any of the various police forces was willing to let the MVSN muscle into its territory.

Clark, M. 2005. **Mussolini.** *London. Pearson. p. 67.*

QUESTION

How significant were the Fascist Grand Council and the MVSN in helping Mussolini to control his own party?

By early 1923, the employers' organisation – the *Confindustria* – had pledged its support for Mussolini. This was largely due to his announcement that there would be no serious measures taken against tax evasion, which was widely practised by wealthy companies and individuals. In March 1923, the small Nationalist Party (a member of the coalition) merged with the Fascist Party. This merger brought the fascists additional paramilitary forces (the nationalists' Blueshirts), but it also confirmed Mussolini's increasing shift to the right, towards the conservative élites. Once again, this disturbed the more militant fascists.

The Vatican

Mussolini also worked to gain increased support from the Catholic hierarchy and to weaken the position of the Catholic PPI (see 3.2, Politics and the Catholic Church), another member of the coalition government. Mussolini announced various measures, including making religious education compulsory and banning contraception. Pope Pius

XI, already a fascist sympathiser, signalled his willingness to withdraw his support from the PPI. In April 1923, Mussolini sacked all PPI ministers from his government; in June, the pope forced the PPI leader to resign. By the summer of 1923, the PPI had lost most of its political importance.

The Fascist syndicates

During their rise to power, the fascists closed down traditional labour-movement trade unions in the areas they controlled. They replaced these with fascist-controlled syndicates, which were still supposed to represent workers' interests. By 1922, a Confederation of Fascist Syndicates had been set up, headed by **Edmondo Rossoni**, who wanted to create corporations that would force industrialists to make some concessions to workers' demands. These corporations would be established for each industry, and made up of government representatives, employers' organisations and representatives from the Fascist syndicates.

Edmondo Rossoni (1884–1965):

Rossoni was initially a revolutionary syndicalist, who was imprisoned for his activities in 1908. He became a socialist and then a nationalist, joining Mussolini's PNF in 1921. Rossoni was the most prominent of the fascist labour leaders and, as head of the Confederation of Fascist Syndicates, he wanted genuine workers' representatives who would share power with employers. After his dismissal in 1928, he continued in fascist politics, serving as under-secretary to the president of the Fascist Grand Council from 1932 to 1935. Later, he supported Dino Grandi's coup and voted against Mussolini in 1943.

However, this 'leftist' fascist aspiration – unlike their attacks on the traditional trade unions – was at first opposed by the *Confindustria*, the organisation that represented the main industrialists in Italy. So, in December 1923, when Mussolini had been prime minister for 14 months, the Chigi Palace Pact was made. In this agreement, the industrialists promised to cooperate with the Confederation of Fascist Syndicates, but they insisted on maintaining their own independent organisations.

Changing the constitution

More secure in his position, Mussolini announced his intention to reform the electoral system in a way that he hoped would strengthen his position even further.

The Acerbo Law

On his instructions, Giacomo Acerbo, the under-secretary of state, outlined a new electoral law that would give two-thirds of the seats in parliament to the party (or alliance) that won at least 25% of the votes cast. According to Mussolini, this would give Italy the strong and stable government it needed. In fact, the law was clearly intended to give the Fascist Party total, but legally acquired, control over Italian politics. Given the intimidation and violence that could be expected from the fascists and the fact that, as minister of the interior, Mussolini could order the police not to intervene, there was little likelihood of the fascists' opponents ever being able to vote them out of office.

To ensure that this law was passed, Mussolini overcame the opposition (who greatly outnumbered the 35 fascist deputies) by threatening to abolish parliament, and by placing armed fascists on the doors to intimidate the deputies. Liberal leaders such as Giolitti and Salandra advised their supporters to approve the law, and Parliament passed the Acerbo Law by a large majority in July 1923. With this law in place, Mussolini now needed to make sure his party won the most votes in the next election. He was helped in this by an event that became known as the Corfu Incident.

The Corfu Incident

In August 1923, an Italian general was murdered on Greek soil. Mussolini took advantage of this situation; he demanded that Greece pay 50 million lire as compensation and make a full apology. When the Greek authorities refused (as they had not been responsible), Mussolini ignored criticism from the League of Nations and ordered an invasion of the Greek island of Corfu. The Greek government paid the fine. Many Italians regarded Mussolini as a national hero after the Corfu Incident, and it increased his popularity for the election he planned to hold early the following year.

Why were the Acerbo Law and the Corfu Incident so important in helping to establish Mussolini's position?

The election of April 1924

Mussolini decided not to hold new elections until April 1924. Before then, in January, he set up a secret gang of thugs and gangsters to terrorise anti-fascists both in Italy and abroad. Known as the Ceka, this group was led by **Amerigo Dumini**, who had his own office within the ministry of the interior.

Amerigo Dumini (1894–1967):

He was born in the USA after his parents emigrated there from Italy. He travelled to Florence at the end of the First World War and became involved in the local *Fasci di Combattimento*. He was soon known as 'Il Duce's hit man'. In 1924, Dumini headed the group that kidnapped and then murdered Giacomo Matteotti, leader of the Socialist Party. In 1943, after Mussolini's overthrow, Dumini gave his support to the establishment of the Salò Republic.

After the date of the election was announced in March, Dumini's gang unleashed a wave of terror against anti-fascists in which over 100 people were killed. In addition to this, fascists voted on behalf of dead people; ballot boxes were stolen in regions where the fascists thought they might lose; and voting certificates were seized. As a result, the fascists (and the right-wing liberals, including Salandra and Orlando, who had formed an electoral alliance with the Fascist Party) won almost 65% of the vote. The number of fascists in the 535-seat chamber rose from 35 to 374. Yet despite the intimidation and vote-rigging, over 2.5 million Italians still voted for opposition parties, mainly the socialists and the communists.

The Matteotti crisis

When the new parliament met for the first time, on 30 May 1924, the much-respected leader of the socialists, **Giacomo Matteotti**, strongly condemned the fascist violence and corruption that had taken place during the election. He even dared to produce evidence, and called the results a fraud.

Giacomo Matteotti (1885–1924):

Born into a wealthy family, he studied law at the University of Bologna. He soon became active in socialist politics, and opposed Italy's entry into the First World War. Matteotti was first elected to the Italian parliament in 1919, and eventually became leader of the United Socialist Party, which was a more moderate socialist group which had split from the PSI. He was an outspoken critic of fascist violence. He was abducted and murdered by fascist thugs in 1924.

Figure 3.7: A cartoon published in 1924 by an Italian underground newspaper, showing Mussolini sitting on Matteotti's coffin.

QUESTION

What is the message of the cartoon in Figure 3.7?

On 10 June, Matteotti was abducted in Rome and then murdered. Although there was no hard evidence, it was widely assumed that he had been murdered by Dumini's fascist thugs, and many people began to distance themselves from Mussolini's regime. For a time, it seemed as though revulsion at Matteotti's murder might actually cause Mussolini's downfall. To win back support, Mussolini ordered the arrest of Dumini and his gang on 15 June and, on 18 August, Matteotti's body was found.

There has been some debate among historians about Mussolini's involvement in Matteotti's assassination. De Felice and Emilio Gentile argued that Mussolini had not ordered the death of Matteotti. De Felice even claimed that Mussolini was the victim of a political plot to threaten his power and frustrate his plans to create a more broad-based government. Other historians, including Denis Mack Smith, thought Mussolini was probably aware of the planned assassination, but that it was ordered and organised by someone else. However, some studies have suggested that Mussolini did order the murder, to stop Matteotti publishing documents containing details of corruption involving the selling of oil rights to a US company.

Although Dumini was found guilty of the murder and imprisoned, some newspapers began to print evidence of Mussolini's involvement in Matteotti's murder. When he suspended parliament in order to prevent a debate about the murder, most of the opposition deputies (mainly socialists and communists) – under the leadership of the liberal Giovanni Amendola – walked out of the chamber in protest. They then set up an alternative parliamentary assembly, claiming they were now the true and democratic representatives of the Italian people.

SOURCE 3.8

The unprecedented – and quite shameless – Fascist violence which had accompanied the [April 1924] election provoked bitter opposition protests when parliament, now with a crushing and exuberant Fascist majority, reopened. Both inside and outside parliament, the Fascists were now bent on making things unpleasant for their critics. One of the most outspoken was Giacomo Matteotti, a moderate socialist... in June 1924 Matteotti was kidnapped by a gang of Fascist thugs and stabbed to death, his body remaining undiscovered until August. When Fascist guilt was exposed, Mussolini's moral if not actual complicity was inescapable... The ensuing 'Matteotti crisis' proved crucial to the development of the Fascist regime. Amidst a wave of anti-Fascist sentiment, much of the... opposition withdrew from parliament in protest: the so-called 'Aventine secession'. Mussolini panicked and would have resigned the premiership had the king required it. The king did no such thing, his inaction exemplifying the unwillingness even now of conservatives to abandon Mussolini.

Blinkhorn, M. 2006. **Mussolini and Fascist Italy**. *London. Routledge. pp. 33–4.*

The Aventine Secession

This protest became known as the Aventine Secession (named after similar events in ancient Rome, when a group of politicians set up a rival assembly on the Aventine Hills above Rome), and was intended to force the king to dismiss Mussolini. However, the king – instead of condemning Mussolini – refused to consider such an action, and instead blamed the opposition deputies (most of whom were republicans, and thus disliked by the king) for 'unconstitutional behaviour'.

SOURCE 3.9

The Aventine [Secession] was undermined by its own contradictions. For the members of the opposition, genuine democrats who had not understood that Fascism represented a radically new element in political life, there was no choice but to await the constitutional monarch's pleasure… Therefore, and as much in order to avoid frightening the king as out of fear of revolution, they rejected the call for a general strike and the proclamation of the Aventine as the sole legal Parliament of the country… They hoped to bring about a Cabinet crisis and the dismissal of Mussolini. It was now December, seven months after the murder of Matteotti, and the Aventine moderates had not yet learned that on the parliamentary battleground Mussolini was bound to win because the king was determined to uphold him.

Gallo, M. 1974. **Mussolini's Italy***. London. Macmillan. pp. 189–91.*

SOURCE 3.10

Mussolini clearly feared his days were numbered. Yet the king declined to act… He had quickly come to value Mussolini…

Mussolini was under considerable pressure, but he was far from resigning. He countered by making changes in the government to reassure moderates… Damage limitation was helped by the Vatican… Many leading members of the clergy were grateful to Fascism for breaking the Left… Industrialists too stayed largely faithful, reflecting their basic satisfaction with government policy.

Eatwell, R. 1995. **Fascism: A History***. London. Chatto & Windus. p. 52.*

The pope also supported Mussolini and condemned the Popolari deputies who had participated in the Aventine Secession. He was joined by Giolitti and Salandra and other leading liberals and conservatives, all of whom saw this as a way of reasserting influence over a now-weakened Mussolini. They also feared that Mussolini's fall might be followed by a revival of the revolutionary left-wing parties. Perhaps most significantly, leading industrialists were opposed to any change of government, especially as Mussolini had begun to reduce state involvement in the economy.

KEY CONCEPTS QUESTION

Causation: What reasons can you give for the failure of the Aventine Secession? Remember: 'reasons' is a term commonly used in history questions: as it requires you to focus on explaining causes, it is thus a causation question, even though the word 'causes' is not used.

In July 1924, industrialists, liberals and conservatives supported Mussolini's moves towards press censorship, and then his ban on meetings by opposition parties in August 1924. When further evidence of fascist violence emerged, Mussolini felt it necessary to promise to get rid of the thugs in the Fascist Party, and he sacked three fascist ministers from the government. However, in November, some leading liberals joined the opposition in criticising the continued press censorship.

Mussolini's actions against fascist thugs provoked a revolt by leading *ras* and some 50 senior officers of the MVSN in December 1924. At a meeting on 31 December, they presented Mussolini with a clear choice: either he had to stop any further investigations of fascist violence and become dictator of Italy, or they would overthrow him and replace him with a more hard-line fascist leader.

Paper 3 exam practice

Question

Examine the reasons for the rise to power of Mussolini's Fascist Party in the period 1918–22. **[15 marks]**

Skill

Writing an introductory paragraph

Examiner's tips

Once you have planned your answer to a question (as described in Chapter 2, Unit 2), you should be able to begin writing a clear introductory paragraph. This needs to set out your main line of argument and to outline *briefly* the key points you intend to make (and support with relevant and precise own knowledge) in the main body of your essay. Remember: *'To what extent...?'* and *'Examine...'* questions clearly require **evaluation/analysis** of opposing arguments, interpretations or explanations, or the relative importance of factors – not simple description. If, after writing your plan, you think you will be able to make a clear overall or final judgement, it is a good idea to state in your introductory paragraph what overall line of argument or judgement you intend to make.

Depending on the wording of the question, you may also find it useful to define in your introductory paragraph what you understand by **key terms** – such as *'trasformismo'*, *'Arditi'*, 'fascism' and *'ras'*.

For this question, you should:

- consider a range of different factors during the period specified by the question
- write a concluding paragraph that sets out your judgement about the relative importance of the different factors.

You will need to cover the following political and economic factors:

- the weaknesses of Italy's liberal political system
- the economic impact of the First World War
- problems arising from the peace treaties of 1919–20

- the growth of left-wing parties and industrial unrest
- the roles of the élites, the Catholic Church and the monarchy
- Mussolini's use of violence and political tactics.

Setting out this approach in your introductory paragraph will help you focus on the demands of the question. Remember to refer back to your introduction after every couple of paragraphs in your main answer.

Common mistake

A common mistake (which might suggest to an examiner that the candidate has not thought deeply about what is required) is to fail to write an introductory paragraph at all. This is often done by students who rush into writing *before* analysing the question and making a plan. The result may well be that they focus on the words 'rise to power' and on the dates – an approach that may simply result in a narrative account of Mussolini's rise. Even if the answer is full of detailed and accurate own knowledge, this will *not* answer the question, and so will not score highly.

Sample student introductory paragraph

The rise to power of Mussolini's Fascist Party in 1922 – the first fascist party in Europe between the two World Wars to be formed and come to power – was the result of many economic and political factors. While there were several long-term factors – such as long-standing claims by Italian nationalists for land in Europe and for overseas colonies – there were several important short-term reasons in the period 1918–22. These include the economic impact of the First World War and the great disappointment many Italian nationalists and ex-soldiers felt concerning the outcome of the peace treaties of 1919–20. Also important were the long-standing weaknesses of Italy's liberal political system – such as trasformismo – and the short-term political manoeuvrings of the mainstream parties in the years 1920–22. In addition, there is the impact of the industrial unrest and the growth of the increasingly-revolutionary Italian Socialist Party. This factor is closely associated with the fears and actions of Italy's economic and political élites – including the Roman Catholic Church and the king. Finally, the growing violence of the Fascists – and Mussolini's political skills – were also important. Overall – as several historians have argued – the élites' fears about the possibility of a Bolshevik-type socialist revolution in Italy immediately after the war was probably the most important factor as, among other things, it led them to finance the Fascist Party and to overlook its criminal violence.

Activity

In this unit, the focus is on writing a useful introductory paragraph. Using the information from this unit, and any other sources of information available to you, write introductory paragraphs for **at least two** of the following Paper 3 practice questions.

Remember to refer to the simplified Paper 3 mark scheme in Chapter 6.

Paper 3 practice questions

1   Discuss the economic and political impacts of the First World War on Italy.

2   To what extent were the weaknesses of Italy's liberal political system the main reason for Mussolini's rise to power in 1922?

3   Evaluate the significance of the Roman Catholic Church in the rise to power of the Fascist Party in the period 1918–22.

4   Examine the role played by fascist violence in Mussolini's rise to power.

5   'The roles played by economic and political élites in Italy were the main reason for Mussolini's rise to power in 1922.' To what extent do you agree with this statement?

6   Examine the actions taken by Mussolini between 1922 and 1924 to strengthen his position.

3

Italy

Unit 2: Establishment and Consolidation of the Fascist State, 1925–39

Introduction

After 1925, Mussolini began to create a Fascist dictatorship. Despite promises to end class conflict and improve life for all Italians, his 'corporate state' mainly benefited the wealthier classes, while independent trade unions and strikes were banned. During the Great Depression of the 1930s, Mussolini's economic policies proved increasingly unsuccessful. He tried to widen support for fascism in a variety of ways – but, as with his economic policies, these measures had limited success. His foreign policy was based on the idea of recreating the old Roman Empire, and eventually brought about his downfall.

TIMELINE

1924 'Battle over the Southern Problem'

1925 **Jan:** End of Matteotti crisis

Jul: Control of press extended

Aug: Fascist *podestà* control provinces

Oct: Vidoni Palace Pact; 'Battle for Grain' begins

1926 'Battle for Land' and 'Battle for Births' announced

Jan: Mussolini takes power to rule by decree

Jul: Ministry of Corporations established

Oct: Trade unions and all opposition parties banned

1928 **May:** New electoral law restricts vote to males belonging to Fascist syndicates; king's powers reduced

1929 **Feb:** Lateran Treaty and concordat with the Catholic Church

1930 **Mar:** National Council of Corporations established

1931 Laws against divorce, abortion and same-sex relations

1933 IRI set up

1935 **Oct:** Invasion of Abyssinia

1936 **Jul:** Italy, along with Nazi Germany, intervenes in Spanish Civil War

Oct: Rome-Berlin Axis formed

1937 Membership of GIL made compulsory

1938 **Jul:** Charter of Race drawn up

Sep-Nov: Racial laws and decrees carried out

1939 **Jan:** Chamber of Fasci and Corporations replaces Chamber of Deputies

Overview

- After surviving the Matteotti Crisis in 1924, Mussolini took steps towards establishing a one-party authoritarian state. These measures included banning trade unions and all opposition parties, and taking control of local government.
- In 1926, as part of his attempts to establish a Fascist dictatorship, he began the creation of what he called the 'corporate state'.
- Mussolini also began to increase his control over the Fascist Party by purging its more radical members. At the same time, repression, censorship, control of the media and various forms of propaganda, all helped to create Mussolini's personal dictatorship by the late 1920s.
- Even the creation of the corporate state – although apparently a concession to party 'radicals' – was carried out in a way that emphasised the power of the Italian state and of employers over employees.
- As well as launching a series of 'battles' to deal with some of Italy's economic and social problems, Mussolini increased support for fascism by making agreements with the Catholic Church in 1929. However, disputes did arise – mainly over fascist attempts to control Catholic youth movements, and then over the introduction of anti-Semitic laws after 1938.
- Women were particularly affected by fascist policies – the 'Battle for Births' attempted to restrict women to the traditional 'housewife/ mother' role.

- Concerted efforts were made to control education and to establish strong fascist youth movements for boys and girls. In 1937, membership of these groups was made compulsory.
- Despite all of Mussolini's measures, he never managed to create a totally authoritarian state. This was confirmed in 1943 when internal opposition led to his dismissal as prime minister.

3.6 How did Mussolini consolidate his power in the period 1925–39?

For a time in 1924, it had seemed that Mussolini might be brought down as a result of the Matteotti crisis. Yet he was able to ride out this political crisis – in large part because the economic and political élites maintained their support. Mussolini made full use of this to begin suppressing opposition and creating a one-party authoritarian state.

Suppressing the opposition

On 3 January 1925, Mussolini addressed the Chamber of Deputies about the murder of Matteotti the previous summer. He denied having set up the Ceka, and condemned the actions of Dumini's gang. Nonetheless, as prime minister and leader of the PNF, he accepted ultimate responsibility for Matteotti's murder, but made it clear that, instead of resigning, he would continue to rule Italy – by force 'if necessary'.

SOURCE 3.11

I declare before all Italy that I assume full responsibility for what has happened… If Fascism has turned out to be only castor oil and rubber truncheons instead of being a superb passion inspiring the best youth of Italy, I am responsible… Italians want peace and quiet, and to get on with its [sic] work. I shall give it all these, if possible in love, but if necessary by force.

Extract from a speech given by Mussolini, 3 January 1925. Quoted in Robson, M. 1992. Italy: Liberalism and Fascism 1870–1945*. London. Hodder & Stoughton. p. 66.*

In February Mussolini became seriously ill, and the newly appointed party secretary, Roberto Farinacci, the notorious *ras* of Cremona, exercised power during Mussolini's illness and recovery. Although Mussolini disliked Farinacci, who favoured a total fascist takeover, his appointment proved to be a shrewd move on Mussolini's part. Almost immediately, Farinacci launched a new campaign of *squadristi* violence against members of the Socialist and Communist parties, and the more radical sections of the PPI. Several people were killed – including **Giovanni Amendola** – and many others went into exile. Farinacci also supervised a purge of PNF members and, especially, of local leaders who were believed to be insufficiently loyal to Mussolini.

Giovanni Amendola (1882–1926):

He was a journalist, professor of philosophy and a democratic liberal politician and minister. He was an outspoken critic of fascism and, despite threats against his life, openly accused Mussolini over fascist violence during the 1924 elections and Matteotti's murder. He died an agonising death in Cannes in April 1926, following an attack by a gang of fascist Blackshirts hired by Mussolini. As a result, his son, Giorgio (1907–80) joined the PCI in 1929 – he was banished for his activities, and joined the armed resistance in 1943. From 1948 to 1980, he was deputy leader of the PCI, and was associated with the reformist Eurocommunist wing of the party.

> ## SOURCE 3.12
>
> For even as Farinacci continued to press for a fascist takeover, his enthusiastic centralization of the party – intended to prepare it for its revolutionary destiny – actually had the effect of undermining the power and autonomy of provincial bosses like himself and neutralizing the squadrismo of which he had previously been chief spokesman. By the time he was manoeuvred into resigning in April 1926 he had fulfilled what Mussolini had expected of him and the PNF was well on the way to being domesticated.
>
> Blinkhorn, M. 2006. **Mussolini and Fascist Italy**. *London. Routledge.* pp. 36–7.

In July 1925, Mussolini, now recovered from his illness, took the first step towards establishing a Fascist dictatorship by imposing a series of laws to control the press. Anti-fascist newspapers were closed down, and other newspapers were only allowed to print articles approved by the government. From December 1925, all journalists had to be on a register drawn up by the Fascist Party.

However, Mussolini's position was still not secure – the king and the Chamber of Deputies still existed, as did the opposition parties. Thus, in October 1926, all parties other than the PNF were banned and their deputies were expelled from the chamber; trade unions were also outlawed. In addition, the Special Tribunal – a new law court – was established to deal with political 'offences', some of which carried the death penalty.

In 1927, Mussolini formed the Organisation for Vigilance and Repression of Anti-Fascism (*Organizzazione per la Vigilanza e la Repressione dell'Antifascismo*, OVRA), a secret police force set up to suppress all political opponents. This was not a specifically fascist organisation, and was essentially an adapted version of the Interior Ministry's existing secret police section. As such, it was under state – not party – control; thus it was different from the Gestapo or SS in Nazi Germany.

ACTIVITY

Carry out some further research on the OVRA and make notes on its methods and activities. Then compare and contrast these methods and activities with those of the Gestapo in Nazi Germany. To what extent were they similar?

Controlling the state

Mussolini also increased his personal power by controlling central and local government. On 24 December 1925, the *Legge Fascistissime* law made him 'head of government' – this was a new official title. He also assumed formal powers over his ministers, who were made responsible to him rather than to the Chamber of Deputies. In January 1926 he assumed new powers that allowed him to issue decrees without parliamentary approval. This effectively meant that Mussolini was responsible only to the king – although the new law stated that the king must obtain Mussolini's personal approval before appointing new ministers. Soon, Mussolini insisted on being called Il Duce ('The Leader'). By 1929, he held eight ministerial posts, thus excluding many fascist leaders from these key positions – although, in practice, it was the traditional conservative civil servants who ran these departments rather than Mussolini or the Fascist Party.

At local government level, in August 1925 Mussolini replaced elected mayors and councils with fascist officials known as *podestà*. Although the *podestà* were members of the Fascist Party, they were mainly conservative and were drawn from landowners and the military. This helped Mussolini further secure control of the Fascist Party.

For the May 1928 elections, Mussolini changed the electoral system so that only men aged 21 or over who belonged to Fascist syndicates could vote. The Fascist Grand Council (the supreme decision-making body within the Fascist Party, which had been formed in 1922) drew up a list of 400 candidates from lists approved by confederations of employers and employees. Voters only had the choice of voting either for or against this list. Fear of fascist violence meant most Italians voted 'yes', as fascist officials in the polling stations were able to identify those who voted 'no' (the voting slips were different colours).

Having secured a clear electoral victory, Mussolini was established as dictator of Italy. The Chamber contained only Fascist deputies, and the king's power was drastically reduced.

The Fascist Party after 1925

This authoritarian regime was not a Fascist *Party* dictatorship – instead, Mussolini deliberately made a series of decisions that increasingly restricted the influence of the party. Despite the existence of the Fascist Grand Council, Mussolini insisted on having sole power over appointments.

However, Mussolini made no serious attempt to 'fascistise' the system of government. Instead of appointing leading fascists, he used members of the traditional conservative élites. After October 1926, the party was purged of the more militant fascists; these purges increased in the 1930s. By 1943, the PNF was a mass party, with almost 5 million (mainly inactive) members, which acted as a loyal basis of support for Mussolini. At the same time, party posts were filled by appointment from above, not through election by party members. Party influence was further reduced in 1928, when the Fascist Grand Council was made part of the state machinery of government.

ACTIVITY

Using the information in this unit, and any other resources available to you, construct a timeline to show the main steps Mussolini took in establishing his dictatorship in the years 1925 to 1939.

Opposition to fascist rule, 1925–39

Although trade unions and all opposition parties had been banned in 1926, there was still limited opposition and resistance. One organised group that remained was the Communist Party of Italy, which had been set up in 1921. In 1924, with many leading Communist Party members already arrested by Mussolini's regime, **Antonio Gramsci** had become its leader, and had even been elected to the Chamber of Deputies.

> ### Antonio Gramsci (1891–1937):
>
> Born in Sardinia in 1911, he went to the University of Turin to study literature and linguistics. In 1913, he joined the Italian Socialist Party, and in 1916 became co-editor of the Piedmont edition of the socialist newspaper *Avanti*. He supported the Socialist Party's decision to join the Communist Third International in 1919, and the establishment of the Italian Communist Party. Gramsci was a highly original Marxist theoretical thinker and wrote various important books, some while he was in prison. One of his most important theories was that of cultural hegemony, the idea that the ruling capitalist classes construct and manipulate cultural norms to maintain a state that protects private property and their own interests.

Gramsci set up a Communist Party newspaper called *L'Unità* ('Unity') and called for a united front to defeat fascism. However, in November 1926 he was arrested and imprisoned under the new emergency laws, and he eventually died in prison in 1937.

During the late 1920s and the 1930s, opposition to Mussolini in Italy, though often courageous, was weak. Such opposition mainly involved isolated individuals, small clandestine groups and remnants of the trade unions. After 1926, political opponents who were caught were often sent into internal exile (known as *confino*) to remote parts of Italy. While fascist treatment of active opposition was brutal, it was not as excessively repressive as in Hitler's Germany or Stalin's Russia, although it became more extreme after Italy's entry into the Second World War in 1940.

Opposition began to increase in the second half of the 1930s, in part as a result of Mussolini's increasingly aggressive foreign policy. The invasion of Abyssinia in 1935, and his military intervention in the Spanish Civil War from 1936 to 1939, caused increasing economic problems. These were made worse when Italy entered the Second World War in 1940 as an ally of Nazi Germany. In the end, the impact of Mussolini's foreign policy on the Italian economy was one of the main factors behind his fall from power in 1943.

Several anti-fascist groups went into self-imposed exile so that they could organise opposition from abroad, particularly in France. They smuggled anti-fascist literature into Italy and, during the Spanish Civil War, over 3000 Italian anti-fascist volunteers fought as part of the

International Brigades on the side of the Republican government against Franco's forces, which included troops sent by Mussolini. Their Garibaldi Legion defeated Mussolini's troops at the Battle of Guadalajara in March 1937 – this greatly angered and embarrassed Mussolini.

Mussolini's Ceka often disrupted the activities of these *fuorusciti* (exiles or 'escapees'), sometimes by assassinating leaders in exile. Those dealt with in this way included **Carlo and Sabatino Rosselli**, two brothers who had established the *Giustizia e Libertà* (Justice and Liberty) group in 1929.

> ### Carlo (1899–1937) and Sabatino (Nello) (1900–37) Rosselli:
>
> Carlo was a journalist and professor of political economy and, along with his brother, Nello, was a supporter of Giacomo Matteotti's reformist United Socialist Party (PSU) and a militant anti-fascist activist. In 1927, Carlo was sentenced to internal exile; but he managed to escape in 1929, and went into exile in France. He fought for the Republican side in the Spanish Civil War, as one of the leaders of the Matteotti Brigade. Nello was a professor of history and he, too, aided the Republicans during the Spanish Civil War. One of those who allegedly planned their murder was Mussolini's son-in-law, Galeazzo Ciano who, at the time, was Fascist Italy's Foreign Minister.

They were brutally murdered in France in 1937, probably on Mussolini's orders, by members of *La Cagoule* (The Cowl), a French fascist group. Once Italy had become involved in the Second World War, though, more serious internal opposition began to emerge in Italy – including an outbreak of strikes.

Figure 3.8: Carlo Rosselli and his brother, Sabatino (Nello). They were brutally stabbed and shot to death in France in 1937.

3.7 What impact did Mussolini's economic policies have on Italy?

One of Mussolini's main concerns was to make Italy a rich and great power, by achieving autarchy (self-sufficiency) in food and in raw materials. To achieve this, Mussolini wanted to modernise industry and agriculture, and conquer a large empire. The effects of the Great Depression led Mussolini to increase this push for autarchy – especially after 1935, when the League of Nations imposed economic sanctions on Italy following its invasion of Abyssinia.

Mussolini's economic 'battles'

To achieve the economic greatness he desired, Mussolini decided to launch a series of initiatives he called 'battles'.

In 1924, Mussolini had launched the 'Battle over the Southern Problem', which aimed to overcome the long-term poverty of southern Italy. This was to be achieved by building thousands of new villages in Sicily and the south. In October 1925, the 'Battle for Grain' began: Italian farmers were encouraged to grow more cereals in order to reduce foreign imports. As well as introducing import controls, more land was made available for growing grain, by ploughing up pasture land, orchards and vineyards. In the more prosperous north, farmers shifted from growing maize to wheat, and adopted more mechanised farming methods.

Figure 3.9: An official government photograph, showing Mussolini helping with the 'Battle for Grain'.

> QUESTION
>
> What are the values and limitations of the photograph in Figure 3.9 for finding out about Mussolini's role in the 'Battle for Grain'?

European States in the Interwar Years (1918–1939)

The 'Battle for Land' – to further increase the amount of available farmland – began in 1926 with the draining of marshes and swamps. This created many small farms, while the work – financed from public funds – created jobs for the unemployed. Attempts were also made to farm on cleared woodland sites and on hillsides. Also in 1926, the 'Battle for the Lira' began when the value of the Italian currency dropped. To restore its value abroad, the lire was revalued. This allowed Italy to continue importing coal and iron for armaments and shipbuilding.

Dealing with the Great Depression

Once the Depression began in 1929, unemployment rose in Italy. By 1933, there were 2 million unemployed, and millions more suffered from under-employment. Mussolini initially resorted to limited state intervention, encouraging job-sharing schemes and forcing many women to give up their jobs so that the positions could be filled by unemployed men.

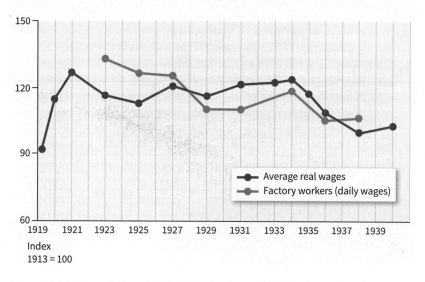

Figure 3.10: A graph showing the impact of Mussolini's policies on real wages and those of factory workers 1919–39.

QUESTION

What, according to the graph in Figure 3.10, happened to average real wages in Fascist Italy?

In 1931, public money was used to help prevent the collapse of banks and industries that were hit by the depression. Then, in 1933, the Institute of Industrial Reconstruction (*Istituto per la Ricostruzione Industriale*, IRI) was established. This took over various unprofitable industries, and by 1939 the IRI was a massive state company controlling many plants, including most of the iron and steel plants, the electrical plants and even the telephone system. However, these industries were not nationalised, and parts of them were regularly sold to larger private organisations.

Success and failure

Mussolini's economic policies achieved some moderate successes. By 1940, industrial production had increased by 9%, and industry overtook agriculture as the largest proportion of Gross National Product (GNP) for the first time in Italy's history. Also, between 1928 and 1939, imports of raw materials and industrial goods dropped significantly. In fact, A. J. Gregor is one historian who claims that Mussolini's regime was a relatively successful 'modernising dictatorship'.

ACTIVITY

Try to find some more information on the historical debates surrounding A.J. Gregor's ideas of 'modernising dictatorships'. Do you think Mussolini succeeded in modernising Italy?

However, many of Mussolini's economic policies, especially his 'battles', were less successful. None of the new villages promised by the 'Battle over the Southern Problem' was built. Although the 'Battle for Grain' succeeded in almost doubling cereal production by 1939, it also resulted in Italy having to import olive oil. Fruit and wine exports dropped, as did the numbers of cattle and sheep.

During the 'Battle for Land', only one area – the Pontine Marshes near Rome – was effectively reclaimed. The 'Battle for the Lira' caused a decline in exports and therefore a rise in unemployment. The revaluation of the currency also undermined the economic policies of 1922 to 1925, and began a recession in Italy. In short, most of Mussolini's 'battles' caused as many problems as they solved.

Overall, the result of fascist economic policy was not a significant modernisation of the economy, or even increased levels of productivity. In fact, it took Italy much longer than most other European states to recover from the effects of the Great Depression.

SOURCE 3.13

Mussolini's economic policies had never been designed simply to increase the wealth of the country… and this became very apparent by the mid-1930s. As the Dictator became increasingly pre-occupied with foreign affairs, living standards and the general welfare of the economy suffered. He believed that war, either in Europe or to further his African Empire, was almost inevitable and that Italy must be prepared. The armaments industry must be promoted, and Italy's economy must become self-sufficient. Italy should be an autarky – able to support itself with all the food and material needed to fight a modern war… Despite [his] efforts the Italian economy was still far from self-sufficient when the Duce declared war in 1940, and indeed it had run into major difficulties.

Robson, M. 1992. **Italy: Liberalism and Fascism 1870–1945.** *London. Hodder & Stoughton. p. 100.*

KEY CONCEPTS ACTIVITY

Change and continuity: Carry out some additional research on the impact of Mussolini's economic policies on the Italian economy. Then write a couple of paragraphs summarising the extent of change and continuity between 1918 and 1939.

3.8 How successful were Mussolini's main social policies?

As well as taking political and economic measures to establish and consolidate his Fascist dictatorship after 1925, Mussolini also adopted several social policies. These were intended to win over and control different sections of Italian society. One of Mussolini's great aims was to unite the Italian people and integrate them into his fascist 'project'. This process of 'coordination' – intended to unite and incorporate the Italian people under fascism – was known as *l'inquadramento*. In particular, there was a concerted effort to expand membership of the party and its associated organisations.

> **QUESTION**
>
> **What is meant by the term *l'inquadramento*?**

Fascism and social class

Mussolini claimed he would replace class conflict with class harmony, and bring equal benefits to employers and employees as they worked in partnership for the good of the nation. The actual results were quite different, however.

The working classes

During the period 1922 to 1925, male industrial workers had benefited from a drop in unemployment, and an improvement in living standards (although this was mainly the result of the general economic revival in Europe in the early 1920s). Throughout 1925 to 1926, however, workers lost their independent trade unions and their right to strike (see 3.6, Suppressing the opposition). Instead of ending class conflict, Mussolini's Fascist state merely suppressed the ability of workers to defend their interests. As the economy began to decline in the second half of the 1920s, employers were able to end the eight-hour day and extend the working week. At the same time, the government cut wages; between

1925 and 1938, the level of real wages dropped by over 10%. As a result, by 1939, working-class standards of living had declined significantly. Some social welfare legislation was passed, including old-age pensions, and unemployment and health insurance, but this 'social wage' did not make up for the decline in real wages and working conditions.

The middle classes

The lower-middle classes, who formed the backbone of the Fascist Party, were affected in different ways. Many small businesses were hit quite hard by the depression as well as by Mussolini's economic policies. However, those who became part of the state bureaucracy or the Fascist Party experienced relative prosperity, with good wages and considerable extra benefits.

The economic élites

The people who gained most from the Fascist corporate state were the industrialists and landowners. Even during the depression, large firms benefited in many ways – either from government contracts or through the IRI (see 3.7, Dealing with the Great Depression), which gave financial assistance and also helped in the creation of huge monopolies. Large landowners also benefited: during the depression, government restrictions on migration kept unemployment high in rural areas, and this meant that landowners could cut wages. Agricultural wages were reduced by over 30% during the 1930s. There was also no attempt to redistribute land, as had been intended by a law passed in 1922. By 1930, 0.5% of the population owned 42% of land, while 87% of the rural population (mainly small landowners) owned only 13%.

Women

Mussolini once said that, as far as higher education for women was concerned, it should just cover what he believed the female brain could 'cope with': household management. Not surprisingly, therefore, women particularly suffered under fascism. The 'Battle for Births', for example, stressed the importance of a woman's traditional role as housewife and mother. Launched by Mussolini in 1927, this campaign aimed to increase the Italian population from 40 million to 60 million by 1950. From this, Mussolini planned to create a large army that would help expand Italy's empire.

The Fascist state offered maternity benefits and awarded prizes to women who had the most children during their lives. Taxation policy was also used to encourage large families – couples with six or more children paid no taxes at all. In 1931, laws were imposed against abortion and divorce, and same-sex relationships were outlawed. The state also tried to exclude women from paid employment. In 1933, the government announced that only 10% of state jobs should be held by women; in 1938, this rule was extended to many private firms.

For all Mussolini's grand plans, though, these government policies largely failed. The number of births actually dropped throughout the 1930s, while nearly one-third of Italy's paid workforce continued to be female.

SOURCE 3.14

The demographic program, the ruralisation of the peninsular, and the effort to revive the traditional female virtues… all appear to have been unsuccessful… Fascism may have been instrumental in removing women from the job market, but the statistics are [inconclusive]… Fascist anti-feminism was not particularly successful and/or may not have been pursued with any special application. In any event, Fascist anti-feminism was, at best, a subsidiary concern of Fascist social policy, and made its appearance largely as a consequence of concerns with a declining birth rate and rising unemployment.

Gregor, A. J. 1979. **Italian Fascism and Developmental Dictatorship.** *Princeton. Princeton University Press. p. 290.*

DISCUSSION POINT

'Fascism – and most other right-wing ideologies – are hostile to equality for women.' Why do you think Mussolini's fascist movement was so hostile to women's rights? Do statements such as this apply to all far-right groups?

The Catholic Church

Mussolini was more successful in gaining support for fascism from the Roman Catholic Church. By the 1929 Lateran Treaty, the pope officially recognised the Fascist state; in return, the state accepted papal sovereignty over Vatican City. In separate agreements, the state gave the pope 1750 million lire (£30 million) in cash and government bonds as compensation for the loss of Rome while, by the concordat, Mussolini agreed that Roman Catholicism should be Italy's official state religion, with compulsory Catholic religious education in all state schools. In exchange, the papacy agreed that the clergy should not join political parties. The pope (and thus the Catholic Church) gave official backing to Il Duce.

Figure 3.11: Mussolini (centre) and his ministers meeting with Catholic leaders at the Vatican in 1932.

However, rivalry between Catholic and fascist youth movements continued even after the Lateran Treaty. In addition, although the Church agreed with several specific fascist policies – such as the invasion of Abyssinia and involvement in the Spanish Civil War, as well as Mussolini's opposition to contraception and abortion – several other disagreements emerged. Thus it was clear that Mussolini never fully controlled the Church.

Young people

Mussolini believed that young people held the key to a great future for Italy, and he particularly targeted them in his efforts to unite all Italians under fascism. Various methods were used to 'fascistise' the young, including indoctrination. In infant schools, the day started with a prayer that began, 'I believe in the genius of Mussolini'. In primary schools, children were taught that Mussolini and the fascists had 'saved' Italy from communist revolution. All school textbooks were inspected by the state, and many were banned and replaced with new ones, which emphasised the role and importance of Mussolini and the fascists.

Attempts to indoctrinate older schoolchildren were less successful. The focus on traditional academic subjects, and the difficult exams they were required to take, prevented many young people from going to secondary school or university. In 1939, **Giuseppe Bottai**, the minister for education, introduced the School Charter: this promised to improve the status of vocational training in schools and colleges, but it came too late to widen the fascists' base of support.

> **Giuseppe Bottai (1895–1959):**
>
> He met Mussolini in 1919 and helped set up a *fascio* in Rome, where he acted as editor of Mussolini's paper, *Il Popolo d'Italia*. He took part in the March on Rome, and his unit was responsible for the deaths of several anti-fascists. From 1926 to 1929, Bottai was deputy secretary of corporations. From 1936 to 1943, he served as minister for education and mayor of Rome. He was responsible for implementing several anti-democratic and anti-Semitic measures, including removing all Jewish students and teachers from schools and universities. In 1943, Bottai sided with Grandi in the coup against Mussolini.

Mussolini also tried to indoctrinate young people by setting up youth organisations. In 1926, all fascist youth groups were made part of the *Opera Nazionale Balilla* (ONB). Within the organisation were different sections for boys and girls, according to age. There was also the Fascist Levy (Young Fascists) for older boys aged 18 to 21. In 1937, the ONB was merged with the Young Fascists to form the *Gioventù Italiana del Littorio* (GIL), and membership was made compulsory for all young people aged 8 to 21. All members of the GIL – and of the GUF (the Fascist University Groups) – had to swear loyalty to Mussolini.

However, the impact on schoolchildren was not as great as Mussolini had intended. Around 40% of 4 to 18 year-olds managed to avoid membership. In particular, private and Catholic schools tended not to enforce ONB membership. Also, because of the entrance exams required for secondary school, many children left school at the age of 11. Contempt for – and even resistance to – fascist ideals was not uncommon in the universities.

Dopolavoro

It was also important to Mussolini to influence the minds of adults. To achieve this, he set up organisations intended to control after-work activities. The *Opera Nazionale Dopolavoro* (OND) – *dopolavoro* is Italian for 'after work' – was established in 1925, and soon comprised a vast network of clubs, libraries and sports grounds. It also organised concerts, dancing and summer-holiday activities in most towns and villages. Overall, about 40% of industrial workers and 25% of peasants were members of the OND. Sport was given a particular emphasis, and Italy began to do well internationally in motor racing, cycling, athletics and football. The main function of the OND was to spread fascist ideology, and although its activities did lead to some popular support – as many Italians enjoyed the subsidised sports, outings and holidays – many local organisers ignored the indoctrination aspects.

To further increase fascist influence among ordinary Italians, concerted efforts were made to expand membership of the Fascist Party and its associated organisations between 1931 and 1939. From 1931 to 1937, during the worst of the depression, the party established its own welfare agencies to provide extra relief – and began to set up women's *fasci* to help run these agencies. Although this led to increased party contact, surveillance and control, party membership did not rise dramatically. According to some sources, by 1939 only about 6% of the population belonged to the party.

Race and the *Romanità* movement

While overt racism had not been a feature of the early fascist movement, a general racist attitude existed within the Fascist Party's plans for imperial expansion. Until the signing of the Rome-Berlin Axis deal with Nazi Germany in 1936, however, anti-Semitism did not play a part in fascist politics. In Italy, this began significantly only in July 1938, when Mussolini issued the Charter of Race, which ruled that Jewish people did not belong to the Italian race.

Further racial laws and decrees were issued between September and November. These excluded Jewish teachers and children from all state schools, banned Jewish people from marrying non-Jews, and prevented them from owning large companies or estates.

An element of racism also existed within the *Romanità* ('Romanness') movement, which was another of Mussolini's methods of broadening the appeal of fascism. As part of the *Romanità* movement, fascist writers and artists portrayed fascism as a revival of, and a return to, the greatness of ancient Rome. The Roman fasces – already adopted as the fascist emblem – was incorporated into the national flag. In addition, much emphasis was placed on the need to establish a second empire – 'the resurrection of empire'. According to *Romanità*, the fascist 'New Man' was a modern version of the idealised Roman centurion. From 1926, Mussolini was increasingly referred to as a new 'Caesar'. In 1937, the *Mostra Augustea della Romanità* exhibition was held to celebrate the

200th anniversary of the birth of the emperor Augustus. Over the entrance to the exhibition was a quotation from Mussolini: 'Italians, you must ensure that the glories of the past are surpassed by the glories of the future.'

Art and culture in Fascist Italy 1925–39

For some time, Mussolini's early regime – unlike that in Nazi Germany – allowed a certain amount of artistic freedom, as long as the symbols of his regime were not criticised. In fact, in 1923, Mussolini stated that he did not want what he called an 'Art of the State'. As a result, the styles of Novecento, Futurism, and Art Deco existed side by side in both art and architecture. However, after the mid-1920s, when Mussolini moved away from a more 'radical' version of fascism, the Futurists' continual attacks on all Italian traditions came to be seen as a bit a liability. Eventually, aspects of Futurism were incorporated into the Art Deco movement which, for a time, became dominant.

After 1939, the impact of Mussolini's imperialist foreign adventures and the looming threat of a new war, led him to increasingly favour an art which was more closely linked to the grandeurs of ancient Rome, and which depicted his regime as one that would recreate that glorious past in the future. In a way, the decline of Futurism and Art Deco paralleled the way Constructivism was replaced by Socialist Realism in Stalin's Soviet Union. In its place, a kind of fascist 'realism' began to emerge.

Figure 3.12: The entrance to the *Mostra della Rivoluzione Fascista* in Rome, 1933.

Ducismo: the personality cult of Il Duce

To create this 'New Man', Mussolini wanted fascism to penetrate every aspect of Italian life and society. To achieve this, he concentrated on building up and projecting his own image, and widely publicised the 'achievements' of fascism.

Almost as soon as Mussolini's dictatorship was established, he began to understand the importance of good publicity. Consequently, a press office was set up to ensure that photographs and newspaper articles projected a positive image of Mussolini and his activities. He was portrayed as youthful, energetic and an expert in a wide range of specialist areas and pursuits. He even gave instructions to the press on how he should be reported. Although initially sceptical of the value of radio, Mussolini eventually established a state radio network in 1924; this expanded rapidly. However, by 1939, there were still only around 1 million radios in Italy – about one for every 44 people. To deal with this, public-address systems were set up in cafés, restaurants and public squares, so that more people could listen to Il Duce's speeches. Free radios were also given to schools.

Mussolini was slow to realise the potential of film, but in 1924, a government agency (*L'Unione Cinematografica Educativa*, LUCE) was established to produce documentaries and newsreels. Soon, Mussolini was making full use of film. He insisted that the state-sponsored newsreel films (from 1926, these had to be played in all cinemas as part of the programme) showed him addressing large crowds of enthusiastic supporters, and that he was filmed from below, in order to disguise his lack of height.

Fascist propaganda

Throughout the 1930s, the Press Office extended its role to cover not just radio and film, but all aspects of culture. In 1933, Mussolini's son-in-law, **Galeazzo Ciano**, took over the running of the office. In 1935, it was renamed the Ministry for Press and Propaganda – in part an imitation of developments in Nazi Germany.

> ### Galeazzo Ciano (1903–44):
>
> He was a founder-member of the PNF, and took part in the March on Rome in 1922. He was briefly a journalist but, after marrying one of Mussolini's daughters in 1930, he rose to prominence as a diplomat. He commanded a bomber squadron during the Italian invasion of Abyssinia and, in 1936, became Foreign Minister. However, he was opposed to Italy's alliance with Nazi Germany and involvement in the Second World War, so Mussolini dismissed him from his post in 1943. Later that year, he was one of the members of the Fascist Grand Council who voted for Mussolini's dismissal as prime minister. In 1944, as a result of pressure from Nazi Germany, Mussolini – now head of the new Salò Republic set up in northern Italy with German assistance – ordered Ciano's execution for treason.

However, unlike the efficient propaganda machine developed by Joseph Goebbels in Nazi Germany, propaganda in Fascist Italy was marked by bureaucratic inefficiency. Mussolini's creation of a fascist propaganda machine was a gradual process. Also unlike Nazi Germany, a number of non-fascist newspapers and radio broadcasts were allowed to continue – including those produced by the Vatican.

Two years later, in 1937, the office was renamed again, this time as the Ministry of Popular Culture (nicknamed Minculpop). This was an attempt to broaden its influence and ensure that all films, plays, radio programmes and books glorified Mussolini as a hero and the fascists as Italy's saviours. However, Minculpop's attempts to regulate the arts were not very successful. Traditional liberal culture proved too strong, and this led to compromises and thus only partial control by the fascists. While Minculpop managed to rally support for the Abyssinian War (1935–36), it failed to gain much popular support for Mussolini's alliance with Nazi Germany, or for the anti-Semitic policies he began to disseminate in 1938.

At the same time, **Achille Starace**, appointed as party secretary in 1930, was also active in projecting an image of Mussolini as a hero.

Achille Starace (1889–1945):

He fought in the First World War, and joined the fascist movement in 1920. He acted as its political secretary and, in 1921, was made vice-secretary of the PNF. He took part in the March on Rome and, in 1923, was put in charge of the MVSN. In 1930, Mussolini made him secretary of the PNF – in that role, Starace helped build up the 'cult of personality' surrounding Mussolini, and pushed through anti-Semitic measures. His attempts to build up the ONB, however, were less successful. In 1939, he was again dismissed as party secretary, and took charge of the MVSN until 1941, when he was dismissed. In 1945, he was captured by anti-fascist partisans and shot after a summary trial – he was one of those strung up along with Mussolini in the Piazzale Loreto in April 1945.

Lights were left on in the dictator's office to suggest that he worked 20 hours a day for Italy, while photographs and posters of Il Duce appeared in public buildings, streets and workplaces. Great prominence was also given to various catchphrases reflecting fascist ideals, such as *Credere, Obbedere, Combattere* ('Believe, Obey, Fight') and 'Mussolini is always right'.

At press conferences, Mussolini was always accompanied by Blackshirt bodyguards, while all public appearances were attended by what soon became known as the 'applause squad', who whipped up 'enthusiasm' for Mussolini's speeches, sometimes even resorting to prompt cards. Public events such as mass rallies and meetings were deliberately turned into political theatre, and full use was made of lighting and music to enhance the drama.

Theory of Knowledge

History, its study and language

According to G. W. F. Hegel (1770–1831), *'The only thing we learn from history is that we learn nothing from history.'* Do you think that, since 1945, people have learned any 'lessons of history' from the study of Fascist Italy and Nazi Germany? Do any fascist movements exist in the 21st century? Also, is it useful to apply labels to, or to stereotype, such political movements?

3.9 What was the nature of the Fascist state in Italy?

When he became prime minister in October 1922, Mussolini had almost immediately taken steps towards the construction of his Fascist state. By as early as 1924, Italy was already on the way to becoming a Fascist dictatorship – as has been seen, this was established and consolidated after 1925 by a variety of means. However – regardless of Mussolini's claims – historians are divided on what was the exact nature of Mussolini's Fascist state.

SOURCE 3.16

The Fascist conception of the State is all-embracing; outside of it no human or spiritual values can exist, much less have value. Thus understood, Fascism is totalitarian, and the Fascist State – a synthesis and a unit inclusive of all values – interprets, develops, and potentiates the whole life of a people... The Fascist State lays claim to rule in the economic field no less than in others; it makes its action felt throughout the length and breadth of the country by means of its corporate, social, and educational institutions, and all the political, economic, and spiritual forces of the nation, organised in their respective associations, circulate within the State.

Extracts from the 1935 edition of **The Doctrine of Fascism**. *pp. 14 and 41.*

The main characteristics of Mussolini's Fascist state

Despite the extravagant claims made in Source 3.16 as to the nature of the state that Mussolini attempted to establish, such claims were often not an accurate reflection of reality. Mussolini was determined to enforce a dictatorship that would be independent of the Fascist Party and the *ras* – thus the regime he established after 1925 was a personal rather than a Fascist Party dictatorship.

Figure 3.13: Mussolini addressing a large crowd in Rome's Piazza Venezia, May 1936.

The declining importance of the Fascist Party

Mussolini made no serious attempt to 'fascistise' the system of government by restricting appointments to leading fascists, as some of his followers wanted. He deliberately restricted the influence of the PNF by using members of the traditional conservative élites to maintain law and order. For instance, in 1927, only about 27% of members of the civil service were said to be fascists: both the Interior Minister (Luigi Federzoni) and the Minister of Justice (**Alfredo Rocco**) were conservative former nationalists. In the 1930s, civil servants often proclaimed loyalty to the Fascist Party merely to retain their jobs.

Alfredo Rocco (1875–1935):

At first, he was associated with the Marxist Radical Party but soon moved to the Italian Nationalist Association (ANI), where he argued that Italy needed to overcome its weak economic power. He developed ideas about a form of economic and political corporatism, which later influenced Mussolini and his Fascist Party. He joined the fascists after the ANI had merged with them. He became president of the Chamber of Deputies in 1924; from 1925 to 1932, was minister of justice and drew up a new criminal code in 1930. Mussolini soon came to see that moderate members of the Italian élites – who supported him because they wished to see a strong Italy and Italian state – were more likely to keep him in power than the more militant fascists. Yet, in 1932, Mussolini dismissed Rocco and, by 1933, all other moderate ministers had been replaced.

However, Mussolini did instigate a purge of the judiciary, and many judges were sacked for lack of loyalty or for following an overly independent line. Mussolini frequently intervened in legal cases, and imprisonment without trial was common. The chief of police was another position filled by career politicians rather than fascists. In the provinces, it was the prefects (the senior civil servants who ran the administration, suppressed 'subversives' and controlled the police) who appointed the *podestà*, or local mayors. The prefects had to be loyal to the government, but also to the local élites. After elected local councils were abolished in 1926, the prefects – whose powers were greatly increased – appointed all the mayors in their provinces. They usually chose 'respectable' landowners or former army officers, rather than local fascists. *Podestà* received no payment, so they needed to be financially independent. Between 1922 and 1929, only 29 of the 86 new *podestà* appointed were fascists. Most were career civil servants.

At first, the *ras* resisted these developments, especially in central Italy. As late as 1927, local fascist leaders were able to insist on some power-sharing. By 1930, however, Mussolini claimed this conflict had been resolved in favour of the prefects. Disputes between prefects and local party leaders still broke out occasionally however.

After Farinacci's forced resignation in October 1926 (ostensibly for another outburst of *squadristi* violence, but really because he had begun to push for a 'second wave' of fascist revolution), the prefects and the *podestà* set about stamping out *squadrismo*. In January 1927, Mussolini issued instructions that all Italians, including fascists, should offer the prefects total obedience.

The 'taming' of the PNF

In 1926, the new party secretary, **Augusto Turati**, began a purge of more militant fascists. At the same time, he opened membership to people who merely wanted to further their career. In just one year, party membership rose from about 640 000 to just under 940 000. For the first time, fascist branches were established in southern Italy.

Augusto Turati (1888–1955):

He was an ex-syndicalist, an irredentist, a supporter of Italy's entry into the First World War, and a journalist. He joined Mussolini's *Fasci di Combattimento* in 1920, and became the PNF boss of Brescia. He was National Party secretary from 1926 to 1930. His purge of party members affected both provincial and non-provincial branches. In 1927, for example, 7000 of Rome's 31 000 members were purged. In his first year as party secretary, Turati expelled 30 000 members, and by 1929 that number had risen to over 50 000. Later, he opposed Italy's entry into the Second World War and did not support Mussolini's Salò Republic.

Most of these new members came from the same local élites that had previously belonged to or supported the liberals. Soon there were very few 'Fascists of the First Hour' left in important positions. At the same time, over 100 000 party members left – many of them disgusted by what was happening to their party.

These developments continued in the 1930s under Turati's successors, Giovanni Giuriati and Achille Starace. The PNF became a party of the masses, with almost 5 million (mainly inactive) members by 1943. However, most were white-collar employees, while the workers and peasants (who had once made up 30% of the party's membership) dropped to a small minority. The Fascist Party thus increasingly became a tame and loyal base of support for Mussolini. At the same time, party posts were filled by appointment from above rather than through election by party members.

This gradual weakening of the PNF was due in part to internal divisions and disunity, which had existed from its foundation. According to the historian Richard Thurlow, there were at least five different factions within the party. These included the militant *ras*, who (like sections of the *Sturmabteilung* in Nazi Germany) wanted a 'second wave' of fascist revolution to replace state institutions with fascist ones, and the 'left' fascists, who wanted to establish a corporativist (see The corporate state, below), or national syndicalist, state.

Opposed to these two factions were the fascist 'revisionists', led by **Dino Grandi**, Massimo Rocca and Giuseppe Bottai, who were prepared to cooperate and merge with the existing political system.

Dino Grandi (1895–1988):

He supported Italy's entry into the First World War and, after serving in the war, joined the fascists' Blackshirts in 1920. He was initially on the violent right of the party, and was one of the 35 fascists elected to the Chamber of Deputies in May 1921. He took part in the March on Rome in 1922 and, in 1929, became Minister of Foreign Affairs. From 1932 to 1939, he acted as Italy's ambassador to Britain. However, he was opposed to Italy's involvement in the Second World War, and attempted to form a pact with Britain to prevent this. As a result, Mussolini removed him from his foreign affairs post, and instead appointed him as Minister of Justice. Grandi's continued opposition to the war led to his dismissal in early 1943. In July 1943, following the Allied invasion of Sicily, it was Grandi who began the successful attempt in the Fascist Grand Council to get the king to dismiss Mussolini as prime minister. Though sentenced to death in 1944 by Mussolini's Salò Republic, he escaped to Franco's Spain.

Mussolini was able to play off these factions against each other to enhance his own power. At the same time, he manipulated different sectors of state personnel to ensure that no one could challenge his authority.

The corporate state

Those fascists who believed that their movement was a 'third way' between capitalism and communism favoured the creation of a corporate state. Sometimes known as the corporative state, the aim of corporativism was to replace the politics of traditional parliamentary democracy with that of corporations representing the nation's various economic sectors. These corporations, each with equal representation for employers and employees, were supposed to overcome class conflict. By thus avoiding strikes and other labour disputes, the corporate state would instead give prime consideration to the interests of the nation. Although there would be elements of increased state control, there was no thought of eradicating private ownership.

SOURCE 3.17

Fascism is therefore opposed to Socialism to which unity within the State (which amalgamates classes into a single economic and ethical reality) is unknown, and which sees in history nothing but the class struggle. Fascism is likewise opposed to trade unionism as a class weapon. But when brought within the orbit of the State, Fascism recognises the real needs which gave rise to socialism and trade unionism, giving them due weight in the guild or corporative system in which divergent interests are coordinated and harmonised in the unity of the State.

Extract from **The Doctrine of Fascism**. *1932. Giovanni Gentile and Benito Mussolini. p. 15.*

Workers and employers

Despite the Chigi Palace Pact of December 1923 (see 3.5, The Fascist syndicates), many employers were not prepared to make any significant concessions to workers, and this provoked a series of strikes in 1925. The resulting Vidoni Palace Pact, in October 1925 confirmed that the *Confindustria* and the Confederation of Fascist Syndicates were the only organisations allowed to represent employers and employees respectively. It was also made clear that workers were not to challenge the authority of employers and managers. All workers' factory councils were closed down and non-fascist trade unions were abolished. In

April 1926, Alfredo Rocco's law made all strikes illegal – even those by Fascist syndicates – and declared that industrial disputes must be settled in special labour courts. The law also stated that there could only be one organisation (a fascist syndicate) of workers and employers in each branch of industry, and identified seven main areas of economic activity.

The corporations

Following these developments, in July 1926 Mussolini established a Ministry of Corporations, with himself as the minister. Each corporation was made up of representatives of employers and workers of the same economic or industrial sector (for instance mining), with the state's representatives acting as referees and final adjudicators. In practice, this new ministry was run by the under-secretary, Giuseppe Bottai, who produced the Charter of Labour (written mainly by Rocco) in April 1927. This document guaranteed fair judgement of labour disputes and promised to carry out social reforms such as improved health care and accident insurance schemes (although none of these measures had the force of law).

In May 1927, Mussolini delivered a speech in which he claimed that a corporate state had been established. He even promised that the corporations would elect half of the members of the next Chamber of Deputies. In May the following year, a new electoral law was passed – a compromise between party and syndicalist views. It allowed for 1000 names to be recommended to the Fascist Grand Council, which would select 400 as candidates for the March 1929 election. In this election, electors could only vote 'yes' or 'no' to the Grand Council's list. Of the original 1000 names recommended by syndicates, employers' associations, former servicemen and a few other groups, the employers had 125 of their nominees 'elected', while the workers' syndicates only managed 89. Mussolini employed his usual methods of 'persuasion', resulting in a 90% turnout, with 98.3% voting in favour of the list presented to them. One of the few politicians to speak out against the new electoral law was Giolitti.

The corporations weakened the Fascist syndicates and, in 1928, Rossoni was dismissed and the Confederation of Fascist Syndicates was abolished. In 1929, Bottai took over as minister of corporations and, in March 1930, he set up the National Council of Corporations (NCC), which represented the seven largest corporations. In 1932, Mussolini resumed control of the Ministry of Corporations, and the number of corporations slowly grew, reaching 22 by 1934.

Despite all of the reorganisation, Mussolini usually made the important decisions himself. In particular, most of the decisions on policies to deal with the effects of the Great Depression had nothing to do with the corporations – including the decision to cut wages. Furthermore, as most trade unionists experienced in industrial negotiations and disputes were socialists or communists (and were therefore either dead, in prison or in exile), the employers had a greater influence in the corporations. Many were 'tame' members of the Fascist syndicates, or even middle-class careerists. In addition, the employers were nearly always supported by the three government-appointed Fascist Party members, who were supposed to remain neutral.

In 1938, in a belated attempt to give more credibility to the corporate state, Mussolini decided to abolish the Chamber of Deputies and to put in its place the Chamber of Fasci and Corporations. Mussolini hoped to establish a new form of politics, in which people were given a voice according to their economic function or occupation, rather than their territorial location. In reality, however, this had little substance or power, being dominated by fascists appointed from above.

Historians are divided over the nature of Italian fascism and its ideology concerning the corporate state. One broad interpretation has tended to examine this in a serious way, largely on Mussolini's own terms. Another has been much more sceptical, considering the ideology surrounding the corporate state to be incoherent, and its declared achievements' mainly unfounded propaganda claims. Since the works of historians Renzo De Felice and Emilio Gentile, a third 'revisionist' strand has returned to the idea of fascist ideology and its stated purposes as relatively coherent and worthy of serious study.

Was Mussolini an all-powerful dictator?

Despite his claims, and despite having established control over the PNF, the reality was that Mussolini had to share power with the traditional groups that had been wielding power in Italy long before 1922. These included the monarchy, the Catholic Church, the civil service and the courts, and the industrial and financial élites and their organisations. For example, after other fascist leaders began moving against Mussolini, it was the king who eventually ordered his arrest on 25 July 1943. Thus came to an end Mussolini's attempt to create a completely totalitarian state, which was largely unsuccessful.

SOURCE 3.18

The existence of autonomous, conservative interests – monarchy, industry, agrari, armed forces and Church – was thus integral to Mussolini's regime as it entered the 1930s. Their continued influence made the regime, in its essential character, less profoundly 'fascist' and less totalitarian in scope than it claimed to be and than outward appearances suggested.

Blinkhorn, M. 2006. **Mussolini and Fascist Italy**. *London. Routledge. p. 52.*

SOURCE 3.19

Mussolini gave the impression of being all-powerful, but he could not rule alone, and the Fascist Party as such was little help to him in running the country. The civil service, the courts, the armed forces and the police remained in the hands of career officials whose commitment to Fascism was usually nominal.

Tannenbaum, E. 1973. **Fascism in Italy**. *London. Allen Lane. p. 93.*

SOURCE 3.20

The new system was a personal dictatorship under Mussolini, yet still legally a monarchy... The government ruled by decree... Local elections were eliminated; all mayors were now appointed by decree. Yet the basic legal and administrative apparatus of the Italian government remained intact. There was no 'Fascist revolution', save at the top.

Payne, S. 1995. **A History of Fascism, 1914–45**. *London. UCL Press. pp. 116–17.*

Theory of Knowledge

History and propaganda

Is it possible to examine Italian fascist ideology and the nature of Mussolini's state with any degree of certainty? Or does the propaganda that surrounded Mussolini's statements and policies put such a 'spin' on these issues that it is almost impossible for historians and students of history to arrive at any accurate and objective judgements?

Paper 3 exam practice

Question

'Mussolini managed to create a totalitarian Fascist state between 1925 and 1939.' To what extent do you agree with this statement?
[15 marks]

Skill

Avoiding irrelevance

Examiner's tips

Do not waste valuable writing time on irrelevant material. If it is irrelevant, it will not gain you any marks. This problem can arise because:

- the candidate does not look carefully enough at the wording of the question (see Chapter 3, Unit 1)
- the candidate ignores the fact that the question requires selection of relevant facts, an analytical approach and a final judgement; instead the candidate just writes down all that they know about a topic (relevant or not), and hopes that the examiner will do the analysis and make the judgement
- the candidate has unwisely restricted their revision, and tries to turn the question into a topic they were expecting instead of answering the question that has been asked; whatever the reason, such responses rarely address any of the demands of the question.

For this question, you will need to:

- examine the different methods used by Mussolini to create his Fascist dictatorship between 1925 and 1939
- evaluate the degree of success achieved by these various policies and actions
- make an overall judgement about whether or not Mussolini was successful in establishing a totalitarian Fascist state.

Common mistakes

One common error with this type of question is for candidates to write about material they know well, rather than material directly related to the question.

Another mistake is to present too much general information, instead of material specific to the person, period and command terms.

Finally, candidates often elaborate too much on events outside the dates given in the question.

Sample paragraphs of irrelevant focus or material

By 1939, Mussolini had succeeded in creating an authoritarian one-party Fascist state in Italy through a mixture of laws, economic policies and repression. However, it was not a totalitarian Fascist state – this was because the king and the Catholic Church still had some powers. This was shown in 1943, when Mussolini was deposed as prime minister and was arrested on the orders of the king.

Mussolini created his Fascist Party in 1921, following two years of violent conflict between his Blackshirts and the political parties of the left. In 1922, local Fascist leaders began to take over various towns and regions. Then, in October 1922, Mussolini organised a Fascist 'March on Rome' and, when the king refused to declare martial law, the prime minister resigned. The king then appointed Mussolini as head of a coalition government in which the Fascists were a small minority. Thus, so far, Mussolini had not created a Fascist dictatorship.

To do this, Mussolini decided to alter the electoral system, to ensure he would gain a majority at the next election, by pushing through the Acerbo Law in July 1923. This new law said that the party or political alliance which won at least 25% of the vote would get two-thirds of the seats in parliament. Mussolini said this was needed to ensure Italy could have a strong and stable government – but it was really his first serious step in establishing a Fascist dictatorship.

[There then follow several paragraphs on the other steps taken by Mussolini before 1925 – such as beginning to moderate aspects of Fascist policies, and obtaining the support of the élites and the Catholic Church – and the political crisis of 1924 which followed the murder of the Socialist leader, Matteotti, who had been an outspoken critic of Fascist violence.]

EXAMINER'S COMMENT

Apart from a good – and promising – introduction, this is an example of a weak answer. Although a brief comment on Mussolini's power before 1925 would be relevant and helpful, there is certainly no need to go into detail about the period 1919 to 1924. Thus, virtually all of the material provided is irrelevant, and will not score any marks. In addition, the candidate is using up valuable writing time, which should have been spent on providing relevant points and supporting own knowledge.

Activity

In this unit, the focus is on avoiding writing answers that contain irrelevant material. Using the information from this unit, and any other sources of information available to you, write an answer to **one** of the following Paper 3 practice questions, keeping your answer fully focused on the question asked. Remember – making a plan *first* can help you maintain this focus.

Remember to refer to the simplified Paper 3 mark scheme in Chapter 6.

Paper 3 practice questions

1   Compare and contrast the extent of opposition and its repression in Nazi Germany (1933–39) and Fascist Italy (1925–39).

2   Evaluate the results of Mussolini's economic policies in the period 1925–39.

3   Examine the extent to which Mussolini's social policies succeeded in widening the basis of support for fascism.

4   'Throughout the period 1925–39, those in the hierarchy of the Catholic Church were collaborators with, rather than rivals to, Italian fascism.' To what extent do you agree with this statement?

Spain

4

Unit 1: From Monarchy to Republic, 1918–30

Introduction

Spain had long been a deeply divided society, and military coups and civil war were not uncommon in Spain. Between 1803 and 1936, there were 19 military coups and three civil wars. The latter – the Carlist Wars – took place between 1833 and 1876, and witnessed considerable brutality between the politically conservative Carlists and their more liberal opponents in the struggle for control of the monarchy. These Carlist Wars also exhibited strong nationalist or regionalist tendencies against a centralised state; and bitter opposition from the traditional Catholic Church to modern liberal or socialist thought.

These 19th century divisions and tensions continued into the 20th century, and many of the roots of the Spanish Civil War of 1936–39 can be found in developments which took place in the period 1918–30. Because of the intense political divisions between left and right, and the fact that the Spanish Civil War was followed within a few months by the start of the Second World War, several historians – notably Ernst Nolte – have argued that the whole period 1936–45 can be seen as a European Civil War. The majority of historians, however, consider the Spanish Civil War to be a separate entity.

TIMELINE

1898 'The Disaster' – Spain defeated by the US, which took Spain's colonial possessions of Cuba, Puerto Rico and the Philippines

1906 Start of colonial war in Morocco

1909 Jul: 'Tragic Week' in Barcelona

1910 Anarchist CNT trade union federation formed

1917 Jun: *Junta Militar de Defensa* formed in Barcelona

Aug: General strike in Barcelona suppressed by military juntas

1919 Bitter struggles between workers and employers in Barcelona

1920 Spanish Communist Party (PCE) formed

1921 Jul: Disastrous defeat of Spanish army at Annual in Morocco

1923 Sep: Military coup; start of Primo de Rivera's dictatorship

1924 Feb: National Economic Council formed

Apr: Rivera forms *Unión Patriótica*

1925 Dec: Formation of Civilian Directorate

1926 Feb: Formation of *Alianza Republicana*

May: End of Rif War

Jul: Plebiscite to approve moves to corporatism

Nov: National Corporations Organisation formed

1927 **Jul:** FAI set up

Sep: First meeting of the National Assembly of *Unión Patriótica*

1929 **Jan:** Failed coup against Rivera

Mar: Student protests repressed

Dec: Primo de Rivera fails to get National Assembly to approve a new constitution to legitimise his rule

1930 **Jan:** Rivera resigns; king replaces him with General Berenguer

KEY QUESTIONS

• What were Spain's main underlying problems before the First World War?

• How did the First World War affect economic and political developments before 1923?

• What were the main developments in Spain from 1923 to 1930?

Overview

• By 1900, Spain was divided by social and economic inequalities, conflict between reformers and conservatives, regional differences and political instability.

• In particular, there were deep divisions between the Spanish monarchy and élites (and the Church and the army which supported them) on one hand, and ordinary Spaniards on the other. From the late 19th century onwards, the latter increasingly turned to anarchist and socialist ideas.

• These political problems had frequently led the army – which often brutally repressed protests and strikes – to intervene in Spanish politics via coups.

• Spanish governments were also faced with problems resulting from its colonial war in Morocco, which began in 1906.

- Spain remained neutral during the First World War, and experienced significant economic growth by exporting to the various combatant countries.
- From 1917, Spain experienced several years of serious political and social unrest. This unrest increased when wartime growth ended with the general slump which followed the end of the war.
- In 1923, another army intervention took place, with Miguel Primo de Rivera establishing a military dictatorship.
- After crushing any opposition, he attempted to establish a stable authoritarian regime under his control. This lasted until 1930, until rumours of plots against him, and the loss of support from most of the army generals, led him to resign.

4.1 What were Spain's main underlying problems before the First World War?

There were several reasons that civil war eventually broke out in Spain in 1936. Some were short-term, but others can be traced back to the 19th century and beyond. One of the main underlying problems was that, in many respects, Spain was still a very divided country in 1918.

The Spanish 'establishment'

By 1900, the political system in Spain was still essentially based on an alliance between the monarchy, the landowning aristocracy, the army, and the Catholic Church. These élites and institutions opposed any modernisation or reform that undermined their privileged position, influence and interests. However, many industrial workers and farm labourers in Spain were encouraged by the 1917 Russian Revolution to challenge these establishments.

The monarchy and politics

Spain had been an absolutist monarchy for centuries but, from 1833 to 1876, rival claims to the throne had led to three civil wars – known as the Carlist Wars. These wars highlighted deep political divisions within

Spain, and were fought with considerable brutality. The Carlists were conservative traditionalists who supported an autocratic monarchy and the Catholic Church. They were opposed to the Queen Regent, Maria Cristina, and her Liberal government, which favoured a more democratic political system and modern secular ideas.

By 1918, the army had intervened in Spanish politics many times. Following a *pronunciamiento* (military coup) in 1874 – which had overthrown the short-lived First Republic of 1873 – the Bourbon family was restored to the throne, in the person of Alfonso XII; his son, **Alfonso XIII**, succeeded him and remained on the throne until he abdicated in 1931. The 'Restoration' period – which lasted from 1874 until 1931 – saw several other military interventions in Spanish politics.

Alfonso XIII (1886–1941):

He became king of Spain the day he was born, as his father had died a few months earlier. He supported Rivera's coup in 1923, and appointed him prime minister. When Rivera resigned in 1930, Alfonso established another military government. Although he left Spain in April 1931, after the declaration of the Second Republic, Alfonso never formally renounced the throne. He supported the Nationalists in the civil war but Franco, after he had won, did not permit Alfonso to return as king.

Spanish politics during most of this Restoration period was marked by the system of *turnismo* (similar to that of *trasformismo* in Italy – see 3.1), with electoral fraud ensuring that the Liberal and Conservative parties – to the exclusion of other political groups – took it in turn to rule. Locally, this led to the rise of *caciquismo*, in which local élite leaders and political bosses – known as *caciques* – ensured they and their clients controlled local and regional politics by appointments and electoral manipulation.

Landowners and industrialists

By 1918, land ownership – as in previous centuries – was largely in the hands of a small number of aristocratic families. In the southern province of Córdoba, for instance, 52% of the land was owned by just 7% of the total population. The owners of the largest estates – known as *latifundia* – kept the wages of the large number of poor landless labourers extremely low. The resulting poverty led to periodic outbursts of rural violence against the landowners, who relied on the Civil Guard and the army to crush these protests – and to prevent any attempts at union organisation. Although, in other areas of Spain, there were more peasant-owned farms, there was still a very uneven distribution of land ownership.

Even before the Wall Street Crash of 1929 and the resulting Great Depression, the Spanish economy was underdeveloped compared with the economies of most European countries. Modern industry only began to appear in Spain in the late 19th and early 20th centuries, and even then it tended to be limited to the north and north-east of the country. There was an important coal-mining industry in Asturias, and a steel industry in the Basque region in the north, while Catalonia had a significant textile industry. However, wages and working conditions were poor, as were living conditions. There was no welfare system for the unemployed, injured or sick. As in rural areas, industrialists relied heavily on the police and army to suppress strikes and protests.

The army

The army had long enjoyed a privileged position in Spain, and had successfully resisted attempts to reform it in the 1880s. Instead of being a modern and effective fighting machine, it was bureaucratic, with a massive top-heavy officer corps: by 1916, there was one officer to every five ordinary soldiers. As a result, some 60% of the entire army's budget went on officers' pay. The General Staff, along with specialised corps such as the artillery and engineers, used officer committees (known as juntas) to ensure promotion was based on seniority. Government attempts after 1900 to reform the army by reducing the size of the officer corps in order to create a smaller but better-equipped army were resisted by the senior officers.

The army, which saw itself as the protector of the nation, was strongly opposed to separatism. In addition, the army was frequently used to crush unrest from agricultural and industrial workers. With officers coming from, or having close connections to, wealthy families, the repressions were often brutal. As strikes and labour unrest increased during the first two decades of the 20th century, army repressions created even deeper hatred among the rural and urban working classes.

The Church

The Catholic Church – like the army – had long held a powerful and privileged position in the life and history of Spain, and had been a strong supporter of the monarchy since the fifteenth century. Unlike in many other parts of Europe in the 18th century, the Catholic Church in Spain had resisted liberal attempts to create a more secular society in which state and church were separated. Much more conservative than in other European countries, the Church was closely identified with the privileged and wealthy classes, and the monarchy and the army which protected their interests.

It also had almost total control over education – but paid little attention to literacy, and secondary education was limited. From the 19th century onwards, the Church waged an increasingly aggressive campaign against political ideas and philosophies which it saw as leading to anti-clericalism, undermining religion belief, or weakening its powerful position. These ideas included liberalism and atheism, as well as socialism and anarchism.

Theory of Knowledge

History, religion and reason

The philosopher Immanuel Kant (1724–1804) once wrote, *'A religion which declares war on reason will not in the long run be able to hold out against it.'* How valid do you think such a statement is in relation to the history of Spain in the early 20th century? Do the increased activities of various fundamentalist faith groups today prove that Kant was wrong?

These factors contributed to increasing discontent among the Spanish people, and affected the Church's influence over the masses. In the south in particular, landless peasants turned away from the Church and towards atheism and anarchism. At the same time, industrial workers grew increasingly attracted to socialism and even communism.

SOURCE 4.1

To appreciate the full intransigeance [sic] of the attitude of the Church one must remember that at all events down to 1910… the Catholic religion and catechism were compulsorily taught in all the schools and that the parish priest had a right to supervise this. So far did this sometimes go that parents used to complain that in State schools the children passed half their class hours in saying the rosary and in absorbing sacred history and never learned to read. The difference between a convent school and a State school was not one of religion but of politics. To put it bluntly, the children in convent schools were taught that if they associated with Liberals, they went to hell. This attitude is expressed very clearly in the complete Church catechism, republished in 1927…

'What kind of sin is Liberalism?' – 'It is a most grievous sin against faith.'

'Why?' – 'Because it consists in a collection of heresies condemned by the Church.'…

'What sin is committed by him who votes for a Liberal candidate?' – 'Generally a mortal sin.'

Brenan, G. 1960. **The Spanish Labyrinth.** *Cambridge. Cambridge University Press. pp. 51–2.*

DISCUSSION POINT

The Catholic Church in Spain during the first half of the 20th century had a privileged position, and clearly felt it had a right to dominate education and intervene in politics. Even today, many religious faiths and churches believe that they should have greater rights, and be treated with more respect, than other self-constituted civil society organisations and ideologies – such as political parties or trade unions. In pairs, draw up arguments for and against such claims.

The emergence of revolutionary groups

The entrenched nature of the traditional establishment in Spain, and the resulting inequalities, led to the emergence of various revolutionary groups. After 1900, there were an increasing number of bitter civil struggles and conflicts.

Socialism

Unlike other countries in the second half of the 19th century, revolutionary political movements, linked to socialism or Marxism, were slow to become established in Spain. In part, this was because Spain was predominantly agricultural, and rural areas were often dominated by the conservative ideologies of the élites and the Catholic Church. In addition, capitalist industrial development was not as extensive in Spain as it was in countries such as Britain and Germany. Nonetheless, in the late 19th century, organised labour movements, opposed to the élites and the old order, began to emerge in Spain. The Spanish Socialist Workers' Party (*Partido Socialista Obrero Espnañol*, PSOE) was formed in 1879: as well as aiming for socialism, it also wanted to replace the monarchy with a republic. In 1888, it founded a national trade union, the General Workers' Union (*Union General de Trabajadores*, UGT) which, by 1913, had over 100 000 members.

Anarchism

Initially, a more serious threat to the old order came from the rise of anarchism. This first reached Spain in 1868, but quickly became widespread. In 1873, after anarchists became involved in a strike in the town of Alcoy and began to spread their revolutionary ideas, the police opened fire on the strikers. The repression which followed drove the anarchist movement underground, and it became largely based in rural areas which were more difficult to police. Because of the repression, anarchism was often limited to individual terrorist acts – intended to spark an uprising, these were met with increased repression and torture.

During the early 20th century, a particularly revolutionary left-wing type of anarchism, known as anarcho-syndicalism, quickly spread in Spain. Anarcho-syndicalists believed that workers' strikes – not individual acts of terror – were the way to achieve a revolution in which all workplaces and land would be under workers' ownership and self-management. They also supported the separatist and nationalist demands of the different regions of Spain, and were opposed to religion and the power of the Catholic Church. In 1900, they formed the Federation of Workers' Societies of the Spanish Region – but the strikes they organised were again suppressed.

Separatism

In addition to the emergence of these revolutionary groups, Spain in 1900 was (and still is) a country that is greatly divided, both geographically and linguistically. The formation of a united country had begun in the late 15th century, with the marriage of the king of Aragón and the queen of Castile – but one of the ways in which this was achieved was via the conquest of the various historic kingdoms which then existed in the Iberian peninsular. These regions and provinces had their own languages, laws and customs which survived their incorporation within a united Spanish kingdom effectively dominated by Castile. To a greater or lesser extent, these provinces resisted further centralising attempts in the ensuing centuries, and nationalist tendencies continued into the 20th century, when significant separatist movements emerged.

Two provinces in particular had strong nationalist aspirations: the Basque country in the north and Catalonia in the north-east. Basque nationalism developed considerably in the early 20th century, but was largely repressed before 1931. Catalonia, too, had resisted full integration: a serious rebellion broke out in the 17th century, and France often helped foster Catalan separatism in order to weaken its rival across the Pyrenees. In the 19th century, serious attempts were made to revive the Catalan language and, during the Carlist Wars, Catalan nationalists threatened to support the conservative Carlists in order to win concessions from the liberals. In the early 20th century, separatist demands for autonomy (self-rule) became increasingly insistent and, by 1913, some measure of self-government had been gained.

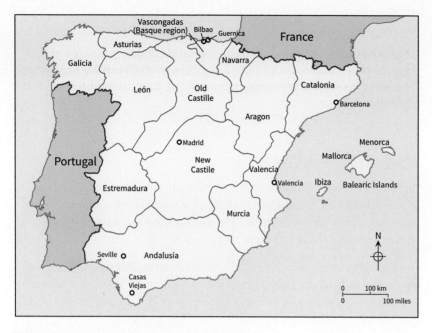

Figure 4.1: The regions and provinces of Spain.

SOURCE 4.2

Just as liberalism could be seen as fracturing the mystical unity of Spain, based upon the Catholic Church, so could cultural and political regionalism appear as a threat to Spain's political unity. Regionalism and localism, the passionate loyalty to birthplace enshrined in the cult of *patria chica*, had long been potent forces in Spain, traditions which sprang in part from a long-established anti-centralism and were nourished by the differing languages and histories of Galicia, the Basque Provinces and Catalonia. Basque and Catalan regionalism were also powered by the vital industrial and commercial traditions of these two wealthy regions, both speaking non-Castilian languages. Catalan regionalism had also been granted some recognition by the Mancomunidad of 1913, which grouped together for local government the four principally Catalan provinces of Barcelona, Lérida, Tarragona and Gerona.

Browne, H. 1996. **Spain's Civil War.** *London. Longman. pp. 4–5.*

The 'Tragic Week'

In July 1909, these factors combined in what proved to be a foretaste of the conflicts to come after 1918. In that year, textile industrialists in Barcelona closed many factories and sacked their workers; those still with jobs were forced to accept wage cuts.

Another important factor was the colonial war in Morocco which had begun in 1906, when Britain and France recognised Spanish influence in northern Morocco, in the area known as er-Rif. However, this had quickly led to a large-scale revolt by the Moroccan people, led by Abd-el-Krim.

To provide extra troops for this colonial war – and to rid itself of rebellious workers – the government called up reserve troops. While those with money could avoid this conscription by hiring a substitute, this was beyond the reach of working-class men. Anti-war protests took place, with workers refusing to fight in a colonial war which they saw as merely being in the interests of wealthy capitalists.

In July 1909, these developments provoked a general strike among workers from various industries, involving both UGT and anarchist members, along with members of the Radical Republican Party. This quickly spread from Barcelona to other Catalan cities. Among other actions, trains carrying conscripted troops were blocked, and churches and convents were attacked; when troops fired on strikers, barricades were erected. The authorities declared martial law but, when local troops refused to fire on the strikers, troops were sent in from other parts of Spain. These responded with typical harshness: about 150 strikers were killed in the fighting, and nearly 2000 were arrested. Afterwards, five leaders were executed, and 59 were sentenced to life imprisonment.

In the repression which followed, unions were banned and newspapers closed down. This repression convinced many anarchists that a stronger organisation was needed. So, in 1910, the anarchists set up their own national trade union, the National Confederation of Workers (*Confederación Nacional del Trabajo*, CNT), which became a powerful rival to the socialist–dominated UGT. Although it was a national organisation, local sections had great autonomy, in line with traditional anarchist opposition to central control and bureaucracy. Very quickly, they called another general strike – once again, this was crushed by the army, and the CNT was banned.

> QUESTION
>
> **How did the colonial war in Morocco help cause the general strike in July 1909?**

4.2 How did the First World War affect economic and political developments before 1923?

Spain's long-standing problems were made worse by the impact of the First World War. In fact, Spain's difficulties arising from the war were not unique: all the southern and eastern European states – with the exception of Czechoslovakia – saw the strains of the Great War of 1914–18 result in the emergence of various forms of authoritarian regime.

SOURCE 4.3

The most immediate effect of the [First World] war in Europe was to divide the [Spanish] political class: Conservatives, army officers, and the right in general supported Germany and 'authority' against 'decadence'; the left, particularly intellectuals, supported 'civilization' against German 'barbarism'. Both raised the political temperature by mass meetings. This division, bitter as it was, troubled the surface of politics: the economic and social effects of the war and its immediate aftermath were deep and lasting.

Carr, R. 1980. **Modern Spain 1975–1980.** *Oxford. Oxford University Press. pp. 81–2.*

QUESTION

How, according to Source 4.3, did the outbreak of the First World War divide Spain's political class?

Economic developments

Because it remained neutral in the First World War, Spain was able to supply goods to both sides. As a result, Spain experienced an export-led economic boom. In particular, the shipping, steel and mining industries prospered. In the Basque provinces, this strengthened the banks, as well as industry; while, in Catalonia, factories worked overtime to supply the French army. Profits also soared in agriculture. Those enriched by war profits tended to spend their new wealth ostentatiously, instead of investing in more modern methods of production.

For ordinary Spaniards, however, the war meant high prices – government attempts to control prices merely led to shortages and a black market where only the rich could purchase what they wanted. However, while non-unionised workers – and the middle classes – had little protection from rising prices, industrial workers in militant unions were able to launch successful strikes in attempts to protect their living standards. With manufacturers desperate to fulfil war-export orders, such strikes were often successful. Similar developments also took place in the agricultural south.

However, with the end of the war in 1918, the wartime prosperity also ended. Basque shipping collapsed and its yards became idle, while mines closed and the new steel mills put their workers on half-time. In Catalonia, 140 textile factories closed down, leaving over 20 000 workers without jobs. In the countryside, landowners who had ploughed up marginal land – in order to meet the demands of combatant countries – allowed these lands to revert to non-use. This resulted in increased unemployment and under-employment, and lowered wages, for agricultural labourers.

These problems were particularly marked in Catalonia where, during the wartime boom, industrialists had formed employers' associations in order to deal with labour militancy and to blunt government attempts to deal with some of the economic problems. For instance, in 1916, the Liberal finance minister had proposed a tax on excess war profits – this had been forcefully resisted by the Catalan and Basque industrialists. Once the postwar slump took effect, Catalan employers reacted with their usual mixture of protectionism and a ruthless offensive against trade unions.

1917: The year of unrest

As well as dividing Spain's political class, the war also led to rising expectations among industrial and agricultural workers – many of whom were inspired by the Russia Revolution which began in March 1917. As a result, support for socialism grew after 1917, and in 1920 the Spanish Communist Party (*Partido Comunista España*, PCE) was formed, although it was much smaller than the PSOE. In these circumstances, the army came to play an increasingly important role, with pressure groups of younger officers claiming to be the political 'saviours of the nation'.

QUESTION

Why did the Russian Revolution of 1917 have a significant impact on working-class movements in Spain?

Army unrest

The colonial war in north Africa had become more serious after Spain's Moroccan areas had been declared a Spanish protectorate in 1912. This war gave ambitious young officers in the Spanish African army – known as the *Africanistas* – a chance to show their military skills. But this began to undermine the tradition of promotion by seniority.

In June 1917, a junior officers' revolt for the retention of promotion by seniority, and for higher wages to cope with wartime inflation, began in Barcelona. This time, the junior officers in the Barcelona infantry garrison formed their own *Junta Militar de Defensa*. When the government attempted to disband this, the Barcelona officers were quickly supported by other junior officers across Spain. All generals were excluded from these *juntas militares* – consequently, the senior officers did not support these *junteros*.

Surprisingly, many civilian politicians – who were critical of the Restoration system – gave their support to these junior officers, who spoke out against '*caciquismo* and oligarchy'. The *junteros* depicted themselves as 'national saviours' who would help reform the political establishment – which the army blamed for Spain's defeat in the Spanish-American War in 1898 (known as 'The Disaster'), and the subsequent loss of its colonies of Cuba, Puerto Rico and the Philippines to the US. Yet the actions of these *junteros* showed once again how the army could use its power to bring down governments.

The Liberal government was forced out of office when it refused to recognise the *juntas*. The Cortes (parliament) was suspended, and a 'renovation' coalition – comprising Francesc Cambó's *Lliga Regionalista* in Catalonia, the Reformist Republicans, and the Radical Republicans led by **Alejandro Lerroux** and Melquíades Álvarez – was formed. These latter two wanted a more democratic constitution and a government which would included the 'new left'. Before the Cortes was dissolved, it agreed to:

- a constituent Cortes to meet in Madrid on 20 October
- a new government which would include some of the renovators
- autonomy for Catalonia.

Although the political regime of the Restoration survived this crisis, it was weakened by it, as a government was forced to resign by a military revolt. In fact, the *junteros*' actions in June 1917 proved to be the first step in what became a generalised crisis in that year.

Alejandro Lerroux (1864–1949):

He formed the Radical Republican Party in 1908; he was anti-clerical, and his militant speeches and writings against Restoration governments won him considerable support among workers in Barcelona. His opposition to government repression during the 'Tragic Week' meant he had to go into exile. In 1930, he was one of those signing the Pact of San Sebastián which united all the main republican and regionalist parties against military dictatorship and the king. However, Lerroux was opposed to Catalan nationalism and radical socialism and, during the Second Republic in the early 1930s, worked with the right-wing CEDA. Lerroux was prime minister of Spain three times between 1933 and 1935 – once as part of the centre-left coalition, and twice following the victory of the right in November 1933. During the Spanish Civil War, he left Spain for Portugal.

The general strike, 1917

Though the PSOE and the UGT supported the renovation coalition, the UGT believed a general strike – in addition to calling for wage increases to overcome wartime inflation – would help achieve more fundamental changes to the political system. Despite advice to the contrary, on 13 August, the UGT launched its general strike, in which CNT members also played an important part. The army – including the *junteros* – supported the government, and this revolutionary general strike was then crushed by police and army units, with over 170 deaths.

SOURCE 4.4

The wonder is not that the constitution was overthrown in the end [in 1923], but that it lasted as long as it did in a country where military intervention had occurred so often during the preceding century. Perhaps it did not really last after 1917: a democracy can hardly exist if several provinces are only kept from revolution by the brutality of the civil guard, and the largest industrial city from civil war by counter-terrorism sponsored by industrialists, and winked at by the police.

During the [First World] war, Spanish employers had expanded their enterprises, but now had to contract. They would fight labour now, since there was a glut of workers; in the war, there had been a shortage. But in the clash of labour and capital, between 1917 and 1923, a class war was to be seen which often came close to outright conflict, and over issues other than economic: employers believed themselves threatened by bankruptcy if not revolution, the anarchists believed they were on the brink of the millennium. Since, whatever the views of the central government, the local military authorities usually agreed with the employers, and often arrested strikers, the character of the conflict became more and more violent. The rule of General Martínez Anido (previously known as the sanguinary governor in Melilla) as civil governor of Barcelona from 1920 to 1922 was notoriously ruthless: a type of repression not seen in Spain for generations.

Thomas, H. 1977. **The Spanish Civil War.** *Harmondsworth. Penguin. pp. 23–4.*

QUESTION

How, according to Source 4.4, did the actions of the Civil Guard and the army make the unrest of the years 1917–23 more rather than less revolutionary?

Figure 4.2: An arrest during the general strike of 1917.

Political problems, 1918–23

After 1917, Spain's parliamentary system faced a series of challenges: for long periods, the Cortes did not meet, the press was censored, constitutional guarantees were suspended and, instead, Spain was often ruled by decree.

When the new Cortes had finally met in Madrid, on 30 October 1917, Francesc Cambó – frightened by the revolutionary general strike in 1917 – formally withdrew his support from the renovation movement. The leaders of the Socialists and the UGT had also begun to move away from outright revolution. A new government composed of Liberals and Conservatives led by García Prieto took over. However, this ended on 22 March 1918 and, after some confusion, was replaced by a national government headed by Antonio Maura. This was essentially a government of the old style – though it did include Santiago Alba, representing the 'modern' wing of liberalism, and Cambó. But, it too, lasted only a short time, as differences quickly emerged between the moderate views of Alba and the conservative separatist aims of Cambó. Following Maura's resignation, from November 1918 to September 1923, Spain had ten short-lived governments, none of which lasted a year.

Yet, during this period, Spain faced two big problems: the violent conflict between employers and employees – especially in Barcelona; and the war in Morocco. Both these issues needed the army to solve them, which further shifted the balance of power between civilian governments and the military, as the army insisted on independence from civilian control if it were to put down industrial conflict.

Continuing industrial unrest

Between 1918 and 1923, Spain experienced some of the most savage social conflicts in postwar Europe. The great increase in membership and militancy during the war had benefitted the CNT, not the Socialists. By 1914, after three years of clandestinity, CNT membership was 14000. By 1919, this had exploded to over 700000: more than three times larger than the Socialists' UGT at 200000.

The two main areas for this conflict were Barcelona and Andalucía – the places where anarcho-syndicalism was strongest. There had been a long tradition of libertarian anarchism and terrorism in these regions, which fed into the CNT's ideas of unions organised for 'direct action' against ruthless employers. CNT leaders preferred a strategy of building up union strength via successful strikes, so that eventually a general strike could be called which would destroy capitalism and usher in a syndicalist structure for Spain. These tended to be opposed to those in *grupos de afinidad* (action groups) who favoured the use of violence to spark off a revolution, rather than working for wage settlements and improved working conditions. These action groups were particularly strong among the lower, often immigrant, lower ranks of the working class.

Barcelona

Despite the repression which had followed the 1917 general strike, political and industrial unrest continued – particularly in Catalonia. This was partly inspired by the Russian Revolution, and was partly a reaction to the depression that followed the First World War. In 1919, yet another general strike took place in Barcelona, following wage cuts imposed on workers at a hydro-electric plant. Soon sympathy strikes and factory occupations by workers in other industries spread rapidly, involving over 100000 workers.

Unlike previous strikes, employers were unable to organise effective repression – even though, as previously, martial law was declared; while the government in Madrid tried, unsuccessfully, to conscript workers. As a result, the strikers won some important concessions: unions were recognised as legitimate representatives of workers, and an eight-hour day was achieved for the whole of Spain. However, political unrest continued, leading many wealthy industrialists and landowners to fear a workers' revolution was not far off. In response, employers hired *pistoleros* (gunmen) to assassinate union leaders and militants – this resulted in the deaths of hundreds of anarchists and socialists. Many anarchists retaliated in kind – in 1921, Catalan anarchists managed to assassinate Prime Minister Dato.

ACTIVITY

Carry out some further research on the use of *pistoleros* by employers in Barcelona after 1918. Then write a short paragraph to show how this made the social conflicts even more bitter.

Andalucía

Unrest in rural areas also spread during the First World War and in the years immediately after it. After the end of the war, a depression ensued which, among other things, hit agriculture worldwide. The demand for Spanish agricultural products declined, and prices fell. At the same time, population increases led landowners – especially those owners of the large *latifundia* – to take advantage of this by reducing wages for the increased numbers of landless labourers, even though postwar inflation meant these workers were faced with rising prices. Although the close alliance between landowners, the police and army, and the government ensured that the increasing unrest and violence were ruthlessly suppressed, these conditions meant socialist and anarchist ideas continued to spread rapidly. In particular, there were increasing calls for land reform – especially in the southern province of Andalucía, where anarchism was strong. As workers migrated from one region to another, they took these political ideas with them.

The army

Also of great significance during this period were developments concerning the army. In an attempt to reduce the influence of the *juntas*, decrees were issued awarding a pay rise, and granting promotion by strict seniority. However, the army – itself split because the senior

225

officers had never approved of the *juntas* – came increasingly under the influence of the privileged corps and, especially, of the African army fighting in Morocco: these latter wanted promotion by merit.

In July 1921, the Spanish army suffered a humiliating defeat at Annual in Morocco, at the hands of Abd -el-Krim's forces – he then declared the Republic of the Rif as an independent state. As with the loss of Spain's colonies in the Americas in 1898, Spain's *Africanista* officers blamed Spain's civilian government for not properly equipping the troops. The Spanish army in Africa was then significantly reformed, and adopted increasingly brutal methods to crush the Moroccan rebels. These *Africanistas* saw themselves as a new élite, and were increasingly hostile to Spain's civilian governments.

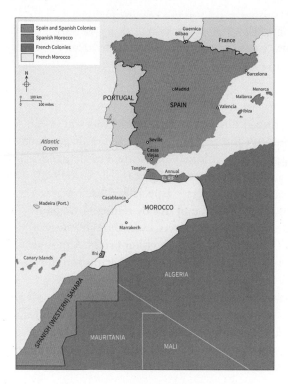

Figure 4.3: Spain and Spanish colonies in Africa.

SOURCE 4.5

Military discontent was related to a division within the army of those who had volunteered to fight in Africa – *Africanistas* – and those who had remained on the mainland – *peninsulares*. For those who had fought in Africa the risks were enormous but the prizes, in terms of adventure and rapid promotion, high. The rigours and horrors of the Moroccan tribal wars brutalized the beleaguered Africanistas, who began to see themselves as a heroic band of warriors who, in their commitment to defending the Moroccan colony, were alone concerned with the fate of the patria. Long before the establishment of the Second Republic, this had developed into contempt for professional politicians, for the pacifist left-wing masses and, to a certain extent, for the *peninsulares*.

Preston, P. 2006. **The Spanish Civil War: Reaction, Revolution and Revenge.** *London. Harper Perennial. pp. 31–2.*

QUESTION

Who were the *Africanistas*? Why did they blame Spain's civilian government for the defeat in Morocco in 1921?

The king was increasingly committed to these *Africanistas*, and public opinion began to turn against the *junteros*. In November 1922, the *junteros* were finally dissolved by Sánchez Guerra's Conservative government.

4.3 What were the main developments in Spain from 1923 to 1930?

After the years of unrest which had existed since 1917, in September 1923 a military coup – led by **Miguel Primo de Rivera**, the captain-general of Catalonia – overthrew the parliamentary government in Spain. Rivera then established himself as dictator. Unlike previous interventions by the military, it was made clear that the army had no intention of passing power over to civilian politicians. Instead, Rivera and the army planned to construct a military regime.

On 14 September, the day after the coup, Rivera declared a state of emergency throughout Spain – this lasted until 15 May 1925.

Figure 4.4: The proclamation of a state of siege in Madrid and the start of Rivera's military dictatorship, 15 September 1923.

Miguel Primo de Rivera (1870–1930):

He was an aristocrat and military officer who had fought in Spain's colonial wars in Morocco, Cuba and the Philippines. With the support of King Alfonso XIII, he seized power in a military coup in 1923 after years of political protests, strikes, revolts and economic decline. He promised to eliminate corruption and to suppress the left-wing unrest. To achieve this, he suspended the constitution, established martial law and imposed a strict system of censorship. The Great Depression affected Spain badly and, in January 1930, Rivera resigned.

SOURCE 4.6

At half past one in the morning of 13 September 1923 the Capitanía General contacted the newsdesks of all the newspapers in Barcelona by telephone. Primo de Rivera wished to announce an 'extremely important document to the press. One hour later reporters filled the office of the dictator. The general… handed over some leaflets with the request – or the order – that they be inserted in all the newspapers. The manifesto, directed to 'the country and the army', declared that the time had come to save the Fatherland, to launch 'on behalf of Spain and the king' a mobilisation that had been demanded by the 'rational population'. Someone had to put an end to the 'social indiscipline' created by murders, terrorist attacks, the impunity for those disseminating communist propaganda, the effrontery of separatism and the 'despicable political intrigues' that used 'the Morocco tragedy' as a justification. In other words, the country faced a set of 'disgraceful and shameful' situations that needed to be 'remedied swiftly and radically'.

Casanova, J. & Andrés, C. G. 2014. **Twentieth-Century Spain: A History.** *Cambridge. Cambridge University Press. p. 85.*

The élites and the coup

The Spanish élites – the army, employers and the Catholic Church – supported Rivera's coup, believing that a strong leader was needed to suppress the working classes and restore order. Like them, Rivera wanted to crush the clearly emerging signs of imminent revolution.

SOURCE 4.7

The apparent backwardness of early twentieth-century Spain led some to conclude, particularly inside the powerful socialist movement, that Spain had not completed its 'bourgeois revolution'. By this they meant that the basis for capitalist development had not been put in place: the emergence of a strong industrial bourgeoisie, the ending of feudal relations in the countryside, the definitive separating of Church and state and the establishment of a liberal parliamentary democracy with its corresponding political and civil rights. The industrial bourgeoisie was indeed weak compared with its British or French counterparts. Its power was very localized: centred on steel, shipbuilding and mining in northern Spain, or the textile industry of Catalonia. Its very weakness had made the Spanish bourgeoisie particularly insecure and deeply conservative in political questions. Labour protest was usually met with extreme intransigence by the employers. But the failure to eliminate the threat represented by the workers' movement or to overcome their economic problems led most industrialists to welcome General Miguel Primo de Rivera's military dictatorship.

Durgan, A. 2007. **The Spanish Civil War**. *London. Palgrave Macmillan. pp. 7–8.*

The king, Alfonso XIII, had never approved of a constitutional monarchy, and had frequently come into conflict with the parliamentary governments of Spain. His decision to postpone any reaction to the coup until he had consulted his military advisers, provoked the prime minister into resigning. The king then voluntarily handed power over to Rivera – even when, after being appointed prime minister, Rivera openly announced he would not form a civilian government or respect the constitution. When, in November, the speakers of the Congress and the Senate called on the king to follow the constitution and reconvene the Cortes, he refused and, instead, dismissed them.

The army, dominated by the conservative and aristocratic élites, upheld the king's decision. After Rivera's coup, the army ruthlessly suppressed any protests or uprisings and, like the Church, it came to be widely despised by Spain's lower classes, who faced a range of social and economic problems such as poverty and poor standards of education. The Spanish élites, on the other hand, flourished under Rivera's dictatorship. In November 1923, the king and Rivera made an official trip to Italy, where they met the pope and Mussolini – the king offered Spain's services to the pope should there be another crusade to 'save' the Catholic Church from its enemies; while Rivera praised Mussolini and was, in turn, advised by him.

The Military Directorate

At first, Rivera only had the support of the military governor of Zaragoza, General José Sanjurjo, and of those generals close to the king in Madrid. The rest of the captains-general and military governors, however, were not prepared to resist fellow officers.

Rivera formed a Military Directorate, made up of eight generals and one rear-admiral: two of these acted, respectively, as under-secretary of the interior, and director-general of public order. However, real power rested with Rivera. Military courts were established to try 'crimes against the unity of the Fatherland'; the constitution and its guarantees of individual rights were suspended; and the press was severely censored: this included banning any criticism of the government or the Church, reporting social conflicts, or comments on the situation in Morocco.

Suppression

There was a surprising lack of immediate opposition to Rivera's coup from many of the left-wing parties – despite Rivera's clear determination to crush 'public disorder', regional nationalism and *caciquismo*, as well as dealing with the war in Morocco. The republican parties either waited to see what Rivera's intentions were, or even gave their support to the coup.

The Socialists and their union, the UGT, urged their members to remain calm and not to join the protests organised by the CNT and by the Communists – even when the repression of the anarchists and communists became increasingly severe. Rivera banned all anarchist organisations, and the CNT's main leaders were arrested – though some went into exile. The harsh repression of the communists resulted in the PCE having fewer than 500 active militants in the whole country.

Rivera was also determined to crush regional separatist movements – he once said he would rather see Spain red with blood than broken up. So the various separatist parties in the Basque part of the country and in Catalonia were harshly repressed – as a result, these organisations went underground. In 18 September 1923, the king signed a decree which forbade the flying of any flag other than the Spanish flag, and only the Castilian language was to be used in official documents, street names, and in schools and churches.

Political centralisation

Rivera was determined to centralise control of Spain's regions and establish military control of civil society. From the start of his dictatorship, a series of decrees were issued by the Military Directorate to achieve this. All civil governors were replaced by army officers, and elected town and city councils were abolished. Instead, Rivera installed officials chosen from among the highest tax-payers – one of their roles was to foster Spanish nationalism and patriotism. In January 1924, Rivera appointed administrators to control the provincial governments, and all municipal courts were abolished.

From 1924, **José Calvo Sotelo**, oversaw steps to reform the entire local and provinical administration.

José Calvo Sotelo (1893–1936):

He was an economist and a member of Antonio Maura's Conservative Party. He supported Rivera's coup in 1923 and, in 1925, became Rivera's finance minister. During the Second Republic, he became one of the most prominent right-wing politicians and, in 1935, tried to gain control of the Falange, Spain's semi-fascist party. After the Popular Front's election victory in 1936, he was leader of the opposition to its reforms. In July 1936, he was murdered in retaliation for the murder of a Popular Front supporter. Sotelo's death was used by the army as one of the justifications for the start of their revolt later that month.

City councils and provincial governments were granted some financial independence and powers to improve services and promote infrastructure and city planning. However, real power remained in the hands of the military governors, who had virtually total control over local corporations and provincial politics. This was despite the fact that in April 1924, Rivera announced that there would be a gradual separation of the posts of civil and military governors. By then however, opposition had been virtually eradicated, and Rivera's dictatorship was firmly established.

The *Unión Patriótica* and the *somatén*

To provide the administrators this new system would need, Rivera set up the *Unión Patriótica* in April 1924. This was supposed to be a national party, based on the ideas of 'Religion, Fatherland and Monarchy', to bring together all Spaniards 'of good faith'. The establishment of a national structure proved slow at first, but soon the new town and city councils began to draw on *Unión* members. By the summer of 1924, Rivera claimed it had almost 2 million members, and that it was now able to defend law and order, private ownership and political authority.

Rivera also quickly encouraged the establishment of local *somatén*. These had been initially set up in Catalonia during the 'gun-law' period (*pistolerismo*) in the early 1920s by the wealthy as a sort of local armed militia that at times had helped the police and the army in repressing left-wing groups and actions. By 1924, there were over 100 000 such somatenistas in Spain. By 1928, numbers had doubled.

On the surface, it seemed as if Rivera's dictatorship was securely established. He had crushed separatist movements in Catalonia. Class conflict and social unrest – and, with it, the threat of revolution – had been reduced to the lowest level for years; and the various institutions established since 1923 seemed to be successfully consolidating his regime.

Success in Morocco

One of the justifications for Rivera's coup had been the need to solve the problem of Morocco. At first, Spanish forces had continued to do badly in the face of several successful attacks by the forces of Abd-el-Krim. Encouraged by this, Abd-el-Krim had decided to attack French Morocco as well. As a result, in July 1925, Rivera signed an agreement with the French to launch a joint military operation. This forced Rivera to reverse his earlier decision to reduce the size of the army and military expenditure. This was successful and Spanish forces performed well; and, in 1926, the Republic of the Rif was ended. Although military mopping-up operations continued until 1927, Rivera was able to announce as early as 1925 that he had solved the Morocco problem.

The Civilian Directorate

Rivera hoped that his political measures, and the success in Morocco, would create mass civilian support for his dictatorship. However, his plan to turn the state of emergency into a long-lasting authoritarian regime was not achieved.

On 2 December 1925, he announced to the king his intention to replace his military dictatorship with an authoritarian civil and economic regime. Alfonso XIII agreed that the work of the Military Directorate needed to be continued and consolidated for 'national salvation'. The next day, Rivera announced the reintroduction of a Council of Ministers, and appointed a civilian cabinet which lasted more-or-less unchanged until January 1930. For this, he relied on Sotelo and Eduardo Aunós who, respectively, were in charge of finance and labour. In addition, the Count of Guadalhorce was put in charge of development. The aim was that these three, with their extensive connections to industrial, banking and agricultural interests, would create economic development, carry out social reforms, and so consolidate Rivera's regime.

However, despite the inclusion of civilian experts, in reality, Rivera remained very much the dictator, with all executive power in his hands. For instance, the Council of Ministers did not deal with political problems – instead, Rivera made such decisions, or left them to General Martínez Anido, who was also deputy prime minister and minister of cabinet affairs. In particular, it was Anido who dealt with civil governors and public order problems. In addition, the cabinet also contained two other high-ranking officers who, as well as being in charge of the ministries of war and the navy, were the only ones to have the power to deal with all crimes related to 'security of the interior' – this included common misdemeanours such as theft.

In practice, the new government, with such strong military influence, had unlimited executive, legislative and judicial powers. This included overruling verdicts of administrative tribunals, appointing special judges and reprimanding magistrates for 'wrong' decisions. Furthermore, there was no right of appeal against their decisions. Thus, despite the surface appearance of change from the Military Directorate set up in 1923, Spanish people had no civil rights or constitutional protections from the dictatorship.

Corporatism

To give his regime more of a legal façade, and to win social support, Rivera developed institutions based on fascist ideas about a corporate state, which Mussolini was implementing in Italy. In July 1926, Rivera started the move towards a corporate parliament and, in September 1926, a national plebiscite was held. The *Unión Patriótica*, with the backing of the Church, urged people to endorse the *Caudillo de Alhucemas* (as Rivera was often known, named after a Spanish victory in Morocco in the summer of 1925). Out of the 13 million entitled to vote, the regime announced that 7 million had voted 'yes' – though there were several 'irregularities' in some of the regions.

Rivera then persuaded the king to agree to the calling of a National Assembly of *Uniones Patriótica* – he agreed, as it was made clear that it would not be a parliament as understood by liberal opinion, and would not have legislative rights or any sovereign powers. Instead, it was an advisory body which 'represented' various 'interests', and was composed of senior state officials, the army, the Church, the judiciary and delegates from *Unión Patriótica*'s municipal, regional and provincial bodies. It also had representatives from national economic interests: employer and trade associations, and members of the academic world.

The assembly first met in September 1927 but, from its very first meeting, it was clearly controlled by the government – even down to appointing its members and what it was allowed to discuss. One of its first tasks was to draw up a new constitution – in the end, the final version of this did not appear until July 1929. Although this included provisions against separatism of the Fatherland, confirmed Roman Catholicism as the official state religion, and gave extraordinary powers to the government, it never became law.

KEY CONCEPTS QUESTION

Change and continuity: To what extent were main features of the Civilian Directorate different from those of the Military Directorate?

Economic and social developments

In March 1924, Rivera set up the National Economy Council to deal with pressure groups, and to regulate protective measures for the national economy. The aim was to prevent strikes and other expressions of social and class conflict by regulating labour relations and passing various forms of social legislation through arbitration organisations and joint employer-worker committees.

The economy

Between 1900 and 1930, Spain experienced a period of significant modernisation and economic growth. In particular, Spanish industry benefitted from the international economic boom of the 'Golden Twenties' – with Spanish industry growing by over 5% a year. This was partly because of Rivera's attempts to increase national production and to protect Spanish industries. Growth was particularly marked in the steel, construction and chemical industries – as a result of city development schemes, the spread of electricity connections, the need for new machinery, increased exports and increased foreign investments. One of Rivera's policies was to promote business concentration and monopolies: such as the petrol, railway, road, port and telephone industries.

Although there was no significant improvement in working conditions during this period, many people appreciated the high employment rate, stable food prices, various social protection measures (such as the provision of cheap housing and the introduction of health services and a six-day working week), and a general improvement in labour relations. In August 1926, the new Labour Code allowed the formation of workers' societies – provided they accepted the corporate framework established by Rivera. In November 1926, a National Corporations Organisation (*Organizacíon Nacional Corporativa*) was created, along with various corporation councils (representing each trade on a national basis), and an advisory Higher Labour Council.

The Socialists' UGT agreed to cooperate with these steps, and gained most of the worker representation posts in the ONC. Its membership grew to over 235 000 by 1928, and it improved its rural base when the *Federacíon Nacional de Trabajadores de la Tierra* (FNTT) was set up. As a result of the Socialist Party's cooperation – and the repression of the anarchists – the number and duration of labour disputes declined.

However, though the national income had doubled since the end of the 19th century, there were still major regional variations. In particular, by 1929, more than half the population of Spain still worked on the land – often in terrible poverty. This was especially true in regions such as Andalucía in the south, where farming was controlled by the owners of large estates known as *latifundia*. These landowners employed landless labourers on a day-by-day basis, and many of these workers lived in conditions of near-starvation.

Spanish society

Between 1900 and 1930, Spain's population rose from 18.6 million to 23.5 million; average life expectancy rose from 35 to 50; and the illiteracy rate went down from 60% to 35% – the latter the result of an expansion of primary education and the emphasis given to scientific and technical training. Additionally, 10 million Spaniards left rural areas to seek work in the larger towns and cities, many of which more than doubled in size. By 1930, while rural areas still dominated many regions, the agricultural labour force was less than 50% of the total working population. At the same time, the agricultural sector's productivity increased; while in industry, over 1 million extra workers were employed in 1930 than in 1900, and production doubled.

Spanish art and culture

The various economic, social and political changes Spain experienced from 1918 onwards naturally had an impact on cultural developments. During the early part of the 20th century, many of Spain's leading artists – such as Pablo Picasso – worked in Paris rather than in Spain itself. These artists either contributed to, or even led, developments in various modernist art movements. However, modernisme (known as art nouveau in most other countries) also developed within Spain, where several cultural movements emerged – beginning with a literary Modernism at the turn of the century. An architectural modernism developed around **Antoni Gaudí** in Barcelona, who created a new style of designing and creating buildings, which flourished until the 1920s.

> **Antoni Gaudí (1852–1926):**
>
> He was a Catalan architect, and was the leading light within Catalan modernism. His best known works are the Sagrada Família (which he was working on when he died, and which is still not quite finished) and Park Güell in Barcelona. However, there are also several Gaudí buildings in places such as León and Astorga.

Around the time of the end of the First World War, the influences of various artistic movements spread to Spain – these included Cubism, Futurism, Surrealism and Dadism. These avant-garde styles shook Spain's cultural and intellectual life, and had a radical impact on literature, art and the new medium of film.

The Generation of '27

One of the most interesting developments in Spain was the appearance of the 'Generation of '27', which was an influential avant-garde group of intellectuals, poets and artists which first began to emerge between 1923 and 1927, during Rivera's dictatorship. In 1927, they had their first formal meeting in Seville. Within this group, Catalan artists and writers often played a leading role.

The group, despite working within a variety of genres and styles, tried to bridge the gap between Spanish popular culture and folklore on the one hand, and the new European avant-garde styles and preoccupations. Among its best-known members were the poet and playwright **Federico García Lorca**, the artist and film maker Luis Buñuel, and the surrealist painter Salvador Dalí.

Federico García Lorca (1898–1936):

He was a leading member of the Generation of '27, and for a time worked closely with Dalí. Partly as a result of the tensions resulting from the need to keep secret the fact that he was gay, he left Spain for the US in 1929. While there, he witnessed the impact of the Wall Street Crash on ordinary people, and wrote poetry which attacked capitalist society. He returned to Spain in 1930, at the time of the creation of the Second Republic, and was appointed director of a university student theatre company – financed by the Ministry of Education – which travelled across Spain and put on free modernist plays. The poverty Lorca saw in rural Spain radicalised him even further, and his Rural Trilogy plays (1932–36) were very critical of traditional Spanish values: especially as regards conventional views about the role of women and issues concerning class and same-sex relationships. Just three days before the start of the civil war, he travelled to Granada in the south of Spain. The Spanish right was strong there and, despite having some contacts among the group, Lorca's socialist beliefs and his sexual orientation made him a potential target. In August 1936, he was arrested and shot by a Nationalist militia group connected to the anti-communist CEDA.

Politically, while they were a very diverse group, most would later fall foul of Franco's Nationalists – Lorca being executed at the start of the civil war. As a result, while a few – such as Dalí – eventually made accommodations with the Nationalists, most went into exile.

Opposition to Rivera

By the summer of 1929, despite all his efforts, Rivera was beginning to lose what support he had from the king and the army. The *Unión Patriótica* and the *somatén* had enjoyed very limited success in building mass support for Rivera's regime. At the same time, some of his opponents had begun to plot against him and his dictatorship.

Growing left-wing resistance

As early as November 1924, several armed anarchists had launched an incursion from France – though this was defeated by the Civil Guard and the *Carabineros*, it was the start of several insurrectional attempts by the anarchists. Ironically, Rivera's decision to ban the CNT led to the growing dominance of those anarchists who had always favoured direct armed action over the trade-unionist strategy of the main anarchist leaders. In July 1927, the more militant anarchist groups set up the *Federacíon Anarquista Ibérica* (FAI) in Valencia. The FAI was a libertarian organisation determined to launch a rebellion against Rivera's dictatorship, and gained increasing influence with the CNT.

In November 1926, the members of the Catalan separatist group *Estat Català*, led by Francesc Macià, adopted a similar strategy. Their plan – like that of the militant anarchists – was to increase subversion via small military actions which would then be followed by a general strike supported by other revolutionary groups and individuals. It was also hoped that such developments might provoke a mutiny within the army.

From 1928, the Socialists – who had always refused to attend meetings of the National Assembly – began to move away from Rivera's regime. In August 1929, PSOE and UGT leaders signed a joint manifesto condemning the dictatorship, and announced their decision to fight for a democratic republic. In part, these moves were linked to the increasingly spirited resistance shown by the anarchists.

Army discontents

A more serious threat to Rivera had already emerged in Valencia in June 1926. There, two generals – Aguilera and Weyler – along with two prominent politicians, had planned to issue a manifesto as part of a traditional *pronunciamiento*, warning that there would be division and insurrection within the army if the king didn't dismiss Rivera. However, this plot – known as the *Sanjuanada* – collapsed after differences among the officers and news leaked out to the press. The ringleaders were either arrested or fined – this plot was so easily dealt with because there was no real support from either the general public or a large section of the army.

Though this army plot was easily put down, another one emerged in September, when the artillery corps staged a protest over promotions by seniority, which the Directorate had removed. This was part of the old conflict between the *junteros* of the army élite corps, such as the engineers and the medical corps, which favoured the old system, and the *Africanistas*, who wanted promotion by merit. Rivera promptly dissolved the Artillery Corps, suspended over 1000 officers, and declared martial law throughout Spain. Though the officers were allowed to return to their posts within a few months, divisions and disputes within the army continued to grow.

Student protests

Rivera also began to face opposition from university students, whose numbers – because of increased economic prosperity and related social changes – had risen from fewer than 20 000 before Rivera's coup to almost 60 000 by 1929. The first student protests had begun in the spring of 1925, and became more widespread after the foundation of the *Federacíon Universitaria Escolar* (FUE), at the end of 1926: in part, to counter the influence of the Catholic associations. From March 1928, student protests moved from specific academic issues to general opposition to the dictatorship. Rivera quickly responded to the growing number of protest demonstrations and student assemblies by ordering the army to occupy the colleges, and by expelling student protesters and closing various universities – such as those in Barcelona and Madrid. However, these actions did not end student unrest, which began to attract the support of intellectuals who began to rally to the demands for a democratic republic.

Republicanism

In February 1926, republicans – who had become divided over how to respond to Rivera's coup and regime – took a step towards greater collaboration. Various radical republicans (such as those led by Alejandro

Lerroux, and the Catalan republicans led by Marcelino Domingo) and more reformist republicans (including *Partido Acción Republicana*, led by intellectuals such as **Manuel Azaña** and Ramón Pérez de Ayala) came together to form the *Alianza Republicana*.

Manuel Azaña (1880–1940):

He was a wealthy lawyer; was strongly anti-clerical, and was initially a member of the Reformist Republican Party. In 1926, he and José Giral founded the *Partido Acción Republicana*, a group largely made up of middle-class progressives. Azaña opposed Rivera's dictatorship and the role of the king, and was one of those forming the Pact of San Sebastián in 1930. Azaña acted as prime minister after Zamora resigned, and continued in that post after the new constitution was approved in December 1931, thus becoming the first prime minister of the Second Republic. He became president in May 1936, just before the Civil War broke out. After Franco's victory in 1939, he fled to France, where Azaña died shortly after.

ACTIVITY

Carry out some extra research on the period 1924–29, and draw up a chart showing which groups were beginning to oppose Rivera's dictatorship, and briefly describing their actions.

Rivera's fall

In January 1929, republicans from the *Alianza Republicana* took part in a plot against Rivera led by José Sánchez Guerra who, in March 1922, had headed a conservative administration. Guerra attempted to unite monarchists who wanted a return to the 1876 Constitution, republicans wanting a new Cortes, and army officers dissatisfied with Rivera's rule into a single party. However, there was a premature uprising and the plan was called off.

Although Rivera survived this attempt to overthrow him, he was becoming increasingly isolated. Even the king was moving away from him, as he wanted to save the crown by getting support from those who would agree to his plan of going back to the political system which had existed before 1923. The final straw for Rivera was the fact that,

European States in the Interwar Years (1918–1939)

from mid-1929, the country's economic situation began to sharply deteriorate. This was made worse by the Great Depression which quickly followed the collapse of the US stock market in October 1929.

This sparked off an international global economic crisis which had never been experienced before – and the scale of which was not seen again until the one begun by the banking crash of 2008. As a result, the number of strikes in Spain greatly increased, with Rivera responding with increased repression. At the same time, landowners' and industrialists' associations ended their unconditional support for the regime – in large part as they disliked aspects of corporatism, and especially the labour arbitration laws.

By then, Rivera's *Unión Patriótica* and the *somatén*, instead of becoming mass organisations supporting his regime, had become filled with *caciques* and opportunists, many of whom mainly acted as paramilitary forces which helped the police in their repression of workers' strikes and student protests.

In December 1929, Rivera announced his decision to transfer power to a transitional government. In January 1930 – with rumours spreading of another military plot, headed by General Goded – Rivera sought the approval of the captains-general for his plan. The only one to clearly support him was Sanjurjo. On 28 January 1930, Rivera resigned and left for Paris, where he died two months later.

The king, who had not been informed by Rivera of his plans, refused to call a new Cortes. Instead, he appointed General Berenguer as prime minister, in the hope of going back to the pre-coup situation. However, many Spaniards believed it would be impossible to return to a constitution which, from 1923 to 1930, had been discarded. In particular, the king's open support of Rivera until near the end of the dictatorship had greatly undermined support for the Restoration monarchy. As will be seen in the next unit, by 1930 the monarchy had become very much a tainted institution as a result of Alfonso XIII's actions since 1923.

Figure 4.5: Primo de Rivera (front row, left), with the King of Spain (front row, centre), and other officers, 1930.

QUESTION

What can you learn from the photograph in Figure 4.5 about the nature of Rivera's dictatorship?

The nature of Rivera's dictatorship

Historians have debated the nature of Rivera's regime, with some seeing it as basically the same as previous military *pronunciamentos*, and others believing it to be something completely different. Up until about 1990, most of these interpretations were either from a Marxist perspective (which stressed socio-economic factors) or a liberal perspective (which focused instead on the political crisis of Spain's parliamentary system as the main explanation for the 1923 coup). The latter approach is, in part, one taken by Raymond Carr.

European States in the Interwar Years (1918–1939)

Since 1990, there has been greater focus on comparative research. Julián Casanova and Carlos Gil Andrés, for instance, see Rivera's 'radical right' coup as part of a general European trend during the interwar years towards authoritarian military or semi-military regimes. José Luis Gómez Navarro takes a similar line, seeing Rivera as just a Spanish version of the dictatorships which emerged in several countries around the Mediterranean (such as Italy) and in central and eastern Europe. Such regimes came to power as a result of political and economic crises which emerged at the end of the 19th century among countries that were late in modernising agriculture and industry and in establishing of liberal political systems. These pressures were greatly heightened by the impact of the First World War which, in these countries, saw the military – with the backing of their respective monarchs – take power in order to eliminate the spectre of workers' revolution.

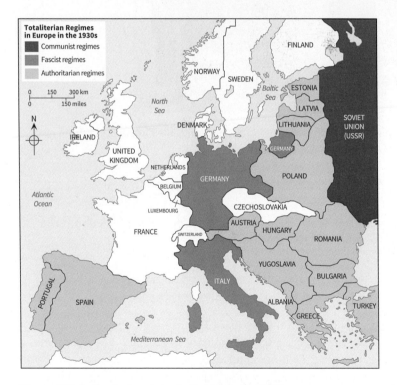

Figure 4.6: Authoritarian states in Europe in the 1930s.

Rivera's coup and his regime certainly had links to Mussolini's fascist movement in Italy. Rivera made no secret of his admiration of Mussolini's March on Rome in October 1922 and, on their state visit to Fascist Italy in 1923, the king actually introduced Rivera as 'his own Mussolini'. Both Rivera and Mussolini were opposed to democracy and parliamentarianism, and both tried to create a corporate state as a way of keeping a lid on revolutionary developments among the workers.

AT THE CAFÉ DES DICTATEURS.

Enter King Alexander of Yugo-Slavia.

Signor Mussolini (*to Señor Primo de Rivera*). "THIS PLACE ISN'T QUITE SO EXCLUSIVE AS IT USED TO BE."

Figure 4.7: A cartoon which appeared in the British magazine, Punch, in 1929, showing Rivera's Spain as just one of several authoritarian regimes in southern and eastern Europe in the 1920s.

There, however, the similarities end – both Mussolini and Hitler came to power after having created mass political movements, not via military coups. Rivera, on the other hand, did not have a mass movement behind him in 1923 – and failed to create one after he came to power. Thus, although Rivera's regime shared some of the features of Mussolini's rule, it was in essence an authoritarian, not a fascist, dictatorship. Unlike fascism, with an ideology which spoke of 'modernism' and dynamism, Rivera's ideas were based on an appeal to traditional values, with no stated objective of building a new society. After taking power, as Shlomo Ben-Ami has pointed out, Rivera – in common with other authoritarian military regimes – attempted to create a party to provide a cloak of legitimacy and popular support, and to pass some social reforms. However, these attempts failed – in part, because the landowners and industrialists resented the concessions made to their employees. Thus, in the end, Rivera's regime was based only on the support of the army and the economic élites – once that was withdrawn, his position became untenable.

However, it has been argued by some historians – such as María Teresa González Calbet – that Rivera did manage to effect some significant changes – even though these were mainly unintentional. These included the disintegration of the old dynastic parties, the elimination of projects which aimed at significant reform within the system, and the discrediting of the monarchy. Eduardo González Calleja sees Rivera as explicitly attempting to end the old Restoration system and, in its place, putting a new national, corporate and authoritarian regime. As a consequence of Rivera's failure, alternative forces – to a greater or lesser extent also authoritarian – emerged, wanting a more fundamental democracy.

Summary activity

Copy the spider diagram below to show the problems facing Spain in 1918, and the main political and economic developments during the period 1918–30. Then, using the information in this unit and any other sources available to you, complete the diagram. Make sure you include, where relevant, brief comments about different historical debates and interpretations.

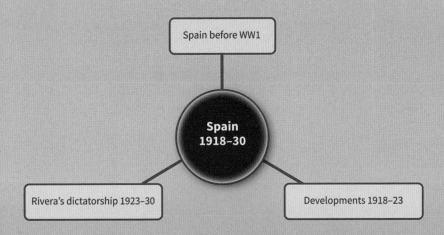

Paper 3 practice questions

1 To what extent, and for what reasons, was Spain a divided society by the time of the First World War?

2 Evaluate the impact of the First World War on Spain's economic and political system before 1923.

3 'The main reason for increasing revolutionary unrest in Spain in the period 1918–23 was the army's suppression of strikes.' To what extent do you agree with this statement?

4 Discuss the reasons for Rivera's decision to organise a coup in 1923.

5 Evaluate the main consequences of Rivera's dictatorship between 1923 and 1930.

4

Spain

Unit 2: The Second Republic and the Spanish Civil War, 1930–39

Introduction

The short-term causes of the Spanish Civil War arose between 1930 and 1936. Rivera resigned in January 1930 – in his place, Alfonso XIII appointed another military dictator. However, in the troubled economic climate the king himself was losing support, and calls for a republic grew louder. In August 1930, the main republican parties joined with the Socialists and the Catalan left to form the Pact of San Sebastián – this called for the overthrow of the military government and the king.

Local elections were held in April 1931, in which republican and socialist parties made sweeping gains. A Second Republic was declared to replace the monarchy, and Alfonso fled the country. A provisional government was then established to maintain control until a new constitution could be drawn up.

TIMELINE

1930 **Aug:** Pact of San Sebastián

1931 **Apr:** Left-wing victories in local elections; Alfonso XIII leaves Spain; provisional government declares Second Republic

May: Law of Municipal Boundaries; Segura's letter

Jun: New elections result in coalition government

Dec: New constitution agreed

1932 **Aug:** Sanjurjo's attempted coup

Sep: Agrarian Reform Law and Catalan Statute

1933 **Jan:** Casas Viejas massacre

Feb: Formation of CEDA

Nov: Right-wing parties win elections; start of *Bienio Negro*

1934 **Oct:** Revolts in Asturias and Catalonia

1935 **May:** Franco appointed chief of general staff

1936 **Jan:** Popular Front formed

Feb: Popular Front wins elections

Mar–Apr: Land occupations and general strike

Jul: Start of Civil War; Nazi Germany and Fascist Italy aid Nationalists

Aug: Non-Intervention Pact

Oct: Soviet aid for Republicans begins

Nov: International Brigades arrive

1937 **May:** Repression of POUM and anarchists in Barcelona

1938 **Oct:** International Brigades withdrawn

1939 **Mar:** Madrid taken by Nationalists

Apr: Civil War ends; start of Franco's dictatorship

KEY QUESTIONS

- Why did the Second Republic face problems in the years 1931 to 1933?
- What were the immediate causes of the Spanish Civil War?
- What were the main features of the Spanish Civil War?
- How important was foreign intervention to the Nationalists' victory in the civil war?

Overview

- In 1931, Spain became a republic once again. From 1931 to 1933, a left-wing government introduced a number of changes, but between 1933 and 1935 a new right-wing government reversed all these reforms and began suppressing left-wing uprisings – this period was known as the *Bienio Negro*.
- Leftist parties united to form the Popular Front, which won a narrow victory in the February 1936 elections. However, civil war broke out after an attempted army coup in July 1936.
- The Spanish Civil War – between Republicans (supporters of the elected government) and Nationalists (opponents of reform) – soon attracted foreign intervention from countries such as Germany and Italy. However, Britain and France followed a policy of non-intervention.
- Many individuals from different countries volunteered to join International Brigades to fight in what they believed was a struggle against the growing threat of fascism.
- The Spanish Civil War was characterised by bombings and atrocities against civilians and political opponents, and was a sign of the

changing nature of warfare – which would become fully evident in the Second World War.

- By April 1939 the Nationalists, led by Francisco Franco, had won the war. Franco then established an authoritarian, reactionary and often brutal regime that lasted until 1975.

4.4 Why did the Second Republic face problems in the years 1931 to 1933?

By 1931, the monarchy had been weakened by its continuing association with unconstitutional rule and military government. In April 1931, local elections resulted in a huge victory for the republicans and Socialists. These declared a new republic, and Alfonso XIII went into exile. A revolutionary committee – made up of the signatories of the Pact of San Sebastián of August 1930 – formed themselves as a provisional government, with the task of drawing up a new constitution.

This provisional government consisted of four parties that spanned the political spectrum: the socialist PSOE, the *Partido Acción Republicana* (Republican Action Party), the *Partido Republicano Radical* (Radical Republican Party) and the conservatives. In June 1931, national elections for a new Cortes saw these parties winning a large majority. Although the Socialists emerged as the largest party, with 115 seats, the conservative **Niceto Alcalá Zamora** became prime minister of a coalition government.

> ### Niceto Alcalá Zamora (1877–1949):
>
> He was a landowner and lawyer, and was a strong Catholic and conservative. He became a deputy of the Liberal Party. He opposed the king's decision to support Rivera's coup in 1923, and refused to work with the dictator's regime. In 1930, Zamora was one of the main leaders behind the signing of the Pact of San Sebastián, and was imprisoned for his part in the failed military uprising which followed. After the municipal elections in April 1931, he acted as prime minister of the provisional government which proclaimed the Second Republic; he then became president. Though he opposed the religious aspects of the new constitution and dissolved the Cortes in 1933, he was also opposed to the right-wing CEDA, and dissolved the Cortes again in January 1936, to prevent the CEDA leader becoming prime minister. In April 1936, Zamora was replaced as president by Manuel Azaña.

Depression and divisions

However, the Second Republic came into being at the worst possible time – as well as trying to cope with significant political reform, it was faced with the economic crisis resulting from the Great Depression. By early 1936, Spanish industrial production was still only 75% of what it had been in 1929. The production of iron fell by over 30% from 1930 to 1935, while that of other metals dropped by 50%. With falling production, unemployment rose; from 400000 in 1931, to 600000 by 1933. Thus, at a time when ordinary Spaniards expected the government to implement reforms to improve their living standards and working conditions as quickly as possible, the government found itself with reduced funds as a result of falling tax revenues.

In addition to the economic inequalities which Spain's industrial and agricultural workers hoped would be ended by speedy and long-overdue fundamental reforms, the long-term problem of separatism remained. Yet right-wing forces did not want to see any significant transformations of the status quo, and were determined to do what they could to resist reforms which would undermine Spain's traditional structures. Thus, in 1931, Spain was still a very divided society.

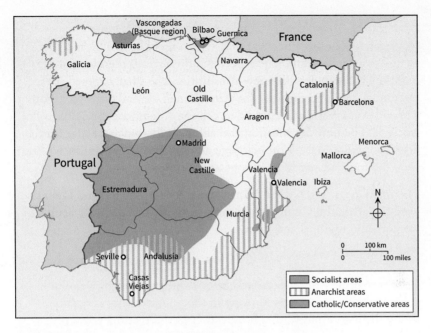

Figure 4.8: Regional and political divisions in Spain in 1931.

SOURCE 4.8

Before 1931, social, economic and political power in Spain had all been in the hands of the same groups, the components of the reactionary coalition of landowners, industrialists and bankers… However, the establishment of the Republic meant that for the first time political power had passed from the oligarchy to the moderate left… Together, they saw themselves using state power to create a new Spain. However, to do so required a vast programme of reform which would involve destroying the reactionary influence of the Church and the army, more equitable industrial relations, breaking the near feudal powers of the latifundio estate-owners and meeting the autonomy demands of Basque and Catalan regionalists… Ultimately, then, the Spanish Civil War was to grow out of the efforts of the progressive leaders of the Republic to carry out reform against the wishes of the most powerful sections of society.

Preston, P. 2006. **The Spanish Civil War: Reaction, Revolution and Revenge.** *London. Harper Perennial. pp. 38–40.*

Second Republic reforms

However, it soon became clear that, with a republic established, there were serious policy differences between the various members of the coalition. Nonetheless, the new constitution was finally agreed in December 1931. Right from the start, though, several of its provisions worried conservatives: including its call for a 'democratic republic of workers'. The new constitution also allowed all women to vote for the first time, and new laws on marriage and divorce were introduced that were the most advanced in Europe at the time.

The main areas targeted for reform at the start of the Second Republic were the army, the Church, the problems of industrial and agricultural workers, and regional autonomy.

The army

The number of army officers and Spain's military budget were both reduced. These steps angered many in the military who, as well as seeing the loss of promotion prospects, believed that the army was Spain's main defence against those groups they – and conservatives – saw as Spain's internal 'enemies'. At the same time, in June 1931, the military academy at Zaragoza was closed, partly to save money, but also because the government suspected it of being a counter-revolutionary centre – this correct suspicion would become clear in 1936, when the Civil War began. The academy's head, since 1927, had been **Francisco Franco**, who strongly believed in the need for the army to act against the 'enemy within'. He had used his position to ensure that his junior officers shared his conservative and reactionary views.

Francisco Franco (1892–1975):

He was an army officer and a supporter of Rivera's dictatorship. He strongly opposed the reforms introduced at the start of the Second Republic, and after Generals Sanjurjo and Mola were killed in two separate plane crashes in 1936 and 1937, Franco became the leader of the army's Nationalist revolt. Although he was not a member of the Falange before 1939, Franco still took the title *caudillo* ('leader') – similar to the titles used by Mussolini and Hitler. After his success in the Spanish Civil War, Franco ruled Spain as an authoritarian leader until his death in 1975.

The Church

Reform of the relations between Church and state was one of the most divisive of the issues in Spain. Because of the Church's strong support for the monarchy and for Rivera's dictatorship, most liberals and the left saw the Church as an obstacle to reform – even though the pope had urged Spanish bishops to obey the new government, this was ignored by Church leaders in Spain.

When, in May 1931, the Church's leader in Spain, Cardinal Segura, issued a letter, urging all Catholics to vote against government parties in the forthcoming June elections, he was expelled. The great anger his statement caused among supporters of the new republic was shown by the number of spontaneous attacks on churches which took place across Spain. The government then issued articles to separate Church and state, and to tax all Church property and assets. It also announced plans to close all religious schools; but even though the government began a massive programme of school building, it did not have the funds to establish public schools to replace all church schools.

DISCUSSION POINT

Should religious schools exist? Is it acceptable that young children should be educated in faith schools? Is this the same as having, for instance, schools which are based on the ideology of a particular political party?

Encouraged by such reforms, local councils in some regions took unofficial anti-clerical actions – for instance, banning religious processions. These reforms – and such actions – eventually alienated most Catholics from the Second Republic. In addition, the decision to phase out the state subsidy to the clergy by 1933 angered many parish priests. Most Spanish priests were often as poor as labourers, and relied on the subsidy to supplement their low income. They had initially welcomed the birth of the Second Republic, but the intention to end the subsidy eventually pushed such priests into supporting right-wing pro-Catholic parties.

These religious reforms – and the strong anti-clericalism of the Socialists and most republicans – also led to Niceto Zamora and the conservatives resigning from the government in October 1931. Zamora was replaced by Manuel Azaña, leader of the Radical Republicans; and Zamora's departure allowed for the implementation of more radical reforms in other areas. However, in December, when the constitution was finally accepted, Zamora was elected president – a post he held until April 1936.

Industrial and agricultural workers

During April to July 1931, decrees established the eight-hour working day and overtime pay for both industrial and agricultural workers. In particular, the Minister of Labour, **Largo Caballero**, addressed the problems of agricultural labourers. Committees of labourers and landowners were established to settle wage disputes and, in May 1931, the Law of Municipal Boundaries stopped landowners from importing migrant workers from other regions in order to break local strikes and keep wages low. In addition, landowners were ordered to cultivate all usable land: if they did not comply, their land could be requisitioned and distributed to landless labourers. At the same time, small tenant farmers were protected against unfair evictions.

Largo Caballero (1869–1946):

From 1925, he was leader of the Spanish Socialist Workers' Party (PSOE) and of the UGT. From 1931 to 1933, he was minister of labour relations under Zamora and Azaña. After the CEDA victory in November 1933, Caballero moved to the left, and headed the Marxist wings of the PSOE and UGT. He supported the workers' armed uprising of 1934 and, between September 1936 and May 1937, was prime minister at the head of the Popular Front. Caballero was forced to resign after the May Days in 1937, in which Republican factions in the civil war fought each other in the streets of Barcelona.

This shift in the balance of power – especially in southern Spain – encouraged many to join the FNTT, the agricultural section of the Socialists' UGT. Landowners, conversely, resented these reforms as they wished to maintain their estates and low wages. Their deep opposition to the Second Republic simply confirmed their traditional support for right-wing parties committed to scrapping these reforms. In the meantime, tensions rose in agricultural areas where many landowners managed to get around these laws – especially when the government seemed to do little to enforce the reforms.

The Agrarian Reform Law, 1932

The reform which did most to anger landowners was the Agrarian Reform Law of 1932, which announced a massive programme of land redistribution – mostly for central and southern Spain. An Institute of Agrarian reform was set up, which would buy any estate of more than 23 hectares – the land would then be allocated to ensure small farmers had holdings large enough to give them a decent income. However, the Institute had very limited funds, and so was only able to distribute land to a few thousand families. While this angered landowners, it also disappointed many agricultural workers and small farmers – many of these began to oppose the leadership of PSOE, the UGT and the FNTT; and there was also an increase in support for the anarchists who called for greater action.

Separatism

Catalonia had been treated harshly during Rivera's dictatorship, and expected the new government to support its call for increased autonomy. In the 1931 local elections, Catalonian separatists won a sweeping victory and proclaimed a totally independent Catalan Republic. In September 1932, the Catalan Statute officially restored a large measure of autonomy for Catalonia, as regards domestic affairs. Decisions about taxation and education would now be made by the *Generalidad*, a new regional government for Catalonia.

SOURCE 4.9

A plebiscite had been held in Catalonia. This had given 592 961 votes for home rule, and only 3276 votes against. In no free elections anywhere, perhaps, has so overwhelming a vote been given. By the summer of 1932, a Catalan statute had become law. The four provincial councils would be reorganised as a Catalan government, with the name of Generalidad, the ancient name for the medieval governorship-general of Catalonia. Catalan and Spanish would both be official languages. Catalonia… would continue to send deputies to the central parliament, as well as to the new local chamber in Barcelona…

Meantime, another bid for home rule was being made by the Basques… A Basque statute was soon brought forward which would have given the Basques the same degree of autonomy as that enjoyed by the Catalans… The growing success of the two separatist parties in Catalonia and the Basque provinces had repercussions elsewhere. A separatist movement in Galicia had been begun during the dictatorship of primo de Rivera. A statute for Galician autonomy was being planned by Casares Quiroga, minister of the interior in Azaña's government. There were similar stirrings among the Valencians, and even among the Castilians. It did seem to some that Spain might be geographically disintegrating. This was yet more cause of fear, and a disposition to sanction force, among those who believed that they might lose from such apparent dismemberment.

Thomas, H. 1977. **The Spanish Civil War**. *Harmondsworth. Penguin. pp. 86 and 90.*

Although this was reform was widely popular in Catalonia, Spanish nationalists and conservatives – and the army – were horrified at what they saw as the possible disintegration of their 'Fatherland'. Especially as other regions – such as the Basque province – demanded similar rights.

Unrest and repression

It was not long before the Second Republic faced opposition from both left and right. Those on the political right strongly opposed rights for women and workers as well as the introduction of secular education and regional autonomy. On the left, anarchist groups strongly re-emerged after the establishment of the Second Republic in 1931.

The anarchists' CNT – and socialists – were frustrated by the government's failure to enforce its reforms against the old élites: the landowners, industrialists, the army and the Church. Left-wing groups organised strikes in urban and rural areas, and called for revolution. The government responded harshly, using the army and the Civil Guard (a paramilitary police force designed to maintain peace in rural areas), commanded by **General José Sanjurjo**, to suppress these rebellions. One of the methods used was the so-called '*ley de fugas*': shooting prisoners, then claiming they had been trying to escape.

General José Sanjurjo (1872–1936):

He served in the Spanish army in Cuba in the 1890s, and fought in Morocco during the Rif War in the 1920s. In 1928, he was appointed by Rivera as head of the Civil Guard; but refused to support the king's attempt to use it against crowds demonstrating in favour of a republic. Although he supported the Second Republic at first, he later fell out with Azaña and, in 1932, was imprisoned for his unsuccessful plot (known as the *Sanjurjada*) against the new government. In May 1936, he joined with Mola and Franco in planning a coup against the Republic. He was killed in a plane crash while trying to return to Spain from exile in Portugal.

In July 1931, a strike of telephone workers – organised by the CNT – was ended after the Civil Guard killed 30 strikers. At the end of the year, a Socialist strike in Badajoz province resulted in the Civil Guard killing 11 people – including several women and children. Although the government dismissed Sanjurjo – who then unsuccessfully attempted to organise a coup against the government in August 1932 – industrial and agricultural workers blamed the government for the harsh repressions. Such attitudes increased after events in the town of Casas Viejas.

In January 1933, farmers in Cadiz province – angry at the slow pace of reform and inspired by anarchist actions elsewhere – killed members of the Civil Guard and began an uprising in the town of Casas Viejas. The authorities sent in reinforcements, including the Assault Guards, which had been formed in 1931 to deal with urban unrest. The Guards set houses on fire, and many people were burned alive; 20 of the rebels were eventually shot – some after prolonged torture. Such acts of repression disillusioned many workers and landless peasants, and deeply discredited Azaña's government.

Figure 4.9: The aftermath of the massacre at Casas Viejas in January 1933.

Eventually, in the autumn of 1933, the lack of serious progress with many of the reforms, and the repressions, led the Socialists to stop cooperating with the Republicans. Zamora then dismissed the government and called for new elections in November 1933.

4.5 What were the immediate causes of the Spanish Civil War?

As early as February 1933, the government's reforms, and the growing unrest, had led to the formation of the Spanish Confederation of the Autonomous Right (*Confederación Española de Derechas Autónomas*, CEDA). CEDA was a coalition of right-wing parties, under the leadership of **José María Gil Robles**. Its purpose was to defend religion, property rights and national unity by forming a right-wing alliance to defeat left-wing political parties. Of particular concern to the left was the fact that the members of CEDA refused to declare their support for the Second Republic.

José María Gil Robles (1898–1980):

He was the leader of *Acción Nacional*, which was later renamed *Acción Popular*. He later formed CEDA, which won the elections in 1933. However, Zamora chose Alejandro Lerroux as prime minister of the new government instead of Gil Robles, although he later served as minister of war. When the civil war began, Gil Robles authorised the donation of CEDA funds to the Nationalists. He dissolved the organisation in 1937.

CEDA gained considerable financial backing from landowners and industrialists, who hoped that it would win the elections and reverse Azaña's reforms. Another significant development in right-wing extremism was the formation of the fascist group the *Falange Española* by Rivera's son, **José Antonio Primo de Rivera**, in October 1933.

José Antonio Primo de Rivera (1903–36):

He was the oldest son of Primo de Rivera, and was a landowner and lawyer; on his father's death, he inherited the noble title. Although he was a member of the *Unión Patriótica* while at university, he also helped create the students' movement which opposed the dictatorship's higher education policies. He was involved in Sanjurjo's failed plot in 1932. The following year, he formed the Falange Española: this adopted a uniform of blue shirts, and the fascist salute. He participated in CEDA, the broadly right-wing front which won the 1933 elections – but made clear his view that violence against left-wing republican reformers was legitimate. He used the election of the Popular Front as an opportunity to take violent action against socialists and anarchists, and against Jewish-owned businesses. In November 1936, he was executed for plotting against the Republic.

The moderate centre and the left – because of the divisions between the Socialists and the republicans – were defeated in the November 1933 elections. However, although CEDA won a sweeping victory and became the largest party in the Cortes, Zamora overlooked its leader, Gil Robles. Instead, he asked Alejandro Lerroux, the leader of the Radical Republicans – the second largest party – to form a government.

The reaction of the Right

Over the next two years – known to the left as the *bienio negro* ('two black years') – the Radical Republicans and their CEDA allies reversed most of Azaña's reforms. Lerroux cut the state education budget and allowed religious schools to continue; he also repealed several laws granting rights and protection to industrial and agricultural workers, and he cut wages significantly. In particular, reforms concerning land redistribution were ended, many peasants were evicted from land that had been redistributed, and the Law of Municipal Boundaries was repealed. In addition, the autonomy rights accorded to Catalonia by the statute of 1932 were ended.

SOURCE 4.10

The result of the second election to be held in the [Second] Republic was a resounding victory for the Partido Radical and the CEDA. There are various ways of explaining this victory and the defeat of the left. Electoral legislation benefited broad coalitions, and the socialists, who stood alone, and the republicans, who were disunited, lost ground. The more conservative forces, directionless and disorganised in 1931, had reorganised and united around the defence of order and religion. The radicals had also moved right, while anarchist propaganda in favour of abstention and confrontation between the two trade union organisations, the CNT and the UGT, took votes away from the republicans and socialists.

Casanova, J. and Andrés, C. G. 2014. **Twentieth-Century Spain: A History**. *Cambridge. Cambridge University Press. p. 125.*

SOURCE 4.11

The CEDA was revealed as a coalition of rigid conservatives which rejected the schemes for agrarian reform, proposed by the handful of social Catholics within the party, as 'Bolshevik' if not a heretical interference with private property rights. Perhaps the most revealing symptom of a period when governments let landowners have their own way was the sharp drop in rural wages and the spate of evictions…

Gil Robles declared himself to be anti-Marxist. To Socialists 'an anti-Marxist Front is a Fascist Front'. With the fate of European Socialists at the hands of Dolfuss and Hitler in mind, in February 1934 the party prepared for armed revolution should the CEDA enter the government. Its instrument would be the Workers' Alliance, to include all proletarian parties and unions. In October three CEDA ministers – scarcely a fascist take-over – entered the government. Ill-prepared (the Workers' Alliance was only a reality in Asturias where it included the CNT, the Socialists, and the Communists), the Socialist party lurched into a revolution.

Carr, R. 1980. **Modern Spain 1875–1980**. *Oxford. Oxford University Press. pp. 129–30.*

Resistance by the Left

Not surprisingly, these attempts to roll-back the reforms of 1931–33 led to increased conflicts in both rural and urban areas. The UGT's FNTT called a general strike in protest, but this was crushed by the Civil Guard. In October 1934, Gil Robles forced Lerroux to form a coalition government that contained three CEDA ministers.

During this period of growing political polarisation, the Socialist Party began to adopt a more revolutionary position, believing that Gil Robles favoured an authoritarian, even fascist, government in Spain – especially given his admiration of Mussolini's Fascist regime and, later, of Hitler's Nazi regime in Germany.

The socialist Largo Caballero called for an armed uprising to oppose the increasing power of the right, and to establish a people's democracy. An even stronger right-wing backlash triggered violent left-wing action in Catalonia and Asturias.

The Asturias Rising, October 1934

The rebellion in Catalonia was not well organised – in part, because the left-wing groups did not cooperate – and was soon crushed. However, the uprising in Asturias – one of the most industrialised parts of Spain – was much more serious. Asturias was a key coal-mining region, and mine owners had responded to the impact of the Great Depression by drastically cutting wages, increasing working hours and sacking many labourers. However, over 70% of the region's workers were members of trade unions – mostly of the UGT.

Encouraged by the calls for revolution, all the left-wing groups in the region – including the communists – decided to cooperate and make plans for an uprising. On 5 October 1934, they began their armed rebellion. Within a few days, they had overcome the Civil Guard and established control over most of the province. Lerroux responded by sending more than 20 000 troops to Asturias – many of them Moorish and Foreign Legion troops sent from Africa. In addition, the navy and air force bombed towns and villages in the region.

After two weeks of bitter fighting, in which over 2000 rebels were killed, the rising was defeated by the army – under the command of General Franco. However, the violence did not end there, as the military immediately began a campaign of savage reprisals and atrocities. Torture and execution without trial became commonplace, and employers took advantage of the workers' defeat and the repression to sack thousands of trade unionists. Such actions were to be repeated many times during the Civil War – at the time, the left-wing resistance and the right-wing repression served to push more and more Spaniards to adopt more extreme views.

Final steps to war, 1935–36

The repression of the Asturias uprising convinced many on the left that they needed to join forces in a coalition to challenge CEDA and confront the rising threat of fascism. This threat seemed confirmed when Gil Robles' CEDA adopted elements associated with fascist parties in Italy and Germany, such as uniforms and salutes – Gil Robles even began to be called *Jefe*, or Chief. In May 1935, he became minister of war and one of his first acts in this post was to appoint Franco as chief of the general staff. He and Franco then began to purge the army of liberal and republican officers.

Such developments worried liberal and left-of-centre parties, and led to attempts to achieve a left-of-centre alliance. One of the main movers behind this was Azaña who, in 1934, founded the *Izquierda Republicana* (Republican Left). Although he had played no part in the 1934 risings, he had indicated that he would act as president if they had succeeded. At a series of massive public meetings, he urged Spaniards to unite in defence of Spanish democracy against the growing threat from the right. In Madrid, over 500 000 attended such a meeting. Although Caballero was at first reluctant to join such an alliance, he changed his mind when the Spanish Communist Party decided that it would join such a coalition.

In September 1935, Lerroux resigned and, in December, corruption scandals led Zamora to dismiss the government. Although Gil Robles assumed he would become the new prime minister, Zamora instead appointed an interim government, and announced that new elections would take place in February 1936.

QUESTION

Why were the years 1934–35 known as the *bienio negro*?

The Popular Front, 1936

The dismissal of Lerroux's government spurred on the left's negotiations for a coalition and, in January 1936, they finally agreed on the establishment of the Popular Front. Socialists, communists and liberals all joined the coalition, although the anarchists refused to participate. Despite attempts by CEDA to retain power by local intimidation of voters and the arrest of leading Socialists, the Popular Front won a narrow victory in the February elections, gaining 48% of the vote, compared with 46% for the right: this resulted in 278 seats for the Popular Front and only 124 seats for right-wing parties in the Cortes. Azaña was once again established as prime minister – this time of a Popular Front government.

After two years of a right-wing reactionary government, the Popular Front coalition – mainly composed of middle-class liberals, and without any Marxists – was determined to undo the work of the *bienio negro*, and immediately announced a political amnesty for the prisoners of the Asturias uprising. It also reintroduced plans for land reform and restored Catalonian autonomy. At the same time, Caballero began calls for a Bolshevik-style revolution in Spain.

These moves naturally caused concern among those on the political right. However, they were even more troubled in April 1936, when the Popular Front found a way of using the constitution to remove Zamora as president and replace him with the more liberal Azaña. More alarming still was the growth of unrest across the country by workers encouraged by the Popular Front victory.

In rural areas, poor peasants – impatient for land reform – seized land from the aristocracy, and Azaña's government did nothing to stop them. In the Extremadura region, in just one day in March, 60 000 peasants took over 3000 farms. In the cities, the UGT and CNT unions organised strikes to protest against low wages, and these often became violent as the Falange militia tried to break them up. As a result, the government banned the Falange, and José Antonio Primo de Rivera was imprisoned. Despite this, the unrest and political killings continued, and the period from February to July 1936 has been described as the 'little civil war'.

Planning the army coup

Although much of the violence was due to right-wing attacks, CEDA called for a military uprising to restore 'order'. **General Emilio Mola** – along with General Sanjurjo – began planning a rebellion, which had CEDA's backing as well as support from the Falange and the Carlists (a political organisation that wanted to restore the monarchy). The Falange and the Carlists were particularly important to Mola's plans, as they both had paramilitary forces that could support the army. The final steps occurred in mid-July: on 12 July, José Castillo (a popular left-wing member of the Assault Guard) was murdered. In retaliation, members of his section murdered José Sotelo, who had returned from exile in 1934 and was a deputy for the right-wing *Renovacíon Española* (Spanish Revival), as well as being associated with the Falange. This provided the excuse for Mola: on 17 July 1936, he gave the order for the coup to begin – thus triggering the Spanish Civil War.

General Emilio Mola (1887–1937):

He was a duke, and fought in the Rif War in Morocco. He was appointed as Director-General of Security in 1930, but his conservative views placed him at odds with the liberals and socialists of the Second Republic. The Popular Front government – worried about his loyalty – made him military governor of Navarre in an attempt to reduce his influence. Yet, once there, Mola plotted with Carlists, and by April 1936 had become the main leader of the right-wing Spanish Military Union in north-west Spain. Although Sanjurjo was seen as the main leader of the army plotters, it was Mola who supervised the planning of the 1936 coup that began the Civil War. After Sanjurjo's death, Mola assumed command of the northern Nationalist zone, based on Burgos; Franco was commander in the southern Nationalist zone. In June 1937, Mola was killed in a plane crash – this left Franco as the main Nationalist leader.

Was civil war in 1936 avoidable?

Most historians agree that a civil war in Spain was not inevitable – nonetheless, there is considerable debate over how it might have been avoided. Certainly, if the Popular Front government had been strong enough to take effective action to stem the political disorder which became increasingly violent, it might have been able to stabilise the situation. Modern neo-Francoist revisionist historians – such as Enrique Moradiellos and Stanley Payne – tend to blame the Popular Front: both for its determination to implement fundamental reforms, and for its alleged toleration of social unrest and even the revolutionary violence committed by some of its supporters. These revisionists argue that the Radical Republicans, the main centre party, lacked leadership when it came to defending constitutional democracy.

Other revisionists, such as Edward Malefakis, argue that the chance of establishing a strong centre was undermined by the alliance that left republican parties made with the Socialists. Antonio Elorza and Marta Bizcarrondo, in particular, blame Popular Front governments for going along with the Spanish Communist Party's intention of crushing right-wing opposition to the Republic. According to these revisionist historians, the army coup took place at a time when democracy had been ended – thus, they argue, there would have been no civil war if the Popular Front government had defended democracy. According to Payne, the only alternatives were either a constitutional monarchy, or a corporatist CEDA dictatorship.

Opposed to this view, other historians, such as Helen Graham, believe that if García Prieto had taken over as prime minister, he could have established a strong, genuinely reforming government which would also have dealt firmly with the generals plotting against the republic. Some historians argue that the role played by Largo Caballero and other PSOE leaders made this an extremely difficult aim. However, Paul Preston – who sees Prieto as an effective politician – nonetheless believes even the creation of a moderate Republican-Socialist coalition would not have prevented the coup, as the Spanish élites were not prepared to make any concessions as regards reform. This intransigence was particularly marked among the big landowning classes. According to Preston, the CEDA – with their destruction during the *bienio negro* of the reforms of 1931–33 – were the main reason why the Republic collapsed. Only if the majority of Spaniards had been prepared to accept the massive social and economic inequalities which had existed before the creation of the Second Republic could civil war have been avoided.

4.6 What were the main features of the Spanish Civil War?

The nature and events of the civil war, which lasted from July 1936 to April 1939, are covered in numerous books, including Hugh Thomas's classic study *The Spanish Civil War*, Paul Preston's *The Spanish Civil War: Reaction, Revolution and Revenge,* and Antony Beevor's *The War for Spain*. In particular, the Spanish Civil War saw the development of deliberate mass bombing of civilians, in a strategy which became known as 'total war'. Perhaps the most notorious example of this was the bombing of the Basque town of Guernica, by Nazi Germany's Condor Legion, on 27 April 1937.

The civil war also saw Spain become the testing ground of the Blitzkrieg method of warfare, which combined land and air forces in a 'lightning war' – this was successfully used by Nazi Germany during the Second World War. Another important feature of the civil war – as in most civil wars – was the use of terror against civilians.

The early phase

At the start of the civil war, large parts of the army in Spain remained loyal to the democratically elected Popular Front government. Many attempts by the rebels to take control of towns were defeated – for instance, one of the army plotters, **General Manuel Goded**, was killed in fighting in Barcelona. As a result, Republican control of Barcelona and Catalonia was established. Overall, after the first few weeks, the rebels only controlled about five towns and less than a quarter of mainland Spain.

General Manuel Goded (1882–1936):

He was, at first, a supporter of Rivera's dictatorship, and fought in the Rif War in Morocco. He led the successful attack in 1925 which marked a turning point in Spain's colonial war against the forces of Abd-el-Krim. As a result, in 1927, he was placed in charge of the Spanish Army of Africa. He lost that position when he began to criticise Rivera's government. In May 1936, the Popular Front government sent Goded to a remote post on the Balearic Islands because he was one of several right-wing officers suspected of plotting against the Republic. He supported the coup of July 1936, but was captured by Republican forces during his unsuccessful attempt to take Barcelona for the Nationalists. His execution in August 1936 removed yet another of Franco's rivals for overall leadership of the Nationalist forces.

However, once Franco's troops – the most experienced and effective in all of Spain's army – began to arrive from Morocco, the Nationalists slowly extended the areas they controlled. This process of gradually eroding the areas controlled by the Republicans was speeded up once troops and equipment from Nazi Germany, Fascist Italy and authoritarian Portugal began to arrive. At first, many of the republic's forces were militia volunteers who had to face the ever-increasing number of professional troops deployed by the Nationalists.

KEY CONCEPTS QUESTION

Significance: Why was the ability to move the Spanish Army of Africa to mainland Spain so important for the Nationalists?

Despite aid from the Soviet Union, and the volunteer troops of the International Brigades, the Nationalists were gradually able to split the various Republican areas from each other. Particularly important was Franco's decision in early 1937 – following the failure to capture Madrid from the Republicans – to move to a war of attrition. Given the massive amount of aid the Nationalists received, while the Non-Intervention Committee prevented the Republicans from obtaining aid, this was an important factor in grinding down Republican resistance. In 1938, the Nationalists succeeded in pushing their forces through Aragon to reach the Mediterranean Sea, separating Catalonia from Madrid. At the end of 1938, Nationalist armies took Catalonia and, in March 1939, Madrid was captured. On 1 April 1939, Franco declared the civil war over.

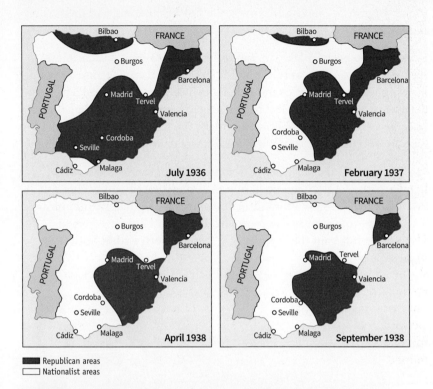

Figure 4.10: The different stages of the Spanish Civil War, 1936-38. The Nationalists' military advantages – including the military aid they received from Nazi Germany and Fascist Italy – enabled them to steadily capture Republican areas.

QUESTION

How did the non-intervention policy applied by Britain and France damage the ability of Republican forces to conduct a defence against the Nationalists' armies?

Franco and the Nationalists

The revolutionary upheavals that had occurred before 1936, and workers' and peasants' revolts after the start of the army rising, ensured

271

that the Nationalist rebels had the support of the established élites in Spain. However, their military support at first was mainly limited on the mainland to parts of Galicia, Navarre and Aragon. In addition, the rebels found support in Spanish Morocco, the Balearic Islands, and the Canary Islands.

Franco was especially keen to win the backing of the Church, as the majority of Spaniards were Catholics. Initially, the army claimed the uprising was in defence of the fatherland, but Franco soon added defence of the Catholic faith to the alleged aims of the war. In addition, once he became aware of how important the Church was to his supporters, Franco made determined efforts to appear religious himself.

On 1 July 1937, the majority of Spanish bishops signed a document known as the Collective Letter, in which they described the civil war as a 'Christian crusade' of good against the evil of 'godless communism'. This letter – and similar statements made by the Church – helped the Nationalists gain the support of Catholics both within Spain and beyond its borders.

Figure 4.11: This photograph, taken in November 1938, shows Franco (centre) and Church dignitaries giving the fascist salute; the support of the Church was an important factor in Franco's victory.

Perhaps most importantly, the attitude of Church leaders in Spain eventually helped win the support of the papacy, which had initially condemned the violence. In 1937, the pope gave in to the calls of the Spanish Church not to support President Azaña's appeal for a negotiated peace. Instead, the pope officially recognised the Nationalist cause.

The republic's military strategy

At the start of the rebellion, support for the Popular Front among ordinary Spaniards meant that, early on, three-quarters of mainland Spain was controlled by the Republicans. In addition, many workers and peasants seized factories and land. However, historians are divided on whether, once the civil war had started, the Second Republic stood a chance of surviving. At the start of Mola's military coup, thousands of working-class members of political and trade union groups demanded that the government issue them with weapons so they could resist the Nationalists.

Figure 4.12: Female republican snipers in Madrid, 1936.

QUESTION

Look at Figure 4.12. Why would those on the right have been particularly angered by seeing these Republican women involved in the fighting?

Initially the government refused, although it later offered weapons to those fighting for the Republican cause. Something which particularly outraged the right was the fact that women also played an important part in the armed resistance to the coup. Conservative Spanish values – in common, for instance, with those in Fascist Italy and Nazi Germany – saw women's traditional roles as being those of housewives and mothers. Women's growing equality and independence was yet another 'evil' which the right-wing blamed on the Second Republic.

Some historians, including Hugh Thomas, believe that the government's reluctance at first to equip its working-class supporters with weapons to fight the Nationalists put it at a disadvantage. They claim that if this had been done immediately, the army coup might have been crushed before a full-scale civil war developed.

SOURCE 4.12

The Republic's military strategy was subordinated to the [Popular Front] government's political orientation. In order to maintain middle-class support at home and win over the democracies abroad, the Popular Army had to be presented as an 'orthodox' army. A restricted use of the navy, to avoid alarming the imperial powers, is one of the clearest examples of the consequences of this orientation. On land, for the Republic to fight a well-equipped regular army such as Franco's, it either had to have at its disposal a similar force or use irregular methods of warfare. An alternative strategy would have been to have fought a largely defensive war punctuated by multiple and rapid incursions by both regular troops and guerrilla units into the sparsely defended parts of an extremely long and under-manned front... It would have tied down large numbers of Nationalist forces and avoided the massive destruction of loyalist troops and material, which undermined the Republic's ability to resist. Guerrilla actions, however limited by repression, could have mobilised political sympathy in the enemy rearguard in support of subversion.

Durgan, A. 2007. **The Spanish Civil War**. *Basingstoke. Palgrave Macmillan. pp. 36–7.*

Terror and atrocities

During the civil war, about 200 000 combatants were killed in the fighting, plus large numbers of civilians in bombing attacks. However, according to historians such as Paul Preston, almost 200000 men and women were either murdered or executed behind the respective lines. On the Nationalists' side, this was a deliberate policy – Mola, for instance, planned the elimination, 'without scruple or hesitation', of all those opposed to Nationalist beliefs.

Figure 4.13: A David Low cartoon about Nationalist atrocities in the early stages of the civil war, 23 November 1936. Note that Hitler and Mussolini are standing behind Franco.

QUESTION

Look at Figure 4.13. Why do you think the cartoonist has shown Franco standing with Hitler and Mussolini?

Behind the Republican lines, the violence and repression in the early days was an unofficial and spontaneous defensive response to the dangers posed by the military coup. For instance, there were many unofficial attacks – mainly by members of anarchist groups – on churches, and on priests, monks and nuns – according to some estimates, there were as many as 7000 deaths. Details of mounting atrocities in the Nationalist zones, and their bombing of civilians – such as in Madrid – only increased fears and retaliations. By December 1936, however, the

Popular Front government succeeded in putting an end to this unofficial violence.

Figure 4.14: This 1937 Republican poster shows eight children killed during a Nationalist air raid on Madrid; it says: 'Murderers! Who, on seeing this, won't seize a gun to crush the fascist destroyers?'

> QUESTION
>
> Look at Figure 4.14. What makes this such an effective propaganda poster?

The 'White Terror'

The wave of savage repression carried out by the Nationalists against Republican supporters was known as the 'White Terror'. Given the large numbers of the urban and rural working classes, the army generals believed a reign of terror was vital if they were to ensure that the reforms of the Second Republic would be forever prevented. Thus

Franco's *Africanistas* – known as the 'Column of Death' – carried out atrocities in every town and village they captured on their way from Seville to Madrid. At the same time, units of the Falange and the Carlists also carried out murders and executions of those believed to be supporters of the Republic. From early 1937, with the Nationalists' failure to capture Madrid, Franco's advance was deliberately slowed, to enable a thorough elimination of those opposed to traditional Spanish values and the interests of the élites.

SOURCE 4.13

The leaders of the rebellion, Generals Mola, Franco and Queipo de Llano, regarded the Spanish proletariat in the same way as they did the Moroccan, as an inferior race that had to be subjugated by sudden uncompromising violence. Thus they applied in Spain the exemplary terror they had learned in North Africa by deploying the Spanish Foreign Legion and the Moroccan mercenaries, the Regulares, of the colonial army... The first of Mola's secret instructions, issued in April [1936], [had] echoed the practice of the Africanistas against the Rif tribesmen, calling for extreme violence to shock the left into paralysis...

[in Villamartín] men and women were tortured and shot without trial for reasons as caparicious as having advocated improved working conditions or for having taken part in a carnival involving a spoof funeral of Gil Robles and songs ridiculing the right. One seventeen-year-old was shot because his father was a socialist and a sixteen-year-old because his anarcho-syndicalist father had fled. Altogether four teenagers were murdered. A couple aged seventy-three and sixty-three were shot because their anarcho-syndicalist son had also escaped... Between July 1936 and February 1937, a total of 102 men and nine women were executed in Villamartín.

Preston, P. 2013. **The Spanish Holocaust: Inquisition and Extermination in Twentieth-Century Spain**. *London. Harper Press. pp. xii, 132–3 and 137.*

In February 1937, after the Nationalists seized the town of Malaga, 3500 Republicans were executed. The Church made no public criticism of such actions. Church leaders later claimed that they were unaware of Nationalist actions at the time, but in fact it is now known that many churchmen took part in acts of repression and, in some cases, even participated in the killing of Republican supporters.

4.7 How important was foreign intervention to the Nationalists' victory in the civil war?

When investigating the reasons why Franco and the Nationalists won the civil war, two factors emerge as being of particular significance: disunity within the Republican camp, and the impact of foreign intervention. Some historians, such as E. Solstein and S. Meditz, see Republican divisions – especially over whether or not to win the civil war first, before moving towards a social revolution – as being the most decisive factor. Others, such as D. Tierney, consider the nature and extent of foreign intervention as the most important factor in determining its result.

Republican disunity

Although the Nationalists were made up of a variety of different groups, the Republicans were more deeply divided.

Civil war or revolution?

Supporters of the Republic were divided at the most fundamental level – they had different views on the purpose of the war as well as the best way of winning it. Middle-class liberals and the centre-right of the PSOE were opposed to the idea of any workers' revolution. They wanted to defend republican democracy, and believed that a centralised and disciplined army was the only way to defeat Franco's forces. This view was shared by the communist PCE, which followed Stalin's orders. Stalin did not want a revolution in Spain in case it prevented Britain and France from forming an alliance with the USSR to oppose the growing threat from Nazi Germany.

However, many left-wing groups did want a revolution, including the anarchists and those on the far left of the PSOE. Also significant – especially in the regions of Catalonia and Valencia – was the Workers' Party of Marxist Unification (*Partido Obrero de Unificación Marxista*, POUM). The POUM, led by **Andrés Nin** and Joaquin Maurin, was formed in 1935 by the merging of two revolutionary groups, and its membership far outnumbered that of the PCE.

Andrés Nin (1892–1937):

He was first a member and then leader of the PSOE in Catalonia, after which he helped form the PCE. He supported the Russian revolutionary Leon Trotsky in his struggle against Stalin, and left the PCE to form a Spanish Trotskyist party. However, Nin's decision to form the POUM led Trotsky to withdraw his support for Nin. After the Republican in-fighting during the Barcelona May Days of 1937, Nin was arrested and tortured to death by communist agents. A plaque in his honour can be found at the former POUM headquarters site on Las Ramblas, Barcelona.

ACTIVITY

Find out more about the various groups that wanted to turn the Spanish Civil War into a revolution. You could read George Orwell's *Homage to Catalonia*, or watch the film *Land and Freedom*. Alternatively, you can find videos on this, and the Spanish Civil War in general, on YouTube. Search for 'Spanish Civil War Chapter 1: The Path to War' and 'Anarchists in the 1936 Spanish Civil War'.

The POUM believed that an immediate workers' revolution would give the ordinary people of Spain something to fight for, boosting support and going some way towards making up for the Republic's relative lack of weapons and experienced troops. For this reason, the POUM favoured the formation of democratic and revolutionary people's militias.

Figure 4.15: Some of the British International Brigade volunteers in Barcelona, September 1936. George Orwell, the British novelist and writer, was a volunteer in one of the POUM militia units based in Barcelona.

In Barcelona, the CNT called a general strike and seized weapons. The CNT and the POUM then formed revolutionary militias that were run on anarchist principles. In areas such as Catalonia and Aragon, these militias encouraged workers and peasants to seize land from landowners and even to set up collective farms. Factories were also taken over by militia groups, and trade unions began organising the production of war materials. Similar developments took place in Asturias, Valencia, the Malaga province of Andalusia, and in and around Madrid. Eventually, on 19 July, the government reluctantly started distributing weapons to the people, and real power in defending the Republic passed to armed workers' organisations and factory committees.

SOURCE 4.14

After the Civil War, Franco claimed that the Rising had been a pre-emptive strike to prevent a left-wing take-over. Except within nationalist propaganda, no such communist conspiracy had ever existed, yet one of the many ironies of Spain's Civil War was that the army rebellion triggered off a Spanish revolution which was broadly anarchist rather than communist. Throughout Republican Spain, except in the Basque Provinces, the established authorities were swept aside and replaced by workers' committees...

During the first year of the war, the Revolution became a key question in the political debates within the Republic. To liberals and many socialists the Revolution was divisive and could endanger success against the common enemy; it must therefore be halted, rolled back even... To most anarchists, however, as to the POUM in Catalonia, the Republic without the Revolution would be void of social content, a liberal political shell whose defence would not win hearts and minds... The revolution challenged, too, the male chauvinism so strongly entrenched in Spain. In some ways, the liberation of women took giant steps forward in Republican towns, although in the countryside attitudes changed hardly at all.

Browne, H. 1996. **Spain's Civil War.** *London. Longman. pp. 54–5.*

However, the government in Madrid opposed this 'dual power' situation, believing it would alienate the middle classes, undermine effective military resistance, and prevent Britain or France from coming to the republic's aid. Consequently, as early as 4 September 1936, the government attempted to reassert its control. Militia groups were broken up and incorporated into regular army units. As the communists became increasingly influential, the police began to repress the more revolutionary organisations, claiming that they were in league with Franco's Nationalist forces. In May 1937, the police and pro-communist troops in Barcelona attacked and defeated anarchist and POUM forces.

Many people in Spain felt demoralised by the obvious divisions among left-wing groups, and this further reduced the effectiveness of Republican forces, making a significant contribution to their eventual defeat.

QUESTION

How did the political differences among the Republicans contribute to the Nationalist victory?

Foreign intervention

The involvement of foreign powers in the Spanish Civil War was a key reason for the Nationalists' victory. In 1936, neither side was expecting a lengthy conflict – nor were they equipped for it. Consequently, both sides sought foreign help. The Nationalist rebels were provided with a large amount of weapons by Nazi Germany and Fascist Italy; the Republicans eventually received aid from the USSR, as well as help from volunteers organised into International Brigades.

Support for the Nationalists

Initially Mola's army uprising achieved little success, and most major towns and cities – as well as the Spanish navy – remained in Republican hands. To gain greater strength, the Nationalists needed to bring in Franco's *Africanistas*, which were currently stationed in Spanish Morocco: these numbered about 35 000 experienced troops. During August and September 1936, Hitler provided planes for air cover to allow Franco to move his Army of Africa to the Spanish mainland, and this assistance early on in the civil war turned out to be hugely important for the eventual Nationalist victory.

The far-right dictator of Portugal, António Salazar, provided some troop support to the Nationalists, but most foreign manpower came from Germany and Italy. Italy supplied 40 000 troops to the Nationalist cause in Spain (more than three times the number Germany sent, according to historian Harry Browne). Germany's most significant contribution was the Condor Legion – a mixed air and tank unit, which developed a method of combined attacks on the Republicans that later became a feature of the *Blitzkrieg* ('lightning war') methods used by Germany in the Second World War. In return for German assistance, Franco joined the Anti-Comintern Pact in April 1939, although he later refused to enter the Second World War on Germany's side.

Support for the Republicans

To begin with, the Republicans hoped to receive aid from France, where a Popular Front government headed by the socialist Léon Blum (see 5.7, Léon Blum and the Popular Front government), had come to power in June 1936. France did not want a fascist-style state allied with Germany on its southern border, so it initially agreed to sell some aircraft and artillery to the Republicans. However, the British government desperately wanted to avoid war breaking out in Europe, so it refused to help the Republican government in Spain, and pressured France into reversing its decision. The French knew that they could not fight a war against Germany without British support, so they proposed a Non-Intervention Pact – by which all nations agreed not to become involved in the events unfolding in Spain. In September 1936, Britain, France, Germany, Italy, the USSR and the USA were among the states that signed this pact.

However, it soon became apparent that the Non-Intervention Pact had failed to prevent foreign interference in Spanish matters. Although British and French naval forces did nothing to prevent supplies from Nazi Germany and Fascist Italy from reaching the rebels, they did prevent supplies of weapons reaching the Republicans – even though their government was the legal Spanish government.

When the USSR realised that both Germany and Italy were sending large amounts of equipment to the Nationalists, Soviet leader Joseph Stalin ordered that humanitarian aid and military equipment, as well as engineers and military advisors, should be sent to the Republicans in Spain. The first consignment of equipment arrived in October 1936, just in time to prevent Madrid falling to the Nationalists. Soviet aid – which later included tanks and aircraft – continued until 1939.

'NEUTRALITY' FRONT **FOR** WAR AND FASCISM.

Figure 4.16: A cartoon about the Non-Intervention Committee, which appeared in the *Daily Worker*, the paper of the Communist Party of Great Britain.

> QUESTION
>
> What is the message of the cartoon in Figure 4.16? What are the values and limitations of this source for a historian studying the operation of the Non-Intervention Committee?

In order to prevent Western governments blocking the Republic's ability to purchase this military equipment, Spain's gold reserves were transferred to Moscow. Stalin also used the Republicans' dependence on the USSR to increase the influence of the Spanish Communist Party (PCE) and Soviet agents working in Spain.

The International Brigades

Foreign assistance for the Republic also came from the International Brigades, which were made up of men and women from around the world who joined together to oppose fascism. These volunteers were mainly organised by the Communist International (Comintern), but they were a mixture of socialists, communists and democrats. In all, there were about 35 000 volunteers, including about 3500 from Italy and 3000 from Germany. The arrival of the International Brigades certainly boosted Republican morale, but in fact there were never more than about 15 000 of their members in Spain at any one time, and most had little or no military experience.

However, the effectiveness of the International Brigades was soon undermined by their communist commanders, who imposed strict military discipline.

SOURCE 4.15

During the course of the whole civil war, between 32 000 and 35 000 men from 53 different countries served in the ranks of the International Brigades. Another 5000 foreigners served outside, mostly attached to the CNT or the POUM... [Al]most 80% of the volunteers from Great Britain were manual workers who either left their jobs or had been unemployed... Some of them were glad to escape the apathy of unemployment, others had already been fighting Mosley's fascists in street battles, as their French equivalents had fought Action Francaise and the Croix de Feu...

Most of the volunteers were very unfit, as well as ignorant of the most elementary military skills... Men who were to be sent against the Army of Africa... could do little except form ranks, march and turn. Many of them had never even handled a rifle until they were on the way to the front.

Beevor, A. 2006. **The Battle for Spain: The Spanish Civil War 1936–1939**. London. Weidenfeld & Nicolson. pp. 157–9 and 162.

SOURCE 4.16

Some members of the English-speaking company had seen action before. In addition to [George] Nathan, there were the five English survivors of the 11th international Brigade's Machine-Gun Company: Jock Cunningham, Joe Hinks, Jock Clarke, Sam Lesser and John Cornford, who was still recovering from the head wound received at [Madrid's] University City, but refused to be left behind. There were also several IRA veterans and the first of a number of Cypriot volunteers to arrive from London. Magdalen scholar Ralph Fox, the author of acclaimed biographies of figures as diverse as Genghis Khan and Lenin, joined the company as political commissar a few days before it left for the front...

On Christmas Eve 1936, No. 1 Company was sent to the Córdoba front in southern Spain... They were part of a response aimed at countering a Rebel offensive, but the action had begun badly... As ever, the volunteers' training was brief at best: 'We wandered over the fields and then we had a long walk and that was the training. We saw the rifles the first time we went to the front.' Almost half of the recruits had not handled a weapon before their arrival at Andújar, when they were presented with turn-of-the-century Austrian Steyr rifles, part of the Republicans' hotch-potch of antiquated weaponry...

Baxell, R. 2012. **Unlikely Warriors: the British in the Spanish Civil War and the Struggle Against Fascism.** *London. Aurum Press. p. 115.*

QUESTION

How far does Source 4.16 support the comments made in Source 4.15?

SOURCE 4.17

Comrades of the International Brigades! Political reasons, reasons of state, the good of that same cause for which you offered your blood with limitless generosity, send some of you back to your countries and some to forced exile. You can go with pride. You are history. You are legend. You are the heroic example of the solidarity and the universality of democracy… We will not forget you; and, when the olive tree of peace puts forth its leaves, entwined with the laurels of the Spanish Republic's victory, come back!

Extract from a speech, made on 28 October 1938, by Dolores Ibárruri, the Communist member of parliament from Asturias. Quoted in: Baxell, R., Jackson, A., and Jump, J. 2010. **Antifascistas: British and Irish Volunteers in the Spanish Civil War**. *London. Lawrence and Wishart. p. 90.*

Franco and the immediate aftermath

After his victory in the civil war, Franco was determined to fully establish his control over Spain, and he remained dictator of Spain until his death in 1975. He refused to restore the monarchy, or to give the fascist Falange any real power after 1939, even though both had provided him with valuable support during the civil war. The police and the Falange militia were placed under military control and, in the early years in particular, Franco oversaw the brutal repression of any groups or individuals who opposed him.

Franco made use of both censorship and propaganda to maintain his personal rule. A Press Law of April 1938 was applied after the Nationalist victory in 1939, by which the government reserved the right to authorise all publications, and to shut down those to which it objected. It also had the right to appoint the editors of all newspapers, and to sack journalists.

Franco also made strenuous efforts to promote his own importance as the 'saviour' of Spain. He was assisted in this by an unofficial alliance with the Church. In 1938 – before the war was won – the Nationalists drew up a series of Clerical Laws, promising to give the Church an important position in the new Nationalist Spanish state. These included granting it a monopoly over primary education and the right to its own independent youth movements, outlawing all non-Christian religions, and severely restricting the rights of Protestants. When the Nationalists won the civil war, Franco implemented these laws. In return, the Church endorsed Franco's continuing crusade against atheists and Marxists, and remained silent about the atrocities and executions committed under his regime.

Theory of Knowledge

History, emotion and bias

The American writer William Faulkner (1897–1962) wrote, *'The past is never dead. It's not even past.'* The Spanish Civil War – at least in part – involved a life-and-death struggle between fascism and its opponents, and seemed to many to be a precursor for the Second World War. Given that Franco's dictatorship only ended in 1975, and neo-fascist groups are still active in several countries, can historians writing about the civil war avoid bias?

Paper 3 exam practice

Question

Evaluate the reasons for the outcome of the Spanish Civil War, 1936–39.
[15 marks]

Skill

Avoiding a narrative-based answer

Examiner's tips

Even once you have read the question carefully (and so avoided the temptation of giving irrelevant material), produced your plan and written your introductory paragraph, it is still possible to go wrong.

By 'writing a narrative answer', history examiners mean providing supporting knowledge that is relevant (and may well be very precise and accurate) *but* that is not clearly linked to the question. Instead of answering the question, it merely *describes* what happened.

The main body of your essay and argument needs to be **analytical and evaluative**. It must not simply be an answer in which you just 'tell the story'. Your essay must **address the demands and key words of the question**. Ideally, this should be done consistently throughout your essay, by linking each paragraph to the previous one, in order to produce a clear 'joined-up' answer.

You are especially likely to lapse into narrative when answering your final question – and even more so if you are getting short of time. The 'error' here is that, despite all your good work at the start of the exam, you will lose sight of the question and just produce an *account*, rather than an analysis. So, even if you are short of time, try to write several analytical paragraphs.

Note that if a question asks you to evaluate/examine/discuss the reasons for something, it expects you to consider a **range** of reasons and, if possible, to reach a judgement about the relative importance of these factors. Very often, such a question gives you the opportunity to refer to different historians' views (see Chapter 5, Unit 2 for more on this).

A good way of avoiding a narrative approach is to refer back to the question continually, and even to mention it now and again in your answer. This should help you produce an answer that is focused on the specific aspects of the question – rather than just giving information about the broad topic or period.

For this question, you will need to examine and evaluate the following aspects:

- the relative military strengths of the two sides at the start of the civil war
- the degree of unity or disunity affecting the two sides
- the military and economic help received by both sides.

You will then need to make a judgement in your concluding paragraph about the relative importance of the factors you have considered.

Common mistakes

Every year, even candidates who have clearly revised well, and who therefore have a good knowledge of the topic and of any historical debate surrounding it, still end up producing a mainly narrative-based or descriptive answer. Very often, this is the result of not having drawn up a proper plan.

The extracts of the student's answer below show an approach that essentially just describes the main features of the Spanish Civil War, without any analysis of why certain factors were or were not important in affecting the eventual outcome.

Sample paragraphs of narrative-based approach

This example shows what examiners mean by a narrative answer – it is something you should *not* copy!

At the start of the civil war, the two sides were fairly evenly matched. The bulk of the army was made up of the Peninsular Army, which had about 100 000 soldiers, and the Army of Africa – based in Morocco – which was the élite force and numbered about 45 000. Although the military plotters had the majority of the professional troops at their disposal, their initial plan to capture Madrid and other main cities failed. In five out of the seven places on mainland Spain that they attempted to seize, their forces were defeated by those police and troops who remained loyal to the republic, and by local militias.

In addition, the republic was able to retain control of the navy, which meant that at first the Army of Africa was unable to reach mainland Spain. However, the Nationalist rebels were able to take control of parts of western Andalusia in the south, and of parts of the north-west centred on Valladolid.

Nonetheless, the republic held the bulk of Spain's industrial centres and ports – important for production and supplies – and, as the legally elected government, was initially recognised by most countries as the legitimate power. However, this situation began to change over the next few months.

During August and September, Franco was able to bring his Army of Africa over from Morocco, to join the mainland forces of the Nationalists. He had been flown from the Canary Islands – where he had been posted by the Republican government in February 1936, as it had doubted his loyalty – to Morocco, in a private plane flown by two British MI6 agents. Once there, he took control of the troops – and then received planes from Nazi Germany, which allowed him to transport these troops to Spain.

While Britain and France set up the Non-Intervention Committee in August 1936, and so gave no supplies to the Republican government, Germany and Italy began to openly increase the amount of supplies they had been sending to help the Nationalists.

The rest of the essay continues in the same way – there are also plenty of accurate and relevant facts about the aid sent by Germany and Italy to the Nationalists, and by the USSR to the Republicans; the contributions made by the International Brigades, and about the divisions among the Republicans. However, there is no attempt to answer the question by **analysing** these factors and **explaining** how they affected the eventual outcome. Such an answer would only gain 10 marks at most.

Activity

In this unit, the focus is on avoiding narrative-based answers. Using the information from this unit, and any other sources of information available to you, try to answer **one** of the following Paper 3 practice questions in a way that avoids simply describing what happened.

Remember to refer to the simplified Paper 3 mark scheme in Chapter 6.

Paper 3 practice questions

1 'The reforms passed between 1931 and 1933 disappointed the left more than they angered the right.' To what extent do you agree with this statement?

2 Examine the reasons for the outbreak of the Spanish Civil War in events between 1931 and 1936.

3 Evaluate the claim that the Popular Front government's refusal to grant independence to Spanish Morocco in July 1936 was the main reason it lost the civil war.

4 Compare and contrast the impact of foreign intervention in the Spanish Civil War for the Republicans and for the Nationalists.

5 Discuss the significance of the policy of non-intervention for the outcome of the Spanish Civil War.

France

5

Unit 1: France, 1918–29

5

Introduction

France was one of the countries that managed to maintain a democratic tradition in the interwar years. Unlike the situation in Italy, Germany and Spain, democratic institutions survived in spite of severe economic and political problems. Economically, France faced the urgent and costly task of reconstruction after a devastating war, much of which had been fought on French soil. Politically, there were frequent changes of government and the growth of political movements on both the left and right wings.

The governments which ran France between the two world wars were part of the Third Republic. This was the constitution adopted after the collapse of the Second Empire of Napoleon III in 1870. The Third Republic lasted for a remarkably long time and only formally ceased to exist in 1946, when it was replaced by the Fourth Republic. However, many historians consider that, in practical terms, it ended in 1940, when France surrendered to Germany in the Second World War. After this Marshal Pétain set up the Vichy government in the southern part of a partitioned France, leaving the northern and western parts under German occupation.

TIMELINE

1918 **Nov:** Armistice ends the First World War

1919 **Jun:** Signing of Treaty of Versailles; Alsace and Lorraine formally returned to France

Nov: *Bloc National* government elected

1920 **May:** General strike prevented by government action

Dec: Congress of Tours – split in Socialist Party and formation of French Communist Party

1923 **Jan:** French occupation of Germany's Ruhr industrial region

1924 **Jun:** *Cartel des Gauches* government under Édouard Herriot

Aug: Dawes Plan ends French occupation of the Ruhr and reschedules Germany's reparations payments for the First World War

1925 **Dec:** Locarno treaties between France, Germany and other powers

1926 **Jul:** Centre-right government under Raymond Poincaré

1929 **Jul:** Building of Maginot Line commences; Poincaré retires

KEY QUESTIONS

- How did the First World War affect France?
- What was the state of the French economy during the 1920s?
- What were the main developments in French politics between 1918 and 1929?
- Which social issues were significant in the interwar years?
- What cultural trends were evident in the 1920s?

Overview

- France suffered severely in the First World War, with a high number of war deaths and extensive material damage. After the war it faced crippling debts and the enormous cost of reconstruction. Although the country received compensation in the postwar settlement, many people in France were disillusioned by the war and believed that the human and economic costs had been too high.

- In spite of the problems involved in the reconstruction of industry and agriculture, the economy recovered remarkably quickly. Nevertheless there were severe financial problems during the decade, most notably inflation. However, by 1929 the franc had stabilised and hopes for a new era of prosperity seemed well founded. There was full employment during the 1920s, but the labour movement was divided, and union membership declined.

- There was a wide range of political parties, making for shifting political alliances and frequent coalition governments. The two main groupings of parties which emerged were the centre-right *Bloc National* and the centre-left *Cartel des Gauches*.

- The *Bloc National* government in power between 1919 and 1924 focused on foreign policy and was determined to ensure future French security by forming alliances with countries in eastern Europe. They shared a common interest in preventing German expansion.

- Between 1924 and 1926 a centre-left coalition government, the *Cartel des Gauches*, faced hostility from conservative business interests and struggled to solve the problem of escalating inflation.
- The return of a centre-right coalition, led by Raymond Poincaré, in 1926 brought economic stability after the government devalued the franc. Until 1929, France enjoyed a few years of political stability and economic growth.
- Social issues in the interwar years included a declining birthrate and population stagnation, made worse by the deaths of so many young men in the war. Women in France did not have the right to vote and there were many restrictions on their legal rights. There were deep class divisions in French society and a small number of the upper-middle classes constituted the social and business élite and had considerable influence in politics as well.
- The aftermath of the war influenced art and literature and led to the emergence of the surrealist movement. Writers and artists from all over the world moved to Paris which became a vibrant centre of creativity in which American jazz became the focus of popular culture. French newspapers, radio and cinemas flourished.

5.1 How did the First World War affect France?

France was involved in the First World War from August 1914, when German troops invaded northern France through Belgium, until 11 November 1918, when the German army signed an armistice at Compiègne in northern France. For over four years, the lines of trenches along the Western Front stretched across north-eastern France, totally disrupting agriculture and displacing communities. In addition, parts of the north-east, the industrial heartland of France, containing 58% of its steel production and 40% of its coal reserves, were under German occupation for much of the war. As a result, the French people and the French economy were directly affected by the daily fighting, probably more so than any other country.

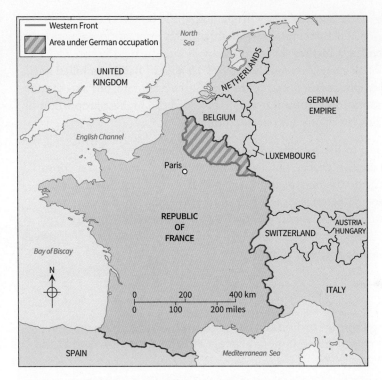

Figure 5.1: France during the First World War, showing the position of the Western Front and the area under German occupation.

War deaths and demographics

The human cost of the war to France was exceptionally high. The country mobilised 8 million men, and 1.3 million (nearly 17%) of them were killed. This was the highest proportion of deaths of any country involved in the First World War. Three million of the soldiers who survived the war were wounded in the fighting or traumatised in battle, and one third of them became permanent invalids who required ongoing disability support.

The loss of life affected all parts of France, where memorials to the war dead were built in every town and village. French peasants made up a larger proportion of the war dead than any other sector of the population. Casualty rates were also very high among junior army officers: for example, 63% of the 1914 class of the Saint-Cyr military academy were among the war dead.

The loss of life also had a serious demographic impact. Even before the war France had a declining birth rate, and this population stagnation was aggravated by a further slump in the birth rate during the war. Over a quarter of all men between the ages of 18 and 27 had been killed and this had implications, not only for the future birth rate, but also the size of the labour force. After the war, France had the highest proportion of elderly citizens of any European country.

In addition to the soldiers who had been killed, there were 200 000 civilian deaths. The loss of life affected all parts of the country, but especially the occupied provinces in the north and north-east, where several *départments* lost half of their population and one, the *département* of Aisne, as many as two-thirds. There were a further 166 000 deaths from the Spanish flu epidemic of 1918–19 which broke out just as the war was ending.

ACTIVITY

Use the internet to find out more about the Spanish flu epidemic. Which countries were most severely affected? Was it linked to the First World War?

After the war, France reincorporated the border regions of Alsace and Lorraine, which had been administered by Germany since the Franco-Prussian War of 1870–71. Although this added an additional 1.7 million citizens to France, it did not offset the loss of population during the war. In 1919 the total population of France was 39 million (including Alsace and Lorraine), whereas in 1914 it had been 39.5 million without these two regions.

Economic effects of the war

The material losses were also immense, especially in the north-east, where whole towns and villages were destroyed. The destruction included 1 million buildings, as well as factories and transport infrastructure, such as bridges and thousands of kilometres of roads and railway lines. In the areas under German occupation, the German army had destroyed many of the French coal mines, by flooding them, blowing them up, filling them with waste materials or setting them alight. Large areas of farmland were scarred with shell holes and trenches and were no longer productive, as the historian Colin Jones explains:

'Ploughed up by endless shelling and irrigated by the ooze of countless corpses, much agricultural land here had become entirely unfertile.' In addition, 1 million sheep, the same number of cattle, and half a million horses had been killed.

The areas under German occupation suffered particular hardships, which left a lasting impression on the local population. Historian Roger Price explains how this prompted people to flee 20 years later when the German army invaded France again at the start of the Second World War:

SOURCE 5.1

In the German zone of occupation over-exploitation and systematic destruction had reduced massively the productive capacity of the railway network. Disruption on this scale, and the harsh treatment of the population of occupied areas deprived of adequate supplies of food and fuel and subject to a reign of terror, deportation and forced labour, would be a major cause of the mass exodus of refugees from the north in 1940. Clearly they were not anxious to repeat the experience of German rule.

Price, R. 2005. **A Concise History of France (Second Edition)**. *New York. Cambridge University Press. p. 252–3.*

ACTIVITY

Explain how Source 5.1 corroborates the information in the text about the impact of the First World War on France.

The French government paid for the war effort by selling off its gold reserves and investments and by massive foreign borrowing. Income tax was introduced in 1916, but paid for only about one-third of the cost of the war effort. Other measures used by the government to finance the war created postwar economic problems: it sold war bonds and printed currency, which, according to historian Robert Paxton were 'two steps that prepared grave postwar economic burdens for the French: a crushing load of debt owed to French middle-class bondholders, and runaway inflation'. Between 1913 and 1920, the value of currency in circulation rose from 6 billion francs to 38 billion.

By the end of the war, the government had built up 30 billion francs worth of war debts, owed mainly to the United States, and also to Britain. During the war, the value of the franc had dropped and by 1919 was worth only half of its prewar value, affecting the livelihoods of many workers and small farmers, and especially those on fixed incomes. All of these factors affected the government's capacity to meet the urgent need to rebuild after the war.

The postwar peace settlement

French losses during the war help to explain French demands at the Paris Peace Conference and also France's attitude towards Germany after the war. At the peace conference France was represented by **Georges Clemenceau**, the prime minister who had led France to victory in the war, and who earned the nickname, among others, of '*Le Tigre*' (The Tiger) on account of his fierce demands on Germany. These demands had two main aims: that Germany should pay for war damages, to help with the reconstruction of France, and that France should be protected against future German aggression.

> ### Georges Clemenceau (1841–1929):
>
> He was a doctor, journalist and politician who became prime minister of France in 1917. He earned the nickname 'Father of Victory' on account of his ruthless pursuit of the war effort. He represented France at the Paris Peace Conference where he clashed with US President Woodrow Wilson and Britain's David Lloyd-George about the treatment of Germany in the Treaty of Versailles. He retired from politics in 1920 after he was rejected as a candidate for the presidency by the *Bloc National*. After the Treaty of Versailles had been signed Clemenceau famously predicted that it was not a treaty that would bring lasting peace but an armistice that would last only 20 years.

He achieved some of these aims:
- the regions of Alsace and Lorraine were returned to France
- France was granted the right to mine the Saar coalfields for 15 years
- the Rhineland was to be permanently demilitarised
- Germany was to pay reparations

- France was given mandates over Syria and Lebanon, formerly part of the Ottoman Empire, and Cameroon and Togo, former German colonies in Africa, enabling France to add to its already substantial colonial empire.

Clemenceau's attitude angered other delegates at the conference, but his willingness to compromise in the end cost him support at home where he was accused of sacrificing French security.

France's post-war attitudes to Germany

Historians have different views about France's attitude to Germany after the war. In 1965, American historian Robert Ergang, commenting on the French attitude to reparations, wrote, 'That an exhausted country [Germany] should pay such vast amounts as the French expected was a preposterous assumption. Nevertheless successive [French] governments were founded on that assumption.' In 1975 fellow American historians, William Langer, John Eadie and others suggested that '[French statesmen] aimed at nothing less than to emasculate Germany internally and to isolate it externally, and they pursued both ends without much regard for their impact on the world at large'. Others, however, are more sympathetic to the French viewpoint. Colin Jones (1994) notes that the 'impact of the war on the social, demographic and moral fibre of France explains why the French call for security was so strident in the war's aftermath' and that 'the quest for security explains much of the apparent French intransigence towards Germany in the interwar period.' Robert Paxton (1997) suggests that Clemenceau had a 'keen awareness that his people had borne the brunt of the Allied war effort and must bear the brunt of enforcing the peace terms on the continent of Europe.'

Theory of Knowledge

History, perspective and time

Does historical perspective change over time? Is the bias of historians affected by the time in which they write? Study the comments made by these historians above and look at when each was written. Why would it be invalid to reach final conclusions based only on these examples?

Despite France's eagerness to reincorporate Alsace and Lorraine, the return was not always widely welcomed in these regions themselves, where residents resented the centralised control that France intended to impose on them. People in Alsace in particular later opposed attempts to extend anti-clerical legislation there and to replace their German-based dialect with French as the language of administration and education. When, in the 1920s, a Home Rule party was formed in Alsace and Lorraine to demand autonomous rule and a separate budget, the central government enforced strict measures to suppress the movement.

Figure 5.2: This 1918 postcard showing a French lesson at a school in Alsace bears a clear pro-government message. The writing on the blackboard means 'France is our Fatherland'.

ACTIVITY

Explain how the postcard in Figure 5.2 reinforces the government's message. Refer to specific details in the picture to support your answer.

The war and the peace settlement seemed to represent a victory for France. It had recovered Alsace and Lorraine and it seemed that the humiliation of the defeat by Prussia in 1870 could finally be overcome. But the price to France in human and economic costs was high, and subsequent postwar reflections revealed deep disillusionment with what had been sacrificed for these achievements.

5.2 What was the state of the French economy during the 1920s?

In the early years after 1918 the focus of economic activity was on reconstruction to repair the damages caused by the war. There was a shortage of labour, and so foreign workers were hired to fill jobs in industry and agriculture. By the late 1920s the economy had recovered, though the problem of inflation remained.

Reconstruction and war debts

The costs of reconstruction were extensive. Repayment of loans, especially to the US and Britain, and the funding of reconstruction were made more difficult by the fact that the government had sold off its gold reserves and overseas assets during the war. It had also incurred considerable losses on account of loans and heavy investments made in pre-revolutionary Russia. After the revolution in that country, it was highly unlikely that the new Bolshevik government would feel any obligation to meet the debts incurred by the tsarist government.

To meet the costs of reconstruction and the repayment of war debts, France was dependent on reparations from Germany. But when it became clear that the German economy would collapse, these reparations were scaled down (see 2.3, Reparations). In the end, France received far less than had originally been anticipated, before reparations payments were suspended altogether in 1931.

Industry

The industries destroyed by the war were rebuilt in a remarkably short time, considering the extent of the damage, and the opportunity was used to modernise some of them. However, many of the 8000 factories that were constructed were simply re-built to what they had been before the war, and many businesses lost the opportunity to modernise. By 1924 industrial production had reached 1914 levels, and there were significant advances in the production of coal and steel. But it was the larger industrial companies that benefitted rather than smaller producers.

New industries also flourished. Of particular note was the growth in the 1920s of the French motor industry. André Citroën adopted Henry Ford's assembly line, and soon companies such as Citroën, Renault and Peugeot were major suppliers of motor vehicles. By 1929 France led the world in motor production with an annual output of 250 000 vehicles.

Agriculture

At the end of the war, agriculture was in a bad state. The peasants had suffered a higher proportion of war deaths than any other section of society. Nevertheless, by 1925, 95% of the farmland left barren after the war was under cultivation again. Although growth was not as great as it was in industry, there was some improvement in production methods after the war. Farmers were also helped by rising food prices during the 1920s, by improvements to the road and rail infrastructure and by the extension of electricity supplies to rural areas.

However, agriculture in general suffered from the low productivity of most small farmers, the low level of mechanisation and the steady drift of labour from rural areas to the towns.

Labour relations

There were no problems of unemployment in France in the 1920s, with a labour shortage resulting in the employment of 1.5 million immigrant workers. Although workers were granted an eight-hour day in 1919, working conditions in general lagged behind those in other countries with a similar social and economic structure. Real wages in 1919 were a fifth lower than they had been before the war, improved slightly during the 1920s, but returned to 1914 levels by the end of the decade. The working class did not benefit much from the relative prosperity of the 1920s. Housing remained poor and wages did not keep up with inflation.

The labour movement received a setback in May 1920 when its calls for a general strike were unsuccessful in the face of strong actions by the government to prevent the strike. Workers had hoped to put pressure on the government to pass more social legislation. Afterwards many employers preferred to employ non-union workers, so union membership declined from 2 million in 1919 to 600 000 in 1921. Trade unionism was also weakened by a split in the Socialist Party in December 1920 and the formation of a separate Communist Party. This development was mirrored by a split in the labour movement as well, with the formation of a separate Communist union, the *Confédération Générale du Travail Unitaire* (CGTU) to rival the Socialist *Confédération Générale du Travail* (CGT).

The unions were also negatively affected by the influence which businessmen and industrialists had in government circles. Employers formed industrial associations and industrialists formed a confederation, and these acted as powerful pressure groups and lobbyists in politics.

Economic recovery

In spite of all the problems, the French economy did remarkably well, and in the early 1920s was growing faster than any of its competitors. By 1929, industrial production was up by 40% and foreign trade up by 66% on prewar levels. Some of the reasons for the economic recovery were the weakness of the franc which favoured French exports, rising consumer demand, and the fact that rising prices acted as an incentive for manufacturers to produce more efficiently. The recovery was also helped by the return of substantial iron ore and potash deposits in Alsace.

Historian Roger Price points out, however, that there were serious structural weaknesses in the French economy, such as the effects of demographic stagnation on demand, inefficiency in agriculture, and the numerous poorly equipped small businesses. Added problems were the unwillingness of many industrialists to invest in new machinery, high production costs, the centralisation of so much economic activity around Paris, and the underdevelopment of other parts of the country, such as the west, centre and south-west.

The biggest economic problem facing France in the 1920s was inflation. In 1919, the franc was worth half of its prewar value, and by 1920 it had lost four-fifths of its value. This continued during the 1920s. A succession of governments tried various strategies to solve the problem, but the issue of inflation was one of the causes of the frequent changes of government during the 1920s.

ACTIVITY

Make a two-column chart. In the left-hand column list the problems facing the French economy in the 1920s, and in the right-hand column list the actions taken by the government to address each one.

KEY CONCEPTS ACTIVITY

Cause and consequence: Explain how the consequences of the First World War became causes in turn of the economic problems facing France during the 1920s.

5.3 What were the main developments in French politics between 1918 and 1929?

A striking feature of France between the wars was its apparent political instability, with 40 different governments and 20 prime ministers between 1919 and 1940. During this period this succession of governments had to cope with a series of political and economic crises. However, some historians explain that although French governments changed frequently, French politics remained stable because there was a high degree of continuity of the people in government. In essence, as Wolfson and Laver note, 'France was ruled by a small group of very experienced politicians from the professional classes'.

The constitutional structure

The constitution of the Third Republic made provision for a two-house legislature – the National Assembly – consisting of a lower house, the Chamber of Deputies, elected every four years by universal male suffrage, and an upper house, the Senate. The Senate was also elected but indirectly, a measure that had been adopted to act as a conservative check on the popularly elected lower house. The head of state was a president elected for a seven-year term of office by the National Assembly. Ministers were appointed by the president from the party or parties which received the most votes in an election.

A key element in the constitution which contributed to frequent political crises was the provision that elections were to be held at regular four-year intervals, and not when a government resigned. This meant that if a government lost the support of the National Assembly it was expected to resign, but another general election would not automatically follow. The government would be replaced instead by another one appointed by the president from the parties which, it was hoped, could command enough support to form an effective government. This was unlike the British system, where a general election would be called if the government lost the support of parliament.

Political parties

There was a wide spectrum of political parties and movements ranging from the Communist Party on the left to the *Action Française* on the extreme right. The large number of political parties led inevitably to the formation of political alliances and coalition governments, many of them short-lived, and made for political expediency, a key factor in the frequent changes of government in the interwar years.

The Radical Party

As in prewar France, the dominant political party was the Radical Party. Despite its name, it had lost any radical focus many years previously when most of the issues which it had promoted were accepted into law, such as universal suffrage (for men), the primacy of parliament over the executive, and the separation of Church and state. It was essentially a centrist party, supported by the *petite bourgeoisie* and generally opposed to state intervention in the economy.

In fact, historians have different views about the Radical Party. Robert Paxton describes it as 'the main political expression of the "little man" in France: anticlerical, egalitarian in political terms, laissez-faire in economic terms, sentimental about the French Revolution, ready to defend the republic if it seemed threatened by bishops, generals, or aristocrats'. Roger Price comments on divisions and differences of opinion within the party as a sign of 'the fundamental instability of the key group in the political centre upon whose support governments depended for survival'. J. M. Roberts notes, 'Radicalism was no longer a progressive force. It was deeply rooted in sections of French society which clung to the past, the independent peasantry and lower bourgeoisie.'

> ### DISCUSSION POINT
> What is the attitude of each of the historians mentioned above towards the Radical Party? Do their views conflict with each other?

Socialists and communists

On the left was the Socialist Party which was weakened by a split in 1920, when, at the Congress of Tours, 67% of members voted to break away to form the French Communist Party. The latter, inspired by the Bolshevik Revolution in Russia, joined the international communist movement, and favoured revolution rather than reform. It chose to remain on the fringes of parliamentary politics, and refused to cooperate with more moderate parties on the left. The remaining members of the party, led by Léon Blum, retained the name of the French Socialist Party or SFIO (the French Section of the [Second] Workers International). It was committed to reform through parliamentary democracy, though still influenced by Marxist ideas. During the 1920s, the Communists lost support to the Socialists and in 1928 won only 11 seats in parliament while the Socialists won 107.

The Radical Party and the Socialist Party frequently cooperated with each other at election time, by supporting each other's candidates. In this way they successfully won majorities in three general elections in the interwar years (in 1924, 1932 and 1936). The two parties did not have a common social policy and they disagreed fundamentally on economic policies. However, they did agree on the importance of political liberties, greater access to education, anti-clericalism and anti-militarism. But although the Socialists were prepared to cooperate with the Radical Party at election time, so as not to split the moderate-left vote, they were not prepared to form a government with them. They preferred to wait until they could win a majority on their own in the hope of introducing socialist reforms.

Right-wing groups

The 1920s also saw the growth of extra-parliamentary right-wing organisations, such as the extreme nationalist and anti-Semitic *Action Française*, led by Charles Maurras. Other right-wing paramilitary groups were also formed, inspired by the success of Mussolini's Fascists in Italy. These fascist leagues were very critical of the failings of the Third Republic. In 1927 a movement of war veterans, the *Croix de Feu* (Flaming Cross), was formed and later attracted 150 000 members and funding from some industrialists. However it was only in the 1930s that these right-wing organisations became important politically.

Significant political coalitions

No single party had enough support to win an election on its own, so two main groupings of parties emerged after the war:

- The *Bloc National* was a centre-right coalition of parties supported by business and finance, as well as favoured by leaders in the army and church. Prominent politicians in the *Bloc National* were Georges Clemenceau, Raymond Poincaré and Aristide Briand. Its main goals were to secure prosperity for French business and stability in domestic affairs, as well as to exact revenge on Germany in order to finance France's economic recovery. To the political right of the *Bloc National* were the royalists, many of whom rejected the republican constitution.
- The *Cartel des Gauches* was a centre-left coalition which was dominated by Édouard Herriot of the Radical Party, and sometimes included the Socialist Party. To the left of the *Cartel* was the French Communist Party, which, under the direction of the Comintern in Moscow, was unwilling to cooperate with other left-wing parties or to form coalition governments.

The shift to conservatism, 1919–24

After the war there was a move towards conservatism and national self-interest. In the 1920 election, many voters, alarmed by the success of the Bolsheviks in Russia, voted for the *Bloc National*. As a result, parties of the centre-right won 450 of the 616 seats in parliament. The *Bloc* victory was also helped by disunity on the left. On this occasion, the Radical Party joined a coalition of parties to form a centre-right government.

European States in the Interwar Years (1918–1939)

The Chamber of Deputies that was elected was essentially very conservative in outlook and contained large numbers of war veterans. The coalition was critical of Clemenceau (the prime minister from 1917 to 1920) for being, from their perspective, too lenient towards Germany in the Treaty of Versailles. They were also opposed to his insistence on the need for austerity and higher taxation, and his attempts to establish a stronger position for the presidency. As a result, they refused to back him when he stood for the presidency in 1920, and he subsequently retired from politics.

The term of office of this government was dominated by foreign affairs. Out of concern for its national security, France signed treaties with Belgium, as well as several countries in eastern Europe. The government's attitude and policies were influenced by a general feeling among the public that France had borne the main cost of the war, certainly in loss of life and war damage, and that it had been betrayed by its former allies.

When Germany defaulted on reparations payments in 1922, the French prime minister, Aristide Briand, agreed with the British view that Germany could not be pushed too hard. For this unpopular view, he was forced to resign and was replaced by the more hard-line **Raymond Poincaré**. His solution was to send French troops into the Ruhr, one of Germany's most important industrial areas, as a means of forcing the German government to resume reparations payments, either by pressure or by direct seizure. France was not supported in this move by its allies, notably Britain, and the occupation of the Ruhr created problems for the French economy. As a result the move proved to be unpopular with the French public and led to the fall of Poincaré's government.

Raymond Poincaré (1850–1934):

He was a lawyer and conservative politician who served as president of France from 1913 to 1920, and three terms as prime minister (1912–13, 1922–24 and 1926–29). As prime minister after the war he adopted an uncompromising attitude towards Germany, which was popular at first but lost support when the French economy was affected, leading to the defeat of his government in the National Assembly. In the financial crisis of 1926 Poincaré was reappointed prime minister and he managed to restore economic stability and prosperity in the late 1920s, mainly by stabilising the franc and basing it on the gold standard.

The *Cartel des Gauches* in power, 1924–26

By 1924, after the disastrous occupation of the Ruhr, voters became disillusioned with the *Bloc National* government and left-wing parties did well in the general election. For this election, the Radical Party switched its support to form a centre-left government, led by **Édouard Herriot**, who served as premier from June 1924 until April 1925.

> **Édouard Herriot (1872–1957):**
>
> He was a writer, intellectual and teacher, who served as mayor of Lyon from 1905 until his death, except for a brief period during the Second World War when he was imprisoned in Germany for opposing moves by the Pétain government in Vichy France. Herriot became leader of the Radical Party in 1919 and was noted for his eloquent and persuasive speeches. He served as prime minister on three occasions (1924–25, 1926 and 1932), most notably as leader of the first *Cartel des Gauches* government in 1924.

Foreign and domestic policies

In contrast to the confrontational approach of the previous government, the *Cartel* adopted a more conciliatory foreign policy, with **Aristide Briand** continuing in the position of Minister of Foreign Affairs – a position he held until 1929 under 14 different governments, four of which he headed himself. Briand's influence on foreign policy steered France towards reconciliation with Germany and international cooperation (a policy referred to as *rapprochement*). In 1924, under the American-sponsored Dawes Plan, France agreed to withdraw its troops from the Ruhr, and to accept a revised plan for German reparations payments, which were coupled with American loans to and investments in Germany. Briand was a major contributor in the drawing up of the Locarno pacts in 1925, which ushered in a new era of better relations with Germany.

> **Aristide Briand (1862–1932):**
>
> He was a politician who served as prime minister 11 times between 1909 and 1929. He also served as foreign minister several times and strongly supported a more conciliatory policy towards Germany. He was a joint winner of the 1926 Nobel Peace prize, with Gustav Stresemann of Germany, as a result of the signing of the Locarno Pacts the year before. In 1928, together with the US Secretary of State Frank Kellogg, Briand drew up the Pact of Paris (or Kellogg-Briand Pact) in which countries agreed to outlaw war.

The new government extended diplomatic recognition to the USSR, and at the same time tried to reduce diplomatic ties with the Vatican. It extended laws intended to reduce Church influence in public schools to Alsace and Lorraine (which had not been part of France when these laws had first been passed in the 1880s), but these policies were not popular there. The government also took steps to improve access to public high schools for working-class children.

Financial problems

However, the main problems facing the *Cartel* government were economic and financial. Postwar reconstruction and the repayment of war debts depended on reparations payments from Germany. But the withdrawal of French troops from the Ruhr implied a reluctant recognition that Germany was simply not able to pay the amounts that the French had anticipated. But there was no agreement among the *Cartel* partners about how the financial problems could be solved, as T.A Morris explains.

SOURCE 5.2

Unable to risk the alienation of their remaining followers by supporting the Radicals too enthusiastically, the Socialists refused positions in Herriot's Radical cabinet, and contented themselves with lukewarm parliamentary cooperation. There could be no cooperation, however, over the second of the Cartel's problems, which was the increasing weakness of the French currency. On this matter, Socialist and Radical philosophies differed fundamentally. The Socialists favoured positive action such as heavy taxation. The Radicals, aware of their support among small businessmen, peasant farmers, and so forth, favoured minimal government intervention. This was a recipe for disaster in the economic climate of the mid-1920s. Uncontrolled inflation ravaged the savings of the average Frenchman and undermined the traditional security of the franc.

Morris, T. A. 1985. European History 1848–1945. Slough. University Tutorial Press. p. 216.

QUESTION

How did the composition of the *Cartel des Gauches* government weaken its effectiveness?

The most serious problem facing the government was inflation. French conservatives were distrustful of the *Cartel* government, which had included nine different finance ministers in two years. Investors were losing confidence in the franc, and speculators began to sell francs for gold or other currencies, causing the value of the franc to decline dramatically. France seemed to be in danger of a complete financial collapse.

As the value of the franc declined, those living on fixed incomes faced real hardship. With conflicting attitudes towards economic policy within the *Cartel* government, Herriot did nothing about higher taxes or implementing the currency controls that might have helped to support the franc and balance the budget. Meanwhile, the Bank of France put pressure on the government to balance the budget by refusing to lend it the current operating sums.

The fall of the *Cartel* government

As the financial situation deteriorated, Herriot lost support and in April 1925 the government resigned. After this there were seven different ministries within 15 months, none of which was able to solve the deepening crisis. The franc declined on world markets until it was worth only one-tenth of its prewar value. As inflation increased, many people lost their savings. The experience of this crisis left many on the left suspicious of business leaders, especially the '200 Families' – the main shareholders in the Bank of France – whom they believed had an undermining influence on money markets and on the political system.

Herriot and the Radical Party blamed conservative financiers for the financial problems facing the government. Robert Paxton supports this view: 'There is no doubt that conservative hostility to Herriot contributed to the run on the franc'. However, he goes on to comment that: 'the real problem lay in the French people's years of refusal to support the expenses of war and reconstruction by taxation, and in the Radicals' horror of state regulation'.

William Shirer, a journalist and historian, provides his view of the reasons for the failure of the *Cartel* government (See Source 5.3). Shirer's book *The Collapse of the Third Republic* was first published in 1969, but it provides one of the most detailed studies of this period of French history that has been published in English.

Theory of Knowledge

History and language

Some people would argue that historians should avoid using judgemental words such as 'selfish', 'greedy', 'ignorant' and 'timid' when analysing the past. How can language reflect bias? Can the language used by historians influence the way we view the past? Or should historians always use neutral words? Should historians have the freedom to use emotive terminology when interpreting the past?

SOURCE 5.3

If the possessor class in France [the wealthy élite] was too selfish, greedy and shortsighted to consent to a fair and decent solution of the State's financial crisis, the leftist Cartel majority in the Chamber of Deputies, representing the Frenchmen of modest means, was at the same time too ignorant, too confused and too timid to impose one on the country, as it had the constitutional right and power to do. The Left too bears a heavy responsibility for keeping the government on the edge of bankruptcy. With its large majority in the Chamber at the beginning of 1924 it could have enacted the laws necessary to give the state the revenue it needed, curb inflation and put a brake on the flight of capital and the widespread evasion of income tax. But it could not make up its mind to do so. By threatening to do something, such as carrying out a forced loan on capital, converting short-term into long-term bonds, raising the income tax and decreasing its evasions, it frightened the rich and drove their money abroad. By doing nothing, despite the threats, it helped to empty the Treasury, weaken the currency and add greatly to the chaos.

Shirer, W. 1972. **The Collapse of the Third Republic***. London, Pan. p. 160–1.*

The return of the centre-right, 1926–29

After the succession of centre-left governments was unable to halt the decline in the value of the franc, a centre-right government returned to power in 1926, with the support of the Radicals. They saw it as a means of restoring stability and confidence. Poincaré led it from July 1926 until July 1929, with Briand serving as foreign minister.

Poincaré was welcomed back as a 'national saviour' and he brought a sense of stability and confidence. Investors started to buy francs back and the pace of inflation slowed down. But Poincaré had to introduce some stringent measures to restore the economy. He returned France to the gold standard (see 5.6, The economic impact of the Depression on France), increased indirect taxation and reduced government spending. He also replaced the 'Napoleon franc' with what was referred to as the 'Poincaré franc', which was revalued at one-fifth of its prewar value. Although this was an unpopular measure, many people, especially the middle classes, welcomed the stability that it brought. The economy was further stabilised by balanced budgets and the steadier flow of reparations from Germany.

The return of a centre-right coalition restored business confidence and stabilised the franc and the economy, creating three years of prosperity and stability. Foreign buyers of French exports were encouraged by the favourable exchange rate which also attracted large numbers of tourists. However it left a bitter legacy, as historians Robert Paxton and T.A. Morris observe (see Sources 5.4 and 5.5).

When Poincaré retired in 1929 on account of ill-health, the pattern of short-lived governments returned.

SOURCE 5.4

The middle class could begin to glimpse the revival of a stable world. The war had been paid for out of their savings, however, and even during the historic high level of prosperity reached in 1929, there remained tender spots on French middle-class consciousness. The franc must never be touched again. And France must never again embark on another war, so costly in gold and blood.

Paxton, R. O. 1997. **Europe in the Twentieth Century (Third Edition).** *Fort Worth. Harcourt Brace College Publishers. p. 254.*

SOURCE 5.5

The advent of Poincaré, with the apparent consent of the Cartel des Gauches, convinced many voters on the left that their democratic will would always be obstructed by the 'Wall of Money' ('Mur d'Argent'), and by the vested interests of bankers and industrialists. They felt that other means of political expression might bring better results. In a period of less economic stability it was to become evident that France had all the ingredients of a 'veiled civil war'. Involved were the remnants of wartime nationalism, the rise of communism, the insecurity of small tradesmen and farmers, and the vested interests of financiers.

Morris, T. A., 1985. **European History 1848–1945.** *Slough. University Tutorial Press. p. 216.*

How do Sources 5.4 and 5.5 suggest that the financial crises contributed to class divisions in French society and polarisation in French politics?

Policies to safeguard French security

Whichever coalition was in power, French governments throughout the 1920s acutely felt the need for security, especially after the United States refused to join the League of Nations and Britain was clearly unwilling to become involved in continental affairs to safeguard French security. For these reasons France constructed a ring of alliances with the states in eastern Europe (Poland, Czechoslovakia, Romania and Yugoslavia), which it hoped would prevent future German aggression. However, the distances of these countries from France, and their comparative weakness, meant that these alliances did not in themselves provide a firm basis for future French security.

The occupation of the Ruhr isolated France from its former allies, mainly Britain, and was unpopular in France too, so the policy of coercion to force Germany to pay reparations was replaced by one of conciliation. This was seen in its acceptance of the Locarno Pacts, Germany's admission to the League of Nations, France's acceptance of the Dawes and Young Plans and the signing of the Kellogg-Briand Pact.

But even when, under Aristide Briand, France followed a policy of conciliation and goodwill towards Germany from 1925 onwards, the country maintained the largest army in Europe. In 1929 it also commenced the construction of the Maginot Line, an elaborate string of fortifications along France's eastern border with Germany. This modern and supposedly impregnable structure ran from the Swiss border to Montmédy near Verdun. However, it did not extend to the Channel coast and cover the Belgian border. It was an ambitious project, and about one-third of the government's 1929 budget was allocated to defence, indicating that the issue of security remained a major priority of French domestic and foreign policy. Ironically, when Germany invaded France again in 1940, the rapid German advance demonstrated the irrelevance of the Maginot line.

France later concluded an alliance with the Soviet Union, after Hitler came to power in Germany. The 1935 Franco-Soviet alliance included a non-aggression pact, commercial treaties and a treaty of mutual assistance, each country pledging to assist its partner if either one was the object of unprovoked aggression.

ACTIVITY

Create a diagram to summarise the developments in French politics during the 1920s under the three different governing coalitions: *Bloc National* 1919–24; *Cartel des Gauches* 1924–26; Poincaré government 1926–29.

KEY CONCEPTS QUESTION

Change and continuity: 'Although there were frequent changes of government, French politics in the 1920s were characterised by a degree of continuity in the political process'. To what extent do you agree with this statement?

5.4 Which social issues were significant in the interwar years?

During the 1920s, there was an improvement in public morale but there were nevertheless significant social issues facing France, such as the low birth rate, the position of women, and the wide gulf separating the élite from other sectors of society.

The low birth rate

France's already declining birth rate was aggravated by the loss of so many young men during the war. After the war, the government tried to solve the demographic problems by encouraging women to stay at home and raise families, as well as to help take care of the three million wounded, many of whom could not return to their prewar occupations and needed home or institutional care. Many women had joined the workforce during the war, in industry and transport, as well as in office work. Many of them were reluctant to give up the new-found independence that their work and incomes gave them. Three years after the end of the war, 42% of adult women were still in employment, and they comprised 40% of the workforce.

Postwar governments made other attempts to increase the birth rate: in 1920 the sale of contraceptives was banned and tough new laws were brought in against abortionists. There was also official government support for the celebration of Mother's Day, and the introduction of state medals for fertility – a bronze medal for five, a silver for eight, and a gold medal for having ten children. The economic recovery during the 1920s led to a boost in the birth rate but this was reversed when the Great Depression reached France after 1929. In 1932, family allowances were introduced as an incentive for having larger families, but this measure was not successful and from 1935 onwards, deaths outnumbered births.

The large number of war dead and the low birth rate resulted in a labour shortage, so the government implemented schemes to attract immigrants. Most of them came from Italy, Spain and Portugal, but there were others too, including Belgians and Russians. There had been about one million immigrants in France before the war, and these numbers increased substantially during and after the war so that by the mid-1930s they numbered 2.5 million, nearly 10% of the adult population, making France 'Europe's melting-pot', according to historian Colin Jones.

The position of women

The position of women in France was still governed by the restrictions laid down in the Napoleonic Code in 1804. Unlike the situation in many other countries where women were granted the right to vote after the First World War, this did not happen in France. Bills to give women the vote were rejected by the National Assembly in 1919, 1929, 1932 and 1935. Both the Radical and Socialist parties were afraid that, if they were given the vote, women would support pro-Church parties. However, education for girls improved in the interwar years, although secondary and higher education was still dominated by middle-class boys.

Figure 5.3: Women in France during the 1920s stage a protest in favour of votes for women.

In 1936 three women were appointed to serve in the Popular Front government by Léon Blum, but they still did not have the right to vote in elections for parliament. In 1938, women were made 'legal majors' for the first time, meaning for example that they could apply for a passport without their husband's permission. Women only won the right to vote in France in 1945, one of the last Western countries to enfranchise women. It was only in 1965 that the surviving restrictions put on women by the Napoleonic Code were lifted, giving a woman the right to open a bank account, own property, and get a job, without her husband's consent.

ACTIVITY

Carry out some research on the restrictions placed on women in the Napoleonic Code. How did policies towards women in France in the interwar years compare with the position of women in Germany and Italy at the same time?

The French Revolution is often seen as an important milestone in the development of democracy in Europe, and France usually saw itself as one of the leading democratic states. How can you reconcile these views with the position of women in France in the interwar years?

The social structure

French society was deeply unequal. It was made up of roughly one-third peasant farmers, one-third workers, and one-third middle class, but wealth and power was concentrated in a small number of the upper-middle class, the *grande bourgeoisie*. They constituted the social élite and were the leaders in banking and business; they had considerable influence over the political establishment as well. The education system contributed to the inegalitarian nature of society.

SOURCE 5.6

Birth, culture, and ultimately wealth determined access to education: the great divider. The vast majority of children attended primary school until the age of fourteen, a small minority received instruction in the primary classes attached to fee-paying *lycées*. The need for professional and cultural qualifications, together with correctness in dress and manners, comfortable accommodation, and the ability to entertain and mix socially continued to severely restrict entry to important decision-making positions in government, administration, and private enterprise. These attributes combined to protect position and to distance the less fortunate.

Price, R. 2005. **A Concise History of France (Second Edition).** *New York. Cambridge University Press. p. 258.*

How useful is Source 5.6 for historians studying class divisions in French society?

Roger Price also comments on the essentially conservative outlook of most of French society, who 'dreamt less of revolution than of social promotion', so that upwardly mobile people from the lower-middle or working classes did not want to reform the existing social system but to conform to it and succeed within its existing boundaries.

> **KEY CONCEPTS ACTIVITY**
>
> **Significance:** Explain why the low birth rate, the position of women and deep class divisions were significant issues in France during the 1920s.

5.5 What cultural trends were evident in the 1920s?

In the decades before the First World War, France and especially Paris were renowned for their flourishing art, music and literature. This era was referred to as the *belle époque*, the 'beautiful era'. In the 1920s Paris once again became a vibrant centre for the arts, but the form and substance of these changed substantially. The 'roaring twenties' in Paris were referred to as '*les années folles*', the 'crazy years'.

The arts

Historians refer to a sense of despair which grew out of the war and affected art and literature, which was evident in the Dada and Surrealist movements. The Dada movement started in Zurich during the war but the ideas spread to Paris and influenced writers and artists there. They rejected bourgeois values and materialism, and mocked conventional attitudes towards nationalism and rationalism, which they blamed for starting the war. They also challenged the conformity associated with traditional art forms.

Surrealism developed out of the Dada movement. It was founded by André Breton, a French medical student, who had been assigned to work in a psychiatric hospital during the war. His experiences there working with shell-shocked patients convinced him of the power of the unconscious and the importance of dreams. He abandoned medicine to become a writer. He believed that art should be used to channel the unconscious and unlock the power of the imagination. In this way he believed art could free the unconscious from the restraints imposed by society and by reason and logic.

In spite of the political instability and financial crises which France faced, writers and artists from abroad were attracted to Paris in the 1920s. It became a vibrant centre of literary activity during this period, and writers from all over the English-speaking world moved there to be part of it, such as Ernest Hemingway, F. Scott Fitzgerald, Gertrude Stein and James Joyce. Paris was the centre too for visual arts and design, and the 1925 Exposition of the Decorative Arts launched Art Deco as a new international style.

Figure 5.4: The 1925 Exposition of the Decorative Arts launched Art Deco as a new international style, and established Paris as the centre for visual arts and design.

Popular culture

The success and skills of African and African-American musicians in Paris in the 1920s inspired an enthusiastic following and had a powerful impact on the development of a jazz culture in Paris. The African American dancer Josephine Baker who appeared in *La Revue Nègre*, which opened in Paris in 1925, became an instant sensation and a national star and was widely admired for the exotic nature of her dance routines. In the jazz craze of the 1920s, many American phrases, such as *un jazz club* and *un cocktail* were adopted into French. Another American, Charles Lindbergh, became a popular hero, when he made the first solo transatlantic flight in 1927, landing his plane, *The Spirit of St Louis*, at Le Bourget airport in Paris.

French cinema remained a popular pastime, and 250 million film tickets were sold in 1933 alone. The popularity of films, radio and gramophone records helped to spread the new trends in popular culture from Paris to a wider audience. French cinema went on to experience a golden age in the 1930s.

Many of the conservative and elderly political élite were totally out of touch with these new developments in culture and fashion, as historian Colin Jones comments: 'The major politicians were an increasingly aged set with their roots in the belle epoque rather than the jazz age'.

The Church

Political leaders were also out of touch with modern attitudes towards religion. In the past, the Radical Party had always managed to drum up support by attacking the Church, but by the 1920s, anti-clericalism had become irrelevant to many French people.

Many of the issues which before had caused rifts between the government and the Church had been settled amicably, such as diplomatic relations with the Vatican. In addition, the government's policies on contraception and abortion found favour with Church teachings. However, church leaders were critical of the more materialist and consumerist popular culture, especially as they saw a decline in church attendance.

The media

Traditionally, newspapers had always done well in France and in the interwar years the press adapted to changing tastes and demand. Two examples of these changes were the emergence of photo-journalism and comic books. A fashion press also developed and the publication of the first *Marie Claire* magazine in 1937 helped to make female fashion less élitist. Sporting newspapers also flourished, and *L'Auto* (the forerunner of *L'Équipe*) sold 500 000 copies a day during the Tour de France in 1923.

ACTIVITY

Choose one area of French culture in the 1920s and research it. In what ways did it reflect the economic, political and social issues of the time?

Conclusion

The First World War had profound consequences for France – economically, politically and socially. Despite initial difficulties and financial crises, the French economy grew in the 1920s and by 1929 had achieved a level of prosperity for some sections of the population. It was also a decade of frequent changes in government but a certain continuity in the political process. However, in the decade that followed this prosperity and continuity were to be severely tested.

5

Paper 3 exam practice

Question

'Fundamental differences between the Radicals and Socialists over economic policy were the main reason for the failure of the *Cartel des Gauches* government in 1926'. To what extent do you agree with this statement? **[15 marks]**

Skill

Using your own knowledge analytically and combining it with awareness of historical debate

Examiner's tips

Always remember that historical knowledge and analysis should be the *core* of your answer – aspects of historical debate are desirable extras. However, where it is relevant, the integration of relevant knowledge about historical debates and interpretations, with reference to individual historians, will help push your answer up into the higher bands.

Assuming that you have read the question carefully, drawn up a plan, worked out your line of argument and approach and written your introductory paragraph, you should be able to avoid both irrelevant material and simple narrative. Your task now is to follow your plan by writing a series of linked paragraphs that contain relevant analysis, precise supporting own knowledge and, where relevant, brief references to historical debate interpretations.

For this question, you will need to:

* give a *brief* explanation of the historical context (the situation of the French economy at the time; divisions between left and right in French politics; the fall of the *Bloc National* government in 1924 and the election of the *Cartel des Gauches*)
* supply an outline of the issues which the *Cartel* government faced while in office between 1924 and 1926
* provide a consistently analytical examination of the reasons for the failure of the *Cartel* government.

Such a topic, which has been the subject of some historical debate, will also give you the chance to refer to different historians' views.

Common mistakes

Some students, being aware of an existing historical debate (and knowing that extra marks can be gained by showing this), simply write things like: 'Historian X says... and historian Y says...' However, they make no attempt to **evaluate** the different views (for example, has one historian had access to more or better information than another, perhaps because he or she was writing at a later date?); nor is this information **integrated** into the answer by being pinned to the question. Another weak use of historical debate is to write things like: 'Historian X is biased because she is American.' Such comments will not be given credit.

Sample student answer

The focus of the French economy in the early 1920s was on reconstruction after the damage caused during the First World War. France also owed huge sums in war debts to the USA and Britain, and the value of the franc had halved during the war. To pay for the reconstruction France relied on substantial reparations from Germany which had been provided for in the Treaty of Versailles.

There were a large number of political parties in France in the 1920s and this led to the formation of political alliances and coalition governments. No single party had enough support to win an election on its own, so two main groupings of parties emerged. A conservative centre-right coalition, the Bloc National, was elected to power in 1919. Its main aims were to secure prosperity for French business and stability in domestic affairs. It also wanted to extract maximum reparations from Germany to pay for France's economic recovery. When Germany defaulted on reparations payments in 1923, the Bloc government sent French troops into the Ruhr, to try to force the Germans to pay. This move was not successful as the Germans launched a passive resistance campaign in the Ruhr and France's actions were criticized by its allies, notably Britain. It also created economic problems in France and the government lost support.

In the 1924 general election support turned to the centre-left parties which formed a coalition called the Cartel des Gauches. The main two parties in the Cartel were the Radical Party and the Socialist Party. Édouard Herriot, the leader of the Radical Party, became prime minister. The new government withdrew the French army from the Ruhr and initiated a conciliatory policy towards Germany. In this way the Cartel government created better relations and cooperation with other European countries. But the main issues facing the Cartel government were economic and financial. The biggest problem was inflation. Many conservative business leaders did not trust the Cartel government and speculators began to sell francs for gold or other currencies. This caused the value of the franc to decline dramatically and investors began to lose confidence in the franc. France seemed to be on the verge of a complete financial collapse. The Cartel government could not agree on what actions to take. The Socialists supported higher taxes and controls on sending out currency but the Radicals did not. So the government took no effective steps to implement policies that might have helped to support the franc and to balance the budget.

As the financial situation got worse, Herriot's government lost support and he was forced to resign after less than a year in office. After this the Cartel formed seven more governments over the next 15 months, but none of them were able to solve the financial crisis. The value of the franc declined so much that it was worth only one tenth of its prewar value. The Radicals believed that the only way to restore stability and confidence was to switch support from the Cartel to the centre-right. So in 1926 a centre-right government under Poincaré took over. The Cartel government had failed.

There are different views of the reasons for its failure. Radical politicians blamed conservative business leaders and bankers for causing the collapse of the franc and for the problems facing the government. Many on the Left thought that the main shareholders in the Bank of France had used their influence to undermine confidence in the government. While some historians, such as Robert Paxton, partly support this view, Paxton also believes that the underlying cause of the economic problems was the unwillingness of the Radicals in power to raise taxes and to regulate the economy. William Shirer believes that the Cartel government was too weak and hesitant to introduce policies, such as raising taxes and introducing currency controls, which might have saved the economy. Instead, by speaking about such measures but not actually implementing them, it contributed to the economic collapse.

The main reason that the Cartel government did not implement effective measures was the fundamental difference in views about economic policy between the Radicals and Socialists. The Radicals supported a laissez faire policy of minimal government intervention in the economy, while the Socialists believed that there should be more government control. The Socialists, who had already lost two-thirds of their supporters to the Communists when the original Socialist Party had split in 1920, were not in a strong position and did not want to lose any more supporters by supporting any measures favoured by the Radicals. The

Radicals, in turn, did not want to lose the support of small businessmen and small-scale farmers, their main source of votes, by introducing government controls so they resisted this. T. A. Morris believes that this attitude was disastrous for the French economy and so led to the failure of the Cartel government.

EXAMINER'S COMMENT

It is clear that this candidate has some precise own knowledge about the topic, and correctly outlines the context and the sequence of events. There is an attempt at a structured approach. However, in parts the answer is superficial and vague, and lacks detail and explanation. Nearly all of it consists of a narrative of the sequence of events and there is little attempt at analysis. Although the candidate has provided some brief knowledge of historical debate, it is not smoothly integrated into the answer but is tacked on at the end. There is also no evaluation of different views. Consequently, such an answer would probably be awarded a mark at the bottom of Band 3 (7 marks).

Activity

In this unit, the focus is on writing an answer that is analytical and well supported by precise own knowledge, and one which – where relevant – refers to historical interpretations and debates. Using the information from this unit, and any other sources of information available to you, try to answer **one** of the following Paper 3 practice questions using these skills.

Remember to refer to the simplified Paper 3 mark scheme in Chapter 6.

Paper 3 practice questions

1 Examine the social, economic and political impact of the First World War on France.

2 Discuss the state of the French economy during the 1920s and the extent to which it had recovered by 1929.

3 Examine the political divisions in France during the 1920s and the extent to which these divisions contributed to political instability.

4 Evaluate the significance of social issues in France during the 1920s, such as the low birth rate, the position of women, and the widening gulf between the social élite and other sections of French society.

5 To what extent was French culture during the 1920s influenced by the experiences of the First World War?

France

Unit 2: France, 1929–40

5

Introduction

The 1930s were a difficult decade for France, as indeed they were for many European countries. The first half of the decade was shaped by the effects of the worldwide economic depression which had a significant impact on France, economically, socially and politically. This led to civil unrest and a revolutionary change in French parliamentary politics with the election of a Popular Front government in 1936.

The second half of the decade was overshadowed by rising international tensions, caused principally by Hitler's actions in Europe, which reignited French fears about security in general and German aggression in particular. The tensions revealed serious divisions in French society and politics, which continued even after France's defeat and partial occupation by Germany in 1940 which effectively ended the Third Republic.

TIMELINE

1929 Oct: Wall Street Crash; start of worldwide Great Depression

1931 Effects of Depression reach France

1932–5 Radical government in power

1934 Jan: Stavisky Affair

Feb: Riots by far-right leagues

1935 Jun: Formation of Popular Front

1936 May: Popular Front government under Léon Blum voted into power

Jun: Matignon Agreements between government, industry and labour

Sept: France abandons the gold standard

1937 Jun: Blum forced to resign

Oct: Popular Front government devalues the franc

1938 Sept: Popular Front breaks up

1939 Sept: Second World War begins

1940 Jun: France surrenders to Germany

Jul: Vichy government replaces Third Republic

KEY QUESTIONS

- How did the Great Depression affect France?
- What was the Popular Front and how successful was it as a government?
- What caused the collapse of the Third Republic?

Overview

- The worldwide Great Depression, which started after the Wall Street Crash in 1929, did not affect France until 1931, when export markets declined, food prices dropped and industrial production slowed down.
- The Depression increased political instability as coalition governments tried unsuccessfully to cope with the crisis by reducing government spending; however, they avoided leaving the gold standard or devaluing the franc, which might have boosted exports.
- Concerns about government corruption surfaced with the Stavisky Affair in 1934, and led to increasing criticism of the government, especially from right-wing groups which had first appeared in the 1920s but now re-emerged as disruptive fascist leagues.
- When right-wing protesters tried to storm the parliament building in February 1934, forceful police reaction resulted in the death of 17 people and over 2000 wounded; after this the government struggled to contain growing political unrest.
- Alarmed by the growth of right-wing groups, the Communists, Socialists and Radicals formed a Popular Front to defend the republic and uphold democracy.
- In 1936 a Popular Front government led by Léon Blum came to power amid a series of nationwide strikes. It introduced sweeping social and economic reforms, which were welcomed by workers but condemned by the conservative middle class.
- The Popular Front was weakened by internal divisions over the Spanish Civil War and the direction of economic policies, as well as

continuing economic problems and financial crises; Blum was forced to step down after only a year in office.

- Although the Popular Front introduced some lasting reforms, it did not solve the economic problems facing France; it also created greater polarisation in French politics and society.
- After the collapse of the Popular Front, governments continued to face financial problems, social divisions and political instability, amid rising international tensions and concerns about French security.
- After the German invasion of France in 1940, the government signed an armistice and the Third Republic collapsed.

5.6 How did the Great Depression affect France?

The start of the Great Depression

The origins of the Great Depression that affected the world economy in the 1930s lay in the collapse of the New York stock market in October 1929. This began a global economic decline characterised by high unemployment, falling production and the almost total collapse of international trade. It resulted in a profound loss of confidence in the capitalist system itself and in the ability of governments to cope with the crisis. The industrial economies of Europe, which had close trade and financial links with the USA, were affected immediately, as investments were withdrawn, banks collapsed and factories closed. This economic crisis also had significant social and political effects, as European governments struggled to solve the problems within a democratic framework. Not all of them succeeded.

The economic impact of the Depression on France

The effects of the Depression reached France later than they did many other countries. In part, this was because France was less industrialised than other countries, and also because it remained on the gold standard longer and so attracted international investors. For the first two years after the Wall Street Crash French industrialists and politicians believed that France had escaped the crisis that had overtaken the world economy. Although exports began to shrink, measures such as price supports and import quotas protected the French economy for a while. However, when the Depression hit, it was more severe and more lasted longer. Historian Robert Paxton refers to it as a 'slow, demoralizing rot rather than a major upheaval'.

Figure 5.5: Hungry people wait outside a soup kitchen in Paris in the winter of 1931–32.

The situation by 1931

By 1931 it was clear that the short-lived prosperity in France was over. Exports were falling, tourist numbers were declining, and industrial output was slowing down. After a decade of labour shortages, there was rising unemployment, with 40 000 jobs per month lost in the first half of 1931. Figures for unemployment in France are lower than those for many other countries at the time, with the official figure of unemployed in 1932 only 250 000. But this number does not reflect the over 1 million foreign workers who left for their home countries, adding to the unemployed in places such as Italy and Algeria. The official figures also do not show the many unemployed from the cities who returned to the countryside where they were supported by their families.

Agriculture was hit hard by the Depression, due mainly to a collapse in food prices, which in turn was due to the oversupply on both the home and international markets. The problem was aggravated by excellent harvests between 1932 and 1935. Prices dropped substantially, for example by 34% for vegetables, 40% for meat and 60% for wine. This meant that farmers' profits, farm-workers' wages and landowners' income from rental all fell. As a result, the rural economy declined significantly.

The situation in the mid-1930s

The Depression was slow to start in France, but it was also slow to end. By the mid-1930s when other industrial economies were starting to recover, France was still grappling with severe economic problems. This was due in part to successive governments' handling of the crisis. Haunted by the memories of inflation in the 1920s, they were determined to maintain the value of the franc. France was one of only four major currencies to remain on the gold standard and the government tried to protect the French economy with protective tariffs and quotas on imports.

The economic crisis affected social groups differently and aggravated existing social and political tensions. Peasant farmers suffered because of the collapse of prices for their products. However, urban workers were not as badly affected, because falling prices meant that the real value of their wages increased. While small businesses and shopkeepers were negatively affected by the downturn in business, many of the wealthy élite retained their wealth and privileged positions.

Economic recovery only really got underway in 1938 and industrial production did not regain 1929 levels until 1939. Historian Colin Jones suggests that the Depression was one of three factors which led to the growth of political extremism in France in the 1930s. The other two were evidence of political corruption and the rise in international tension.

Gold standard	a fixed link between the value of a currency and the price of gold
Inflation	a general increase in prices and a fall in the value (or purchasing power) of money
Deflation	reducing government expenditure to balance the budget
Devaluation	reducing the value of a currency
Exchange controls	government restrictions on the movement of capital out of a country
Protective tariffs	high customs duties on imports to protect local producers
Price supports	government controls on minimum prices to protect producers
Import quotas	government restrictions on imports to protect local producers by reducing imports

Table 5.1: Governments tried various strategies to cope with the economic problems. This table will help you to understand the terminology associated with these economic policies.

Theory of Knowledge

The role of the historian

In commenting on the fact that economists and politicians do not seem to have learned from the mistakes that caused and prolonged the Great Depression, historian Eric Hobsbawm suggests that this *'provides a vivid illustration of society's need for historians, who are the professional remembrancers of what their fellow citizens wish to forget'*. Critically examine this view of the role of historians. What other functions do historians fulfil?

The political impact of the Depression on France

The depression years intensified deep divisions in French society, and many people lost faith in the French republic and democratic principles.

The large range of parties on the left, centre and right, could not reach agreement on how to solve the problems. This undermined popular confidence in the democratic system and led to a bitter polarisation between left-wing and right-wing parties. Historians Peter Gay and Robert Webb suggest that while the few years of prosperity of the late 1920s may have 'plastered over deep divisions in French society, the old debates had been adjourned but not forgotten.'

Political instability in government

The economic crisis was in turn aggravated by political instability. Between 1929 and 1932, André Tardieu headed three governments. He wanted to reform the electoral system and give more power to the executive but these measures were defeated in the Chamber of Deputies. In the 1932 election, the right was defeated and a centre-left government was elected. Herriot became prime minister once again. The government had the support of the Socialists, although they did not form part of the coalition government. Between February 1932 and February 1934 eight different governments failed to find solutions. They tried to balance the budget by raising taxes and reducing public spending, for example by cutting civil servants' wages and reducing military pensions. The quick succession of governments meant that cabinets did not view problems from a long-term perspective. Deputies focused more on local issues of concern to their own constituencies rather than on seeking solutions for the economy as a whole. Because of this, they were reluctant to support meaningful social reforms or economic measures that might have helped the situation.

The financial crisis and government policies

At the same time the unbalanced budget and the general economic situation caused a drain on the gold reserves of the Bank of France. However, all French governments were determined not to leave the gold standard or, especially, to devalue the franc.

SOURCE 5.7

The passionate strength of opposition to devaluation as a 'swindle', which threatened the value of savings, meant that it was an option politicians proposed at their peril. There was much more political mileage in denouncing it in the most apocalyptic terms possible… As a result of this determination to preserve the international value, status and purchasing power of the currency and to avoid a return to the inflation of the 1920s, French products became increasingly uncompetitive in world markets.

Price, R. 2005. **A Concise History of France (Second Edition).** *New York. Cambridge University Press. pp. 265.*

ACTIVITY

Explain how public attitudes towards devaluation were shaped by what had happened in France during the 1920s.

As a result, France's share of international trade between 1929 and 1935 plummeted by 44% in volume and by 82% in value. France tried to compensate for the loss of trade by promoting exports to its own colonial empire. But although the volume of these exports increased, they did not compensate for the loss of markets in industrialised countries. Governments continued to apply deflationary policies by reducing government spending in order to balance the budget, but this reduced demand even further, and created a downward spiral of falling prices, falling wages and falling demand.

DISCUSSION POINT

Why is there often a link between economic problems and political instability? Apart from France in the 1930s, what other situations can you think of where this has been the case?

Concerns about corruption

At the same time as the economy was declining, there were suspicions about corruption involving political leaders. These concerns surfaced with force in 1934 with the 'Stavisky Affair'. Serge Alexandre Stavisky, a Ukrainian Jewish immigrant and a French citizen, was a shady financier who had been suspected of involvement in corrupt municipal deals before, but never prosecuted. His schemes involved selling worthless bonds to the public, with the apparent collusion of government officials. His sudden death in January 1934, in mysterious circumstances, led many to believe that he had been murdered to protect people in positions of power who had benefited from his deals in the past. In fact, the cause of Stavisky's death was most probably suicide, but it was widely suspected at the time that it was a political murder to cover up the involvement of corrupt politicians and police.

The affair led to increased criticism of the government. Many ordinary people believed that Radical Party politicians were involved in corrupt dealings that they were now trying to hide. Both the Communist Party and right-wing groups used the opportunity to attack the government, while the right-wing press promoted xenophobic and anti-Semitic messages. The Stavisky scandal brought the government down: it lost support in the Chamber of Deputies and was forced to resign. A new government led by another Radical politician, **Édouard Daladier**, ordered investigations into the affair but these were not properly instituted and this led to protests in the streets.

Édouard Daladier (1884–1970):

He was a Radical politician who served as prime minister several times during the 1930s, and was leader of the Radical Party when it formed the Popular Front with the Communists and Socialists. After the German invasion of France in 1940, he escaped to French North Africa where he tried to set up a government-in-exile. However, he was arrested and taken to Vichy France where he was put on trial and imprisoned in Germany until the end of the war.

The rise of the right

The weakness of parliamentary politics encouraged the formation of extra-parliamentary groups. Right-wing groups which had first appeared in the 1920s now emerged again displaying, as Peter Gay and Robert Webb describe, 'an openly fascist aura and program and demanding the regeneration of a corrupt nation'.

The oldest of these organisations was the *Action Française*, a reactionary movement which received support from right-wing writers and intellectuals. The most prominent group was the *Croix de Feu*, originally an organisation of military veterans. Under the leadership of Colonel François de la Rocque its membership rose to 300 000, and it became dangerously political, holding secret meetings to plan the overthrow of the government. Another right-wing group, the *Jeunesses Patriotes*, wore fascist-style uniforms and were financed by François Coty, the controversial perfume millionaire. None of these organisations had enough support to take power, but they had the capacity to cause political disruption.

ACTIVITY

Use the internet to research some of the right-wing groups active in France in the early 1930s. To what extent did they pose a threat to the government?

The protests of 6 February 1934

The Stavisky Affair gave these organisations the opportunity to demonstrate against the shaky coalition government. On 6 February 1934, right-wing parties and fascist groups staged a protest march in Paris and tried to force their way into the parliament buildings, threatening to overthrow the government. A violent police reaction to the protests resulted in 17 dead and over 2000 wounded. The left saw the events as a threatening attempted coup by right-wing groups, but Colin Jones offers an alternative explanation, saying that it was simply 'a deliberately ostentatious gesture of protest and exasperation'.

T. A. Morris sums up some of the conflicting views about the significance of this event.

SOURCE 5.8

Were the riots of 6th February 1934 a serious attempt to seize power? It has been the consistent claim of the French left that they were, and as late as 1947 an official enquiry described the events as 'a genuine insurrection, minutely prepared'. Others have seen them merely as a spontaneous outburst of anger and frustration against the 'invertebrate republic'… Whatever the case, the 6th February marked a hardening in the political divisions within the nation, and a significant stage in the decline of the Third Republic.

Morris, T. A., 1985. **European History 1848–1945.** *Slough. University Tutorial Press. p. 218.*

KEY CONCEPTS ACTIVITY

Significance: Explain the significance of these right-wing protests for the political situation in France at the time.

Figure 5.6: Right-wing protestors clash with police guarding the approaches to the Chamber of Deputies in the Place de la Concorde, 6 February 1934.

Growing political unrest

Communist demonstrations led to more bloodshed, as rival groups confronted each other on the streets. For the next two years France was on the brink of civil war. Successive governments tried to cope with the crisis but seemed unable to solve the economic problems or suppress the social and political unrest. Daladier resigned in favour of a national unity government led by former president, Gaston Doumergue.

Doumergue formed a broad coalition government in which almost all political parties were represented. Doumergue tried to alter the constitution to strengthen the executive over the Chamber of Deputies (such as a requirement to call for an election when the Chamber turned out a government). His government collapsed when the Radicals withdrew over what they considered his increasingly authoritarian style. The next government tried to attain special powers to deal with the growing financial crisis. In both cases the Chamber was unwilling to support measures which they felt would pose a threat to democracy. From May 1935 to January 1936, the government of **Pierre Laval** tried to counter the economic decline with unpopular measures such as increased taxes and sharp cuts in government spending, but these measures were ineffective in solving the mounting political and economic crises.

Pierre Laval (1883–1945):

He served as prime minister of France in 1931 and again in 1935 to 1936. After the German invasion of France, he was a member of Pétain's government which signed the armistice. Laval helped to persuade the Chamber of Deputies to disband, thus ending the Third Republic in July 1940. Convinced of a German victory in the war, he supported collaboration with Nazi Germany, and agreed to send French labourers to work in German industries. After the war he was tried for treason, found guilty and executed.

QUESTION

What were the economic and political effects of the Great Depression on France?

5.7 What was the Popular Front and how successful was it as a government?

At this stage a new development on the left changed the political landscape in France. A new political alliance, the Popular Front, was voted into power in 1936, and it tried to implement a new approach to the social and economic problems.

The formation of the Popular Front

So far, the French Communist Party had refused to work with other parties, such as the Socialists. Now the growing danger of fascism at home as well as the threat posed by Nazi Germany, led the Communists to reconsider their previous refusal to form political alliances with other left-wing groups. From 1934 the Communist Party started to call for the formation of a Popular Front to resist fascism and introduce political and social changes. The Socialists and many Radicals supported the call, and in 1935 the left-wing parties made gains in local municipal elections. The breakaway Communist trade union, the CGTU, rejoined the Socialist-dominated CGT, and they also supported calls for a Popular Front government. The reunited trade union strengthened the labour movement significantly and within two years the CGT had four million members.

The change in policy was influenced by a change in Moscow. Previously, communist parties throughout Europe, under directions from the Comintern, had refused to cooperate with other left-wing parties, a factor which had helped the Nazis to come to power in Germany. Now Stalin was concerned about the growing threat of fascism and Nazism in Europe and so he ordered a complete reversal of Comintern policies. He directed communist parties throughout Europe to ally themselves with socialists and other left-wing parties. This went one step further in 1935 when the Comintern directed communist parties to cooperate not only with socialists, but also with liberals, moderates and even conservatives who were opposed to fascism in order to create a united 'popular front' against the right-wing threat.

ACTIVITY

Popular Front governments came to power in Spain in February 1936 and France in June 1936. Research the results of Stalin's call for a 'popular front' in other European countries. Did the concept find support elsewhere? Did a Popular Front come close to being voted into power anywhere else?

At the same time there was an increase in support for far-right parties in France in the face of what was perceived as a growing communist threat. Alarmed by this growth of right-wing groups, the Communists, Socialists and Radicals formally decided to form a Popular Front (*Le Front Populaire*) in June 1935. They agreed to support a single candidate in each electoral district in the second round of voting in the forthcoming general election. But there were fundamental differences between the Radicals, Socialists and Communists over economic policy. So the Front was essentially a compromise agreement in which the main focus of the election campaign would be the defence of republican institutions.

Figure 5.7: A pamphlet cover urging voters to support the Popular Front against Misery, War and Fascism, in support of Bread, Peace and Freedom.

Explain why the election message in Figure 5.7 would appeal to many voters in France at the time.

The 1936 election

The Popular Front election campaign was designed to appeal to a range of voters, and it:

- promised benefits to workers, such as a shorter working day, higher unemployment relief payments and greater trade union rights
- offered measures to stimulate the economy, such as reducing unemployment, reforming the taxation system and increasing spending power
- suggested government intervention to stabilise prices for agricultural products in order to assist rural recovery
- pledged to defend the Republic (which would involve suppressing the right-wing leagues)
- proposed nationalising the armaments industry as a means of accelerating rearmament
- announced its intention to modify the powers of the conservative minority who controlled the Bank of France.

The manifesto was by no means a radical socialist programme, which disappointed some of its supporters. Historian Roger Price describes it as a 'moderate programme which offered genuine social reform while seeking to re-assure the small-property-owning supporters of the Radical Party'.

The 1936 general election was held at a time of high unemployment and continuing street violence. It was a bitterly fought election. When the Popular Front won, it was hailed as a victory by the French working classes, who hoped that the new government would provide a socialist alternative to the collapsing capitalist system. The number of Communists elected to parliament jumped dramatically from 10 to 72, and the Socialist Party, led by Léon Blum, emerged as the strongest party with 147 seats. Altogether the Popular Front parties won 386 of the 608 seats in the Chamber of Deputies, compared with 222 for the conservative and far-right parties.

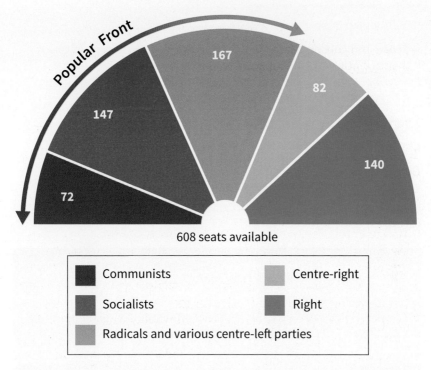

Figure 5.8: The composition of the Chamber of Deputies after the 1936 general election.

Explain why it could be said that the Radicals held the balance of power in the Chamber of Deputies.

Historians have interpreted the significance of these election results in different ways. Robert Paxton suggests that the results did not indicate a massive swing to the left but that the two-stage electoral system favoured the most united coalition. Previously Communists and Socialists had competed against each other in the run-off second stage of the election, but this time they supported a single candidate. McKay, Hill and Buckner suggest that the results reflected the growing polarisation in French politics. On the left, the moderate Radicals lost support to the Communists and Socialists, while on the right, the conservatives lost support to the far right.

Cause and consequence: Explain the causes and consequences of the formation of the Popular Front in France.

Léon Blum and the Popular Front government

Léon Blum headed the new government which was a coalition of Socialists and Radicals. Although they had cooperated with the other two parties in the election, the Communists were still unwilling to be part of the government.

> ### Léon Blum (1872–1950):
>
> He was an intellectual, writer and lawyer. He was the first socialist leader to be elected in France. He was also the first Jewish prime minister and was almost beaten to death in a brutal anti-Semitic attack by members of *Action Française* shortly before the Popular Front came to power. During the Second World War, Blum was imprisoned by the pro-Nazi Vichy government and sent to Buchenwald concentration camp in Germany. After the war, he successfully negotiated loans from the US for postwar reconstruction in France, and served briefly as prime minister of a coalition government.

There were vastly divided reactions to the election of Blum as prime minister from different sections of French society.

SOURCE 5.9

Blum was confronted from the outset with a wave of anti-Semitism such as France had not seen since the days of the Dreyfus affair. It was directed against him personally because he was a Jew, the first to become Premier in the history of France… No one who was not in France in those days can comprehend the hatred of Blum by Frenchmen on the Right. They loathed him as a Jew, as a socialist, as the head of a Left government and even as a subtle intellectual… On the Left the new Premier was venerated as a man who would save France from Fascism, lighten the burdens of the poor, conquer the Depression and preserve Peace.

Shirer, W. 1972. **The Collapse of the Third Republic.** *London, Pan. pp. 319–20 and 321–2.*

QUESTION

How useful is Source 5.9 for historians wanting to find out why there were such divided opinions about and attitudes towards Léon Blum?

ACTIVITY

Use the internet to research information about the Dreyfus Affair. Find out the links between it and the former French leader, Georges Clemenceau, and also the links between it and Charles Maurras, the leader of the right-wing *Action Française*.

The Popular Front in power

The victory of the Popular Front created as a sense of expectancy among voters that things were about to change. Working-class supporters wanted reforms to be implemented as soon as possible, while right-wing opponents were apprehensive about what these changes would entail.

European States in the Interwar Years (1918–1939)

The strikes of 1936

As the new government took office, there was an outbreak of sit-down strikes across France as 2 million workers occupied factories and workplaces and locked management out. The strikers were peaceful and orderly and there was no damage to property. The strikes affected not only industrial workplaces, but shops, banks, insurance companies, magazine offices and restaurants as well. Workers called for the reforms promised by the Popular Front to be implemented quickly, such as higher wages, shorter working hours and paid holidays. Blum refused to order the use of force to evacuate the workers as he feared that this might create political unrest or even revolution.

Figure 5.9: Strikers in a factory in the Parisian suburbs after the victory of the Popular Front, June 1936.

Historian Robert Paxton comments on the significance of the strikes and conservative fears about them in Source 5.10.

SOURCE 5.10

In retrospect, we know that the workmen and department store clerks who occupied the premises and sometimes danced in them were celebrating Blum's victory. The strikes were a grassroots release of steam after years of pent-up resentment at deflationary wage cuts; they were not a concerted effort to expropriate property. Trade union leaders struggled to channel the movement into traditional wages and hours negotiations. At the time, however, it looked very much like revolution to French conservatives already unsettled at the prospect of France's first Jewish, socialist premier.

Paxton, R. O. 1997. **Europe in the Twentieth Century (Third Edition)**. *Fort Worth. Harcourt Brace College Publishers. p. 329.*

QUESTION

How does Source 5.10 corroborate the information in Source 5.9?

At the time, the right-wing press in France labelled the strikes as sinister and dangerous and as the forerunner to revolution. Historians, however, see them differently. Tim Blanning refers to the movement as a 'colossal spontaneous general strike' and adds that the strikes took place 'in an optimistic spirit of carnival with concerts in the factories'. Colin Jones describes them as a 'touching expression of working-class fraternity in the context of long-deferred hopes for change.' Roger Price sees them as 'euphoric outbursts by workers for whom suddenly everything seemed possible. There were assertions of the dignity of labour, protests against harsh factory discipline, and a demand for better living and working conditions and enhanced security.'

KEY CONCEPTS QUESTION

Perspective and significance: How does the perspective of a writer, journalist or historian influence his or her interpretation of the significance of events? Use the 1936 strikes in France as a starting point but think of other examples from history or current events.

The Matignon Agreements and other reforms

The government moved with commendable speed, and organised a meeting between government officials, labour leaders and employers to discuss changes to social policy. The results of the meeting were the 'Matignon Agreements' (*Accords de Matignon*) of 7 June 1936, where workers and employers agreed to back the government's progressive labour reforms which included:

- wage increases averaging 10%
- compulsory collective bargaining, plus the machinery for arbitration and conciliation of labour disputes
- a 40-hour working week (to replace the existing 48-hour week)
- the principle of two weeks' paid holiday annually for all workers.

The government introduced other reforms as well:

- Grain prices were stabilised to help farmers.
- The school leaving age was raised from 13 to 14.
- The railways were nationalised with the creation of the SNCF (*Société nationale des chemins de fer français*).
- The arms industry was also nationalised.
- The Bank of France was placed under government control.

At first only the 12 biggest armaments factories were nationalised, but the rest were put under government supervision. At the same time the government implemented a costly rearmament programme. The Bank of France, which had been set up by Napoleon in 1801, had a great deal of influence and control over the French economy, for example by having the right to issue currency. Its 200 largest shareholders had enormous power to influence any decisions made. These shareholders were now left with their shares, but they could no longer dictate policy as the bank was placed under firm government control.

The fascist leagues were also outlawed or driven underground. However, further reform bills initiated by the Popular Front government failed to be approved by the Senate, which remained more conservative than the Chamber.

The measures introduced by the Popular Front government were welcomed by workers and the lower-middle class. The two-week annual paid leave proved to be especially popular.

Figure 5.10: The first paid holidays in France in 1937: a campsite along the sea.

QUESTION

What message is the photographer trying to put across in the photograph in Figure 5.10? What symbolism is used to achieve this?

Problems faced by the Popular Front government

Although the reforms introduced by Blum's government were popular with workers, there were problems within the ruling coalition.

The Spanish Civil War

The issue of the Spanish Civil War presented a particular dilemma for Blum. It started in July 1936, just a month after the Popular Front came to power in France. Blum favoured supporting the Republicans in the war, at least with supplies, but to do so would have risked losing the support of the Radical Party. He also faced pressure from the British government of Stanley Baldwin and the right wing in France, which labelled his plans to help the Republicans as 'irresponsible warmongering', according to historian Tim Blanning. So he opted instead for non-intervention, which angered the Communists and many Socialists as well. The Popular Front began to disintegrate, partly because of these disagreements over the Spanish Civil War. The left accused Blum of allowing the Nationalists under Franco to triumph in Spain, as Germany and Italy blatantly ignored the non-intervention agreement they had been party to and assisted the Nationalists.

Economic problems

There were economic difficulties as well. Some of the reform measures did not produce the results the government had anticipated. Increased wages were offset by higher prices, so the hoped-for increase in spending to boost the economy did not happen. Many critics also saw the higher wages as inflationary. Small businesses could not afford the increased costs involved in higher wages and a shorter working week, so they raised their prices. Efforts to reduce unemployment by limiting the working week were unsuccessful because industry was disrupted. The shorter working week was initially interpreted rigidly to mean that factories operated for only 40 hours a week, without a system of shifts, with workers refusing to work on Saturdays and Sundays. As a result, productivity fell. For example, France was producing fewer cars in 1937 than it had been in 1929. Food prices rose too as a result of the new higher prices set by the Wheat Board.

There were disagreements over economic policy within the Popular Front too. Many on the left were disappointed as they had hoped that the election of a Popular Front government would pave the way for important social and economic changes. They wanted the government to exercise more central control, but Blum resisted more extreme measures to control the economy. He knew that he would lose the support of the Radicals if he did so, and he needed their backing to maintain a majority in parliament. As a result, the Popular Front disappointed its Communist and Socialist supporters who had hoped for more sweeping reforms.

At the same time the reforms alienated many business and banking leaders and conservative middle-class voters, and alarmed many Radicals, their allies in parliament. Wealthy people sent their money out of the country and right-wing critics accused the government of promoting dangerous revolutionary policies. Blum was reluctant to alienate businessmen even further so he did not impose strict exchange controls to prevent the movement of capital. The government also resisted devaluing the franc and so lost the chance to benefit from lower export prices. However, rumours about devaluation led to a flight of currency and further inflation. In September 1936 France finally left the gold standard. In January 1937, in an effort to boost business confidence, Blum announced a 'pause' in the social reform programme, which angered the Front's left-wing supporters. When Blum asked for the authority to rule by decree to deal with the crisis by imposing exchange controls, the Senate refused and so he was forced to resign in June 1937.

ACTIVITY

Draw up a two-column chart to summarise the reforms introduced by the Popular Front. In the left-hand column list the measures introduced, and in the right-hand column make notes on the economic or political effect of each.

Theory of Knowledge

History and economics

How do events in France in this period demonstrate that historians need to examine the link between economics and politics in order to understand historical events?

The end of the Popular Front

The Popular Front government remained in office after Blum's resignation, but faced mounting political problems. In October 1937 it was finally forced to devalue the franc but this action came too late to benefit France's export trade. Blum returned to office briefly in 1938, but by then the Popular Front had virtually ceased to function as a political alliance. It was only formally dissolved after the Munich Conference in September 1938 in which the Radical prime minister, Édouard Daladier, together with Britain's Neville Chamberlain, capitulated to Hitler's demands over Czechoslovakia, a move that was angrily condemned by the Communists.

Daladier remained in office until 1940, with Paul Reynaud as his finance minister. Reynaud suspended many of the Popular Front reforms. In 1938 the Communist Party's call for a general strike, over modifications to the 40-hour week, was unsuccessful, but the left lost support as a result.

In the political instability and international uncertainty of the late 1930s, some of the disbanded fascist leagues re-emerged as right-wing political parties, such as the *Parti social français* (French Social Party) (formerly the *Croix de Feu*) which had 1 million members. There was also a radical left-wing party, the *Parti populaire français*, which Colin Jones describes as 'dangerous and rabble-rousing'.

Historians' views of the Popular Front

The achievements and legacy of the Popular Front government are a subject of intense debate among historians.

Social reforms

Some historians believe that the Popular Front legislation brought lasting benefits to the position of workers in France. Employers could no longer hire workers on their own terms but had to recognise their rights. Although some of the reforms were modified by later governments, much of the labour and social legislation remained in force. Annual paid holidays meant that working-class people could now go to the coast, 'shocking the middle-class people who had always had these resorts to themselves' according to Findley and Rothney. Paxton comments that the Popular Front government was the first to recognise leisure as a basic social need, and that the annual exodus of French families to the coast or the mountains every summer 'remains the most substantial monument to Blum's humanitarian vision'.

Economic policies

However, the Popular Front did not restore the economy and some of its reforms were costly and controversial. Productivity declined and unemployment did not improve. It certainly did not achieve all that its supporters hoped that it would. The measures it introduced were very moderate and did not stretch to the radical reforms that could have modernised the structure of the French economy, so that, for example, it would be less reliant on small-scale businesses and farms. Some historians think that the Popular Front did not use the opportunity that it had to carry out major reforms in the distribution of wealth and the power of private corporations in the economy and for these reasons they see the Popular Front as a failure.

Other historians point out that the time at which the Popular Front came to power has to be taken into account. It was a time of great political instability verging on civil war, and the economy was in a state of crisis which successive governments had failed to solve. It also came to power three months after Hitler remilitarised the Rhineland, causing grave concerns about French security. The Popular Front implemented a costly rearmament programme which France could ill afford, as Martin Roberts suggests that, 'Only a flourishing economy could have paid for both radical reform and rearmament and the French economy was far from flourishing.'

Blum's leadership

Some historians see Blum's leadership as partly responsible for what they see as the failure of the Popular Front. They think he was too cautious. He knew how suspicious of a Socialist government most conservative businessmen were, and he was careful not to implement anything that would antagonise them further. So, for example, he did not impose exchange controls or devalue the franc when these measures might have made a difference, and then only did so once the economic situation had deteriorated considerably. Findley and Rothney argue that, 'Blum's efforts to conciliate all groups in French society ended by satisfying none.' Paxton suggests that his caution made no difference anyway: '[Blum's] effort to reassure conservatives by exercising moderation was his greatest failure. The French right reacted as bitterly as if Blum had actually tried to make the major changes his left urged him to make.'

Political divisions

Another view is that the Popular Front increased the polarisation in French society as Roger Price explains: 'The hopes aroused on the left and among workers had created an apocalyptic vision of revolutionary anarchy on the right and among the property-owning classes, feeding on a resentment of a government whose policies seemed to favour the workers at the expense of the middle class.'

Martin Roberts argues that the Popular Front threatened the way of life of the French élite who had wealth and property. They saw communism as the greatest threat to France, and some even began to wonder whether Hitler might be the best obstacle to a Bolshevik takeover of Europe.

SOURCE 5.11

Among the middle classes, and especially the more wealthy and influential, this continuing air of crisis and mounting anxiety concerning income and status, together with an awareness of the deterioration of the country's international status, resulted in a growing conviction that democracy had failed. Strong authoritarian government appeared to many to be the answer to the nation's problems. Once again, the call for 'moral order' came from the right, uniting nationalism, clericalism, economic liberalism, and anti-Bolshevism. Anti-parliamentary feeling was re-kindled by every electoral success the left enjoyed. The élite, those with economic power and substantial influence over governments, the civil service, and the media, found it hard to accept that people whose objectives conflicted with their own might hold political power.

Price, R. 2005. **A Concise History of France (Second Edition).** *New York. Cambridge University Press, p. 270.*

Was the Popular Front a failure?

Historians differ in their views about whether the failures of the Popular Front outweighed its achievements. Those who see it as a failure have different views about the reasons for this. Some believe that international events aroused a climate of suspicion and prevented the Popular Front from carrying out its agenda. Others, such as William Shirer, argue that it was not strong enough to stand up to the forces against it, while T. A. Morris suggests that its failure was caused by a number of factors.

SOURCE 5.12

[The Popular Front] had not been strong enough to overcome its own divisions and to stand up to the determined opposition of industry and finance, the onslaughts of the reactionary Press, and the fierce enmity of the upper and middle classes. The government, which by its promulgation of mild and long overdue social reforms had inspired so many fears, did not have the force to justify them.

Shirer, W. 1972. **The Collapse of the Third Republic**. *London, Pan. p. 360.*

SOURCE 5.13

The left-wing interpretation of the undermining of the Popular Front, by capitalists exporting bullion and refusing investment, obviously has some validity. The continued stagnation of production, at about 86 % of the 1929 level, suggests however that the government was also let down by the very workers that placed such faith in it…

Secondly, far from bridging the rifts in French political society by the introduction of greater social justice, the Popular Front increased the polarisation of extreme political views. The Communist Party increased its membership from 30 000 to 300 000 between 1933 and 1937. Its credibility was re-established, and it benefited from the failures of Blum's Socialists. The legal dissolution of the fascist leagues by the government resulted either in their re-emergence as legal political parties… or in their crystallization into sinister secret societies… Just as the Popular Front had declared fascism to be the true threat to France, so the right now retaliated by claiming that anti-bolshevism was the truest form of patriotism, and coining the insidious slogan 'Better Hitler than Blum'.

Morris, T. A., 1985. **European History 1848–1945**. *Slough. University Tutorial Press. p. 219.*

QUESTION

QUESTION

Study Sources 5.11, 5.12 and 5.13. How useful are they to other historians researching the extent of right-wing opposition to the Popular Front as a factor in its failure? What other factors do the sources suggest were also important?

QUESTION

Was the Popular Front responsible for its failure to achieve what it had set out to do, or did other factors outweigh this?

5.8 What caused the collapse of the Third Republic?

After the collapse of the Popular Front, the government was led by Édouard Daladier, who remained in office from 1938 to 1940. The economic situation was so serious by this time that parliament allowed him the right to rule by decree in the hope that this would give the government the power to solve the crises. One emergency measure passed was to permit paid overtime and a system of shifts so that armaments factories could remain open for six days a week. This was part of a greater push for rearmament after the Munich Conference (see 5.7, The end of the Popular Front).

Increasing international tensions

The construction of the Maginot Line lulled France into a false sense of security. However, it did not go all the way to the coast as had originally been planned. The decision not to extend it any further had been made by the government in 1932 because of the costs involved at the time when France was suffering the first effects of the Depression.

Developments in Europe, especially Germany, during the 1930s had made France increasingly uneasy. At a conference in Lausanne in 1932 the major powers had made two decisions which directly contributed to this. They recognised Germany's inability to continue to pay reparations and they acknowledged its right to rearm. The first decision affected the French economy and the second French security. French security was threatened further when Hitler came to power in Germany in 1933, withdrew from the League of Nations, introduced conscription, denounced the Locarno Pacts and remilitarised the Rhineland.

At the same time, France was paralysed by financial crises, social unrest and political instability. The divisions in French society that deepened at the time of the Popular Front government added to the absence of an urgent and unified response to the threats against French security which Hitler posed. Indeed, many on the right openly admired Hitler and thought that he offered a preferable alternative to communism. As the situation in Europe moved towards war, there was a mood of pessimism and defeatism among many people in France. As a result of all of these factors, the Third Republic was considerably weakened by the time that the Second World War started in 1939.

The outbreak of war

When war broke out in September 1939, the government outlawed the Communist Party. There were doubts about its loyalty to the Republic after the bombshell of the announcement of the Nazi-Soviet Pact in August 1939. During the first eight months of the war there was no military action involving France, as Hitler turned his attention eastwards into Poland and northwards into Denmark and Norway. The French referred to the months of expectant wait as *la drôle de guerre* (while the British called it 'the Phoney War'.) But on the political front in Paris, dissension and indecisiveness continued, and was aggravated by personal rivalries between ministers and military leaders. Daladier was forced to resign in March 1940 and was replaced by Paul Reynaud.

The interwar years effectively ended for France in May 1940, when Hitler attacked, bypassing the Maginot Line and invading from the north. The Allied armies were trapped at Dunkirk on the Channel coast, from where 140 000 French soldiers were evacuated, along with the British Expeditionary Force. Taking advantage of the situation, Mussolini declared war on France and sent his army to occupy the south-east.

When the German army invaded, ten million French civilians tried to flee southwards from the German advance, in what became known as 'the Exodus'. The government left Paris and fled southwards as well. Reynaud tried to prop up the authority of the government by appointing the 84-year-old war hero, **Marshal Philippe Pétain**, as vice premier. The government fled first to Tours, then Bordeaux, before ending up in the small town of Vichy. Pétain arranged an armistice with the German forces on 25 June 1940. The Chamber of Deputies voted overwhelmingly to give Pétain the authority to write a new constitution and create a new state. This, effectively, was the end of the Third Republic, although it was only formally dissolved after the war. Colin Jones comments on the significance of the occasion: 'The virtues of the Third Republic – its capacity for soaking up bitter social and political tensions within a democratic framework – were forgotten in the shocked recognition of utter defeat.'

Marshal Philippe Pétain (1856–1951):

He was a hero of the First World War who succeeded Paul Reynaud as prime minister of France in June 1940. He signed an armistice with Germany and led the reactionary Vichy government in central France until 1944. Under his leadership Vichy France was notorious for its cooperation with Nazi Germany, although Pétain did not support collaboration as actively as his vice premier, Pierre Laval. After the war Pétain was tried for treason in a French court and sentenced to death, although this was commuted to solitary imprisonment for life.

During the war the Vichy government ruled over the southern part of a partitioned France as a separate non-occupied area. Alsace and Lorraine were incorporated once again into Germany, while the northern part and the Atlantic coastal regions were placed under direct German occupation. The Vichy government was authoritarian, right-wing and anti-Semitic, and targeted some of the politicians who had held office in the late 1930s. Blum, Daladier and Reynaud were tried for treason in Vichy France before they were handed over to the Nazis and sent to Germany where they were imprisoned until the end of the war.

Historians and *La Décadence*

Blum, Daladier and Reynaud were accused of not doing enough to prepare France for war. In public statements at the time, Pétain claimed that the defeat of France was punishment for its moral failures. This concept developed into a historiographical debate after the war about *La Décadence* (the decadence) of France. Supporters of the theory argued that the French defeat in 1940 was due to decadence, corruption and incompetence. In his book *La Décadence* (1979), French historian Jean-Baptiste Duroselle, condemned the politicians of the Third Republic as weak and cowardly. This view was shared by the English historian, A. J. P. Taylor, and the American historian, William Shirer. Since then, other historians have challenged this view and suggested that the defeat was due to military factors and the impact of the Great Depression on arms production, rather than on moral weakness.

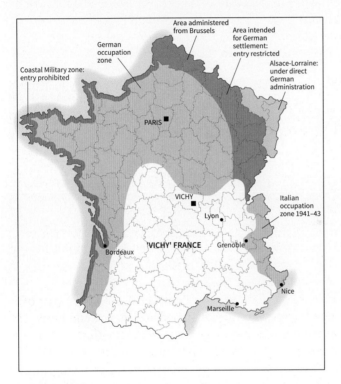

Figure 5.11: The partition of France during the Second World War.

QUESTION

Compare Figure 5.11 with Figure 5.1, a map of France during the First World War. What observations can you make from these maps about the comparative impact of the two world wars on France?

Conclusion

The impact of the Great Depression in the first half of the decade, and the international tensions in the latter half, created serious problems for France. However, in spite of the economic crises, social divisions and political difficulties before and after the term of office of the Popular Front, France survived the Depression years of the 1930s without succumbing to civil war or to either left- or right-wing revolution. It was the military defeat by Germany in 1940 that caused the collapse of the Third Republic.

Paper 3 exam practice

Question

Evaluate the achievements of the Popular Front government.
[15 marks]

Skill

Writing a conclusion to your essay

Examiner's tips

Provided you have carried out all the steps recommended so far, it should be relatively easy to write one or two concluding paragraphs.

For this question, you will need to cover the following aspects of the Popular Front's policies:

- reforms to working conditions and other social changes
- measures to stimulate the economy
- stabilisation of agricultural prices
- suppression of right-wing leagues
- nationalisation of the arms industry
- control over the Bank of France.

This question requires you to consider a range of different policies and issues, and to support your analysis with **precise and specific** supporting knowledge – so you need to avoid generalisations. Such a question implicitly offers you the chance to consider different views, and to come to some kind of **judgement** about the successes and failures of the Popular Front.

Common mistakes

Sometimes, candidates simply rehash in their conclusion what they have written earlier – making the examiner read the same things twice. Generally, concluding paragraphs should be relatively short. The aim should be to come to an overall judgement or conclusion that is clearly based on what has already been written. If possible, a short but relevant quotation is a good way to round off an argument.

Sample student conclusion

The Popular Front was successful in implementing many of the measures which it had set out to do. It introduced some lasting benefits for workers as well as other social reforms, such as raising the school-leaving age. Farmers also benefited from the stabilisation of agricultural prices. It nationalised key elements in the economy such as the railways and the armaments industry, making more effective re-armament possible, and put measures in place to end the control of the Bank of France by a handful of private shareholders. It outlawed the extremist right-wing leagues, in a bid to end the political violence that had been evident in 1934–35.

However, the new measures failed to stimulate the economy. Some measures were costly and controversial and productivity declined. In this way it failed to reverse the economic problems caused by the Depression. The Popular Front also failed to satisfy its left-wing supporters by introducing more far-reaching reforms, such as greater central control over the economy. But at the same time the new measures alienated conservative business leaders who saw the changes as too radical. In its efforts to please both groups, the government failed to use the opportunity that it had to carry out meaningful reform. As Findley and Rothney have noted: 'Blum's efforts to conciliate all groups in French society ended by satisfying none.'

EXAMINER'S COMMENT

This is a fairly good conclusion because it briefly pulls together the main threads of the argument. In addition, there is an apt final quotation that rounds off the conclusion – and no doubt the core of the essay – in a memorable way. However, in parts there is a tendency to summarise what has already been covered in the essay, and there is no clear conclusion. There should also be some reference to the context in which the Popular Front was operating.

Activity

In this unit, the focus is on writing a useful conclusion. Using the information from this unit, and any other sources of information available to you, write concluding paragraphs for at least two of the following Paper 3 practice questions. Remember: to do this, you will need to create full plans for the questions you choose.

Remember to refer to the simplified Paper 3 mark scheme in Chapter 6.

Paper 3 practice questions

1 Examine the economic impact of the Great Depression on France.

2 To what extent did the Depression, evidence of political corruption and a rise in international tensions contribute to the growth of political extremism in France in the early 1930s?

3 Discuss the reasons for and consequences of the formation of the Popular Front in France in 1935.

4 Examine the reasons for the failure of the Popular Front government to achieve its objectives.

5 To what extent did rising international tensions and fears about security affect domestic politics in France after 1938?

6

Exam Practice

Introduction

You have now completed your study of the main economic, political and social developments in four European countries during the period 1918–39. You have also had the chance to examine some of the various historical debates and differing historical interpretations which surround these developments.

In the previous chapters, you have seen examples of Paper 3-type essay questions, with examiner's tips. You have also had some basic practice in answering such questions. In this chapter, these tips and skills are developed in more depth. Longer examples of student answers are provided, accompanied by examiner's comments that should increase your understanding of what examiners are looking for when they mark your essays. Following each question and answer, you will find tasks to give you further practice in the skills needed to gain the higher marks in this exam.

IB History Paper 3 exam questions and skills

If you are following Route 2, HL Option 4 – *History of Europe* – will have studied in depth **three** of the 14 sections available for this HL Option. *European states in the interwar years 1918–39* is one of those sections. For Paper 3, two questions are set from each of the 14 sections, giving 28 questions in total; you have to answer **three** of these.

Each question has a specific mark scheme. However, the 'generic' mark scheme in the IB *History Guide* gives you a general idea of what examiners are looking for to be able to put answers into the higher bands. In particular, you will need to acquire reasonably precise historical knowledge so that you can address issues such as cause and effect, and change and continuity. This will be required in order to explain historical developments in a clear, coherent, well-supported and relevant way. You will also need to understand relevant historical debates and interpretations, refer to these and critically evaluate them.

Essay planning

Make sure you read each question *carefully*, noting all the important key or 'command' words. You might find it useful to highlight them on your question paper. You can then produce a rough plan (for example, a spider diagram) for *each* of the three essays you intend to attempt, *before* you start to write your answers. That way, you will soon know whether you have enough own knowledge to answer them adequately. Next, refer back to the wording of each question – this will help you see whether or not you are responding to *all* its various demands and aspects. In addition, if you run short of time towards the end of your exam, you will at least be able to write some brief condensed sentences to show the key points and arguments you would have presented. It is therefore far better to do the planning at the *start* of the exam; that is, before you panic if you suddenly realise that you don't have time to finish your last essay.

Remember that your answers need to be relevant and focused on the question. Don't go outside the dates mentioned in the question, or write answers on subjects not identified in that question. Also, don't just *describe* the events or developments. Sometimes students simply focus on one key word, date or individual, and then write down everything they know about it. Instead, select your own knowledge carefully, and pin the relevant information to the key features raised by the question. Finally, if the question asks for 'causes/reasons' and 'results', 'continuity and change', 'successes and failures', or 'nature and development', make sure you deal with *all* the parts of the question. Otherwise, you will limit yourself to half marks at best.

Examiner's tips

For Paper 3, examiners are looking for well-structured arguments that:

- are consistently relevant and linked to the question
- offer clear and precise evaluation and analysis
- are supported by the use of accurate, precise and relevant own knowledge
- offer a balanced judgement
- refer to different historical debates and interpretations or to relevant historians and, where relevant, offer some critical evaluation of these.

Simplified mark scheme

Band		Marks
1	**Consistently clear understanding of and focus** on the question, with **all main aspects addressed.** Answer is **fully analytical, balanced** and **well-structured/organised.** Own knowledge is **detailed, accurate and relevant**, with events placed in their **historical context.** There is **developed critical analysis**, and **sound understanding of historical concepts.** Examples used are **relevant**, and used effectively **to support analysis/evaluation.** The answer also **integrates evaluation of different historical debates/perspectives.** All/almost all of the main points are **substantiated**, and the answer reaches a **clear/reasoned/consistent judgement/ conclusion.**	13–15
2	**Clear understanding of the question**, and most of its **main aspects are addressed.** Answer is mostly **well-structured and developed**, though, with **some repetition/lack of clarity** in places. Supporting **own knowledge mostly relevant/accurate**, and events are placed in their **historical context.** The answer is **mainly analytical**, with relevant examples **used to support critical analysis/evaluation.** There is **some understanding/evaluation of historical concepts and debates/perspectives.** Most of the main points **are substantiated**, and the answer offers a **consistent conclusion.**	10–12
3	**Demands of the question are understood** – but some aspects **not fully developed/addressed. Mostly relevant/accurate supporting own knowledge**, and events generally placed in their **historical context. Some attempts at analysis/ evaluation but these are limited/not sustained/ inconsistent.**	7–9
4	**Some understanding** of the question. **Some relevant own knowledge**, with some factors identified – but with **limited explanation. Some attempts at analysis**, but answer **lacks clarity/ coherence**, and is **mainly description/narrative.**	4–6
5	**Limited understanding of/focus on** the question. **Short/generalised** answer, with **very little accurate/ relevant own knowledge.** Some **unsupported assertions**, with **no real analysis.**	0–3

Student answers

The following extracts from student answers have brief examiner's comments throughout, and a longer overall comment at the end. Those parts of student answers that are particularly strong and well-focused (such as demonstrations of precise and relevant own knowledge, or examination of historical interpretations) will be highlighted in red. Errors/confusions/irrelevance/loss of focus will be highlighted in blue. In this way, you should find it easier to follow why marks were awarded or withheld.

Question 1

Examine the strengths and weaknesses of the Weimar Republic between January 1919 and October 1929. **[15 marks]**

Skills

- Factual knowledge and understanding
- Structured, analytical and **balanced** argument
- Awareness/understanding/evaluation of historical interpretations
- Clear and balanced judgement

Examiner's tips

Look carefully at the wording of this question, which asks you to evaluate the strengths and weaknesses of the Weimar Republic and also provides very specific dates for consideration. You will not only need to consider what strengths and weaknesses the republic possessed, you will also have to decide whether the strengths outweighed the weaknesses or vice versa.

You would also be advised to go further and consider the relative importance of the various strengths and weaknesses that you refer to. Remember to stick closely to the dates given in the question. It is important not merely to describe features and events, but to use them to support an argument. In making your plan, you will be able to decide whether you can produce more evidence on one side than the other, and thus decide what that argument will be. It does not matter what view you adopt, as long as you have a 'thesis' and can write analytically and convincingly.

Student answer

The Weimar Republic was set up in Germany at the end of the First World War. Its home was in Weimar rather than Berlin because Spartacist riots there made the capital too dangerous for the government. However, it established a new constitution for Germany that was one of the most democratic in Europe, and thus the Weimar Republic started out with many high hopes. However, many historians have suggested that it was 'doomed from the start', because the constitution contained flaws and the new republic had many enemies. This essay will consider whether or not that was true.

EXAMINER'S COMMENT

This is a poor introduction and suggests limited reflection before writing. It shows some knowledge of the establishment of the Weimar Republic and so identifies the topic that the question is asking about. However, it fails to offer a view in relation to the question and also becomes slightly sidetracked by a related, but slightly different question – 'Was the Weimar Republic doomed from the start?' The final sentence is unnecessary and the reference to 'many historians' suggests a lack of precise knowledge.

The Weimar Republic had a poor start. It was the product of a revolution that never really quite succeeded. The socialists in the SPD wanted to bring about change in Germany at the end of the war, but they were horrified at the outbreaks of mutiny and communist-inspired rioting that occurred throughout the country in October/November 1918. The risings and establishment of workers' councils frightened the socialists, who believed things were going too far. So, when they proclaimed the republic and the kaiser was forced to abdicate, they made a pact with the army called the Ebert-Groener Pact. This was both a strength and a weakness.

It gave Ebert, the socialist leader of the new government, the power he needed to crush the rebellions. He was also able to use the army and the Freikorps when the Spartacists rebelled in January 1919. However, it made the socialists reliant on the right-wing army. This was a weakness, because Noske, who commanded the troops, behaved brutally towards the communists, whose beliefs were actually nearer to those of the socialists than the nationalist views of the army were. The

SPD was therefore accused of 'selling out' by some of its own supporters and the more left-wing USPD.

EXAMINER'S COMMENT

These paragraphs offer some useful information, but the candidate has made the mistake of ignoring the question dates and providing too much pre-1919 detail. This also gives a rather narrative feel to the answer. Mention of the Ebert-Groener Pact is relevant, and its part in crushing the Spartacists is important to any consideration of the republic's strengths and weaknesses. The knowledge given at the end of this paragraph is excellent, but what this candidate fails to do is to offer any judgement. This merely sets out views on both sides.

The Weimar Republic was 'doomed from the start' because of its constitution. This gave a lot of power to the president, who appointed and dismissed the chancellor, could dissolve the Reichstag, commanded the army and could, in emergencies, rule by decree under Article 48. This was a major weakness, which allowed for the use of dictatorial powers. However, the constitution also had its strengths. Everyone over the age of 20 could vote every four years, and there were both local state assemblies and a central government, thus dispersing power. They also had the right to arrange plebiscites, giving still greater people-power. Having a Reichsrat that could give advice and reject new laws (even though it could be overridden by the Reichstag) provided a check on what laws were made, and the Supreme Court was kept separate from the legislature and executive. Although the proportional representation system was in some ways a weakness, because it produced coalition governments and allowed extremist parties into the Reichstag, it was also a strength because it allowed all voices to be heard. Finally, the constitution guaranteed the basic rights of German citizens.

The Weimar Republic has been criticised by historians such as Lee because the underlying social, administrative and judicial structures remained unchanged. Big business and the large landowners, for example, continued much as before and the judiciary were notorious for favouring the right wing. When left-wing opponents were brought to trial they were treated very harshly, but members of the right wing were given lenient sentences and treated sympathetically. The army was also unchanged and hostile to the republic and so were many of the civil servants and teachers, especially in the universities. However, Carr says that all of this was also a strength because by leaving the key structures and people alone, the republic could function. Had most of the civil servants been dismissed, for example, the republic might have collapsed immediately.

EXAMINER'S COMMENT

These paragraphs shows some excellent knowledge and understanding, but the candidate still fails to advance any particular view. While the link to historians in the second paragraph shows further awareness, it is a shame that no individual judgement is offered. The first paragraph perpetuates the mistake of focusing on words that are different from the question at the beginning (probably trying to adapt a previously prepared answer), but there is also some consideration of strengths and weaknesses, which could have gone further. Article 48, for example is alleged to be a 'major weakness' but this is not fully explained – or questioned – and the final sentence of the first paragraph is undeveloped. The second paragraph shows some depth of awareness, but is again a little limited in development. It would have been relatively easy to add a specific case of right-wing judicial leniency, or left-wing prejudice.

In June 1919, the German government was forced to sign the Treaty of Versailles. This was regarded as a 'diktat' because there had been no German representatives invited to Versailles, where the negotiations took place. The Germans had expected a lenient peace based on Wilson's Fourteen Points, but what they got was extremely harsh on their country and they were horrified and humiliated. The Weimar politicians who signed it were soon known as the 'November Criminals' (because they had also agreed the armistice) and they were accused of 'stabbing Germany in the back' by agreeing to a peace while the German army was still undefeated.

The treaty weakened the Weimar Republic because Germany lost land, including Alsace-Lorraine and the Polish Corridor, as well as all its colonies. It was also left with a tiny army of 100 000, no air force and only six battleships. The war guilt clause and reparations were particularly hated. The treaty encouraged opposition to the republic. The only strength of the treaty was that it ended the war and there were hopes among some politicians who believed that it could be changed in future years if Germany cooperated with it. Not all Germans understood this idea though, and many remained hostile.

[There then follow several paragraphs considering the attempted risings of both left and right wings, and the economic problems and hyperinflation 1919–23. Both show how the republic displayed strengths and weaknesses in their handling of these developments.]

Between 1924 and 1929, the republic showed more strengths than weaknesses. Politically, the country became much more stable and the democratic parties performed better in the elections; there were no more putsches or assassinations. Inflation was cured and thanks to the Dawes Plan of 1924 and the Young Plan of 1929, reparations were made easier to cope with. American and other foreign money flowed into Germany to aid the development of industry, and this also helped the government to set up an extensive welfare system. Furthermore, the country gained greater credit internationally in the hands of Stresemann, who negotiated the Locarno Treaty and oversaw Germany's entry into the League of Nations. As well as an economic revival there was a flowering of culture, which has led to this period being known as a 'golden age'. These years of Weimar Germany produced exciting new 'modernist' art, architecture and thought-provoking literature and plays. Berlin became the centre for a liberating new night-life and young people enjoyed greater freedom. Feuchtwanger has described the 'feel-good factor' of these years. However…

EXAMINER'S COMMENT

This paragraph introduces another major factor weakening the republic, although the way it is presented offers detail followed by comment rather than directly addressing its strengths and weaknesses for the republic. There is an admirable attempt to identify some strengths at the end, however, and the knowledge and overall understanding are again good.

[This is followed by a paragraph considering the limitations of the 1924–29 period, with specific reference to the views of the historians Layton, Nicholls and Peukert. The essay ends with a conclusion that emphasises that the republic had both strengths and weaknesses – it was not entirely 'doomed from the start' but had problems that would make it difficult to cope in a crisis like that experienced after 1929.]

Overall examiner's comments

This answer displays a good understanding of the strengths and weaknesses of the Weimar Republic, addressing all aspects of the question and providing a good deal of accurate supporting knowledge: there is little that is irrelevant, for example. The essay also shows an awareness of historiography and differing historical interpretations, although there is scope for the range of interpretation to be developed further. The answer is, on the whole, well-structured and there are some attempts at evaluation, even though the synthesis of views in support of an individual judgement is limited. The essay is not without its faults. It has a weak introduction, it provides a little too much background information, sometimes the comment on strengths and weaknesses grows out of the information supplied rather than being presented first and then supported by the detail and, most importantly, the conclusion is rather bland. However, there is definitely enough here for an award at the top of Band 2, with 12 marks.

ACTIVITY

Look again at the simplified mark scheme and the student answer. Now draw up your own plan and rewrite the answer in a way that would reach the criteria for Band 1, and so obtain the full 15 marks. You will need to offer a clearer judgement, provide a little more supporting detail and evaluate a greater range of alternative interpretations. Make sure your introduction (theses) and conclusion match.

Question 2

'The Nationalists won the Spanish Civil War because of the divisions among their opponents.' To what extent do you agree with this statement? **[15 marks]**

Skills

- Factual knowledge and understanding
- Structured, analytical and **balanced** argument
- Awareness/understanding/evaluation of historical interpretations
- Clear and balanced judgement

Examiner's tips

Look carefully at the wording of this question, which asks you to examine the reasons for the victory of the Nationalists in the Spanish Civil War. Not only will you need to consider a **range** of reasons, you will also have to decide to what extent you agree or disagree with the statement.

To do this, you will need to evaluate the **relative** importance of the various reasons you identify. Remember – it is important not merely to identify and explain reasons, but to use them to support an argument. In making your plan, you will be able to decide whether you can produce more arguments and evidence to agree or disagree with the statement. It does not matter what view you adopt, as long as you have a clear argument, write evaluatively, and make an explicit judgement.

Student answer

There are several reasons why Franco and the Nationalists eventually won the Spanish Civil War in 1939. One very important reason was the amount of aid the Nationalists received from the very start of the Civil War from Nazi Germany and Fascist Italy, and which the Nationalists continued to receive throughout the Civil War. Another important reason was the fact that, compared to the Republicans, the Nationalists were soon strongly united under Franco's leadership. Whereas the Republicans were increasingly divided between those who thought that the main objective was to fight a conventional war against the Nationalists, and those who thought it necessary to carry through a revolution at the same time as conducting the military struggle. An additional important factor was the role played by the Non-Intervention Committee set up by Britain and France. All of these reasons help explain why the Nationalists eventually won.

EXAMINER'S COMMENT

This introduction identifies a number of valid reasons for the Nationalist victory in the Spanish Civil War. However, there is no explicit reference to the view set out in the question, and there is no indication – so far – as to which reason or factor is seen as being more important than the one identified in the question. With questions like this, it is important to engage directly with the exact wording of the question – otherwise, there is the risk of producing an answer which is merely a list of factors.

In July 1936, both sides in the Spanish Civil War were fairly evenly matched so, to gain an advantage, both sides quickly sought help from other countries. Compared to that received by the Republicans, the Nationalists received much more – and much more effective – foreign aid. As the Nationalists' ranks included the Falange – Spain's fascist party – and because the Nationalists were violently anti-socialist and anti-communist, it was no surprise that both Nazi Germany and Fascist Italy backed them. With the Nationalists' forces within Spain largely unsuccessful at first, the rebels were desperate to get Franco's experienced army in Morocco across to the mainland. However, this seemed a very problematic aim, as the Spanish navy remained loyal to the elected Popular Front government. Fortunately for the Nationalists, Hitler provided German planes which gave Franco the necessary air cover and transport to move his Army of Africa across to Spain during the months of August and September 1936. This early help played a big part in the Nationalists' eventual victory in 1939.

EXAMINER'S COMMENT

This paragraph offers a relevant factor, with some explanation, and provides a little supporting information. However, as shown by the introduction, there is no real indication yet of the answer moving beyond simply presenting a list of reasons.

In addition, the help provided to the Nationalists by the fascist countries gave valuable military support. Both Nazi Germany and Fascist Italy gave vast sums of credit, to enable them to buy vital supplies – many of these imports reached the Nationalists across the border with Portugal which, since 1932, had been ruled by Salazar and his far-right authoritarian party. In addition, Fascist

Italy sent almost 40 000 troops and over 700 planes; while Nazi Germany sent 16 000 troops and the 5000-strong Condor Legion, which was a mixed air and tank unit. The Condor Legion developed the Blitzkrieg method of 'lightning war' which caused the Republican side great problems. In particular, German and Italian planes carried out effective bombing raids on Spanish cities in the Republican areas, which disrupted supplies and reinforcements at crucial times, and which began to undermine civilian morale. The Nationalists also got valuable help from Salazar's dictatorship in Portugal which, as well as allowing materials to cross the border, also supplied some troops.

Compared with this, the Republicans received relatively little effective help. At first, the Popular Front government in Spain hoped to receive aid from France. There, a Popular Front government had come to power in June 1936, with the socialist Leon Blum as prime minister. As France was worried about a fascist-type regime – allied to Nazi Germany – coming to power in Spain, they agreed to sell some planes and artillery to Spain's democratically elected. However, this offer was eventually withdrawn as a result of British pressure.

Eventually, in October 1936 – three months after the rebellion had begun, and after Franco had been able to bring his army across from Morocco – the Soviet Union sent about 3000 'advisers', 400 tanks and 1000 planes. This, however, was much less than the Nationalists received. While it is true that the Republicans were also supported by about 35 000 male and female civilian volunteers from various countries – organised in the International Brigades – there were rarely more than about 15 000 of them in Spain at any one time. In addition, most of these International Brigaders – though they fought bravely – had little military experience, and were hampered by communications problems and the lack of sufficient modern weapons. In 1938, before the Civil War was over, they were withdrawn.

Another reason for the victory of the Nationalists was their unity behind General Franco. At the start of the Civil War, the army coup was headed by a group of generals, which included Sanjurjo, Goded and Mola – Franco, at first, kept some distance from the coup. However, Sanjurjo was killed in a plane crash early on, and Franco soon established himself as the main leader. He then quickly subordinated all the various anti-republican groups – such as the Falange – under his sole command, and became known as Caudillo (leader).

This was very different for the democratically elected Popular Front government, which was increasingly divided between liberals, republicans, regional separatists, anarchists, socialists, Trotskyists and communists. In particular, many of the anarchists – along with the semi-Trotskyist POUM – wanted to organise a social revolution during the Civil War, as they believed that this would help balance the greater military advantages of the Nationalists. In many areas, workers occupied factories while, in rural areas, peasants and landless agricultural labourers seized land from the larger landowners. They also quickly set up workers' and peasants' militias, which often had a loose command structure.

These developments were opposed by the Popular Front government, which wanted to fight a conventional war with a centralised army (as opposed to relying on the various workers' militias), and to postpone any major social reforms until after the Nationalists had been defeated. This view was supported by the Spanish Communist Party, and in Barcelona 1937, fighting broke out between the two sides. The forces of the Popular Front won, and revolutionary groups were increasingly suppressed – this civil war within the Civil War undermined the morale of many among the Republican ranks.

Another reason for the Nationalists' victory was the political help which, in practice, they received from Britain and France. Britain was headed by a Conservative-dominated National Government – this government was following the policy of appeasement towards Nazi Germany, and so did not want to get involved in a dispute over developments in Spain. So it refused to help the democratically elected government in Spain in any way – and, instead, put pressure on France to withdraw its offers of help. France – which knew it was not strong enough to risk a war with Nazi Germany without British support – reluctantly agreed.

Instead, in September 1936, Britain and France set up a Non-Intervention Committee, which was supposed to be an agreement by which all the important countries in Europe agreed not to intervene in the Spanish Civil War. Those countries which signed this agreement included Nazi Germany, Fascist Italy, the USA and the Soviet Union, as well as Britain and France. When it became clear that Italy and Germany were both sending troops and equipment to help the Nationalists, the Soviet Union decided to help the Republicans.

In practice, although the Non-Intervention Committee did little to interfere with the aid coming from Nazi Germany and Fascist Italy – even when British and French ships were attacked – it did take considerable effective action to prevent supplies reaching the democratically elected government in Spain. In addition, many firms in the democratic countries which signed the Non-Intervention agreement actually sold military supplies to the Nationalists. This included US oil companies and various British firms – according to the historian Robert Whealey, in July 1938 alone, Franco bought over 30% of his supplies from British companies – without any attempts by the British government to prevent this.

> ### EXAMINER'S COMMENT
> These paragraphs show some excellent knowledge and understanding, and there is a brief mention of one historian. However, the candidate still fails to make any judgement about which reasons they consider to be more important – and, in particular, has continued to make no reference to the view expressed in the question. As well as reading like a list of reasons, some sections are beginning to take on a narrative approach.

[There then follow several paragraphs on the military course of the Civil War. Although these paragraphs provide accurate details of the various battles and increasing Nationalist successes, they are essentially narrative in approach. This is something which often happens when, instead of *evaluating* the *relative* importance of a range of reasons or factors, a candidate just presents a list of reasons and illustrative details.]

Thus there are clearly several reasons why the Nationalists won the Spanish Civil War. Many of these are to do with Nationalist advantages, but several are the result of Republican weaknesses and divisions.

> ### EXAMINER'S COMMENT
> This short conclusion essentially continues with the approach adopted at the start of the essay: which was based on just identifying several different reasons. If the question had been borne in mind from the start, this mistake could have been avoided. It is a shame that, nowhere in the answer, does the candidate say whether they agree or disagree with the statement that, ultimately, the Nationalists won because of Republican divisions. As a result, the answer fails to make the clear judgement about the statement which is required.

Overall examiner's comments

The candidate's answer has shown good understanding of the various factors behind the Nationalists' victory in the Spanish Civil War. A range of reasons is identified, and a fair amount of accurate supporting knowledge has been provided. Although there is little that is irrelevant, the treatment of the course of the Civil War – which could have been used to show how the Nationalists were able to take advantage of Republican weaknesses – was essentially narrative in approach. Also, apart from one brief reference, there is little sign of awareness of the historiography and differing historical interpretations relating to the reasons for the outcome of the Spanish Civil War. A serious weakness is that, although the answer is generally well-structured, there are no attempts at evaluation, and no attempt to explicitly address the question. In addition, the conclusion is rather bland – it is here that a final judgement should have been made indicating whether or not the candidate agreed or disagreed with the view expressed in the question. Consequently, this answer, at best, is likely to be awarded a mark towards the bottom of Band 3.

ACTIVITY

Look again at the simplified mark scheme and the student answer. Now draw up your own plan and try to answer the question in a way that would reach the criteria for Band 1 and so obtain the full 15 marks. You will need to offer a clear judgement, linked to the view given in the question, provide a little more supporting detail and, in particular, explain and evaluate some relevant historical interpretations.

Further Reading

Sources and quotations in this book have been taken from the following publications.

Baxell, Richard. 2012. *Unlikely Warriors*. London, UK. Aurum Press.

Beevor, Antony. 2006. *The Battle for Spain: The Spanish Civil War 1936–1939*. London, UK. Weidenfeld & Nicolson.

Blanning, T.C.W. 1998. *The Oxford Illustrated History of Modern Europe*. Oxford, UK, OUP.

Blinkhorn, Martin. 2006. *Mussolini and Fascist Italy*. London, UK. Routledge. Browne, Harry. 1996. *Spain's Civil War*. London, UK. Longman.

Carr, William. 1991. *A History of Germany, 1815–1990*. London, UK. Bloomsbury Academic.

Casanova, Julián and Gil Andrés, Carlos. 2014. *Twentieth-Century Spain: A History*. Cambridge, UK. Cambridge University Press.

Clark, Martin. 2005. *Mussolini*. Harlow, UK. Pearson.

Durgan, Andy. 2007. *The Spanish Civil War*. Basingstoke, UK. Palgrave Macmillan.

Eddy, Steve and Lancaster, Tony. 2004. *Germany 1866–1945*. London, UK. Causeway Press.

Findley, Carter Vaughan and Rothney, John. 1986. *Twentieth Century World*. Boston, USA. Houghton Mifflin Company.

Graham, Helen. 2002. *The Spanish Republic at War, 1936–1939*. Cambridge, UK. Cambridge University Press.

Gregor, A. J. 1979. *Italian Fascism and Developmental Dictatorship*. Princeton, USA. Princeton University Press.

Haffner, Sebastian. 1973. *Failure of a Revolution: Germany 1918–1919*. Berne, Switzerland. Andre Deutsch.

Henig, Ruth. 1995. *Versailles and After, 1919–1933*. London, UK. Routledge.

Henig, Ruth. 1998. *The Weimar Republic 1919–1933*. London, UK. Routledge.

Hiden, John. 1996. *The Weimar Republic*. London, UK. Longman.

Hite, John, and Hinton, Chris. 2000. *Weimar and Nazi Germany*. London, UK. John Murray.

Hobsbawm, Eric. 1994. *Age of Extremes*. London, UK. Abacus.

Jones, Colin, 1994. *The Cambridge Illustrated History of France*. Cambridge, UK, Cambridge University Press.

Kershaw, Ian. 1993. *The Nazi Dictatorship*. London, UK. Arnold.
Kindleberger, Charles P., 1992. *The World in Depression 1929–1939*. Berkeley, USA. University of California Press.

Kissinger, Henry. 1995. *Diplomacy*. New York, USA. Touchstone.

Laver, John. 1991. *Nazi Germany 1933–1945*. London, UK. Hodder & Stoughton.

Layton, Geoff. 1992. *Germany: The Third Reich 1933–45*. London, UK. Hodder.

Layton, Geoff. 2005. *Weimar and the Rise of Nazi Germany 1918–1933*. London, UK. Hodder Murray.

Lee, Stephen J. 1987. *The European Dictatorships, 1918–1945*. London, UK. Routledge.

Macdonald, H. 1999. *Mussolini and Italian Fascism*. Cheltenham, UK. Nelson Thornes.

McDonough, Frank. 2001. *Conflict, Communism and Fascism*. Cambridge, UK. Cambridge University Press.

McKay, John, Hill, Bennett and Buckler, John. 1988. *A History of World Societies*. Boston, USA. Houghton Mifflin Company.

McKichan, Finlay. 1992. *Germany 1815–1939*. Edinburgh, UK. Oliver and Boyd.

Mommsen, Hans. 1998. *The Rise and Fall of Weimar Democracy*. Chapel Hill, USA. University of North Carolina Press.

Morris, T.A., 1997. *European History 1848–1945*. London, Collins.

Nicholls, A. J. 2000. *Weimar and the Rise of Hitler.* Basingstoke, UK. Palgrave Macmillan.

Overy, R. J. 1994. *The Inter-War Crisis 1919–1939.* London, UK. Longman.

Paxton, Robert O. 1997. *Europe in the Twentieth Century (Third Edition).* Fort Worth, USA. Harcourt Brace College Publishers.

Preston, Paul. 2006. *The Spanish Civil War.* London, UK. Harper Perennial.

Price, Roger. 2005. *A Concise History of France (Second Edition).* 2005, New York, Cambridge University Press.

Robson, Mark. 1992. *Italy: Liberalism and Fascism 1870–1945.* London, UK. Hodder.

Shirer, William. 1972. *The Collapse of the Third Republic.* London, Pan Books.

Simpson, William. 1991. *Hitler and Germany.* Cambridge, UK. Cambridge University Press.

Tampke, Jürgen. 1988. *Twentieth Century Germany: Quest for Power.* Southbank, Australia. Thomson Learning Australia.

Waller, Sally. 2009. *The Development of Germany, 1871–1925.* Cheltenham, UK. Nelson Thornes.

Weitz, Eric D. 2007. *Weimar Germany: Promise and Tragedy.* Princeton, USA. Princeton University Press.

Welch, David. 1998. Hitler. London, UK. UCL Press.

Wolfson, Robert and Laver, John. 2001. *Years of Change: European History 1890–1990 (Third Edition),* London, Hodder & Stoughton.

Wood, Anthony. 1986. *Europe 1815–1960.* London, UK. Longman.

Index

European States in the Interwar Years (1918–1939)

Acknowledgements

The authors and publishers acknowledge the following sources of copyright material and are grateful for the permissions granted. While every effort has been made, it has not always been possible to identify the sources of all the material used, or to trace all copyright holders. If any omissions are brought to our notice, we will be happy to include the appropriate acknowledgements on reprinting.

Text

Part 3 unit 1 source H, Part 3 unit 2 sources B and H: excerpts from *Mussolini and Fascist Italy* by M. Blinkhorn, Routledge, 2006, pp. 33–4. Copyright © 2006 Routledge. Reproduced by permission of Taylor & Francis Books UK; Part 4 unit 1 source B, Part 4 unit 2 source G: excerpts from *Spain's Civil War* by H. Browne, Longman, 1996, pp. 4–5. Copyright © 1996. Reproduced by permission of Taylor & Francis Books UK; Part 4 unit 1 source C, Part 4 unit 2 source D: excerpts from *Modern Spain 1975–1980* by R. Carr, Oxford University Press, 1980, pp. 81–2. By permission of Oxford University Press, www.oup.com; Part 4 unit 1 source D, Part 4 unit 2 source B excerpts from *The Spanish Civil War* by Hugh Thomas, Penguin Books, 1977, pp. 23–4. Copyright © 1989 Hugh Thomas, used by permission of The Wylie Agency (UK) Limited; Part 4 unit 1 source E, Part 4 unit 2 source A: excerpts from *The Spanish Civil War: Reaction, Revolution and Revenge* by P. Preston, Harper Perennial, 2006, pp. 31–2. Reprinted by permission of HarperCollins Publishers Ltd. Copyright © Paul Preston, 1986, 1996, 2006; Part 4 unit 1 source F, Part 4 unit 2 source C: excerpts from *Twentieth Century Spain: A History* by J. Casanova and C. G. Andres, Cambridge University Press, 2014, p. 85. Copyright © Cambridge University Press. Reproduced with permission from Cambridge University Press and the author; Part 4 unit 1 source G, Part 4 unit 2 source E: excerpts from *The Spanish Civil War* by A. Durgan, Palgrave Macmillan, 2007, pp. 7–8. Reproduced with permission of Palgrave Macmillan; Part 4 unit 2 source F: excerpt from *The Spanish Holocaust:*

Images

Photo12 / UIG; Figure 4.5 TopFoto: World History Archive; Figure 4.7 TopFoto; Figure 4.9 Agencia Efe: lafototeca.com; Figure 4.12 Getty Images: Keystone; Figure 4.13 Solo Syndication: David Low / University of Kent / British Cartoon Archive; Figure 4.14: TopFoto; Figure 4.15 Getty Images: Universal History Archive / UIG; Figure 4.16 Getty Images: Universal History Archive / UIG; Figure 5.2 Mary Evans Picture Library; Figure 5.3 REX /Shutterstock: Roger-Viollet; Figure 5.4 The Art Archive: Kharbine-Tapabor / Coll. Perrin; Figure 5.5 Topfoto; Figure 5.6 TopFoto: The Granger Collection; Figure 5.7 The Art Archive: Private Collection / CCI; Figure 5.9 TopFoto: Roger-Viollet; Figure 5.10 Getty Images: Succession Willy RONIS / Diffusion Agence RAPHO / Gamma-Rapho.